"LET THE EAGLE SOAR AGAIN"

"LET THE EAGLE SOAR AGAIN"
A Guide to a Better Democracy and Society

Allan LeTourneau

iUniverse, Inc.
Bloomington

"Let the Eagle Soar Again"
A Guide to a Better Democracy and Society

iUniverse books may be ordered through booksellers or by contacting:

iUniverse
1663 Liberty Drive
Bloomington, IN 47403
www.iuniverse.com
1-800-Authors (1-800-288-4677)

ISBN: 978-1-4620-5620-0 (sc)
ISBN: 978-1-4620-5621-7 (hc)
ISBN: 978-1-4620-5622-4 (e)

Library of Congress Control Number: 2011917339

Printed in the United States of America

iUniverse rev. date: 10/06/2011

Preface

This book is a collection of perspectives, solutions, and ideas that may contribute to the betterment of our world, our nation, and our society. It is primarily targeted toward empowering the middle class of America. If the middle class adopts the strategies outlined in various chapters, Americans will build the greatest society and strongest economy ever imagined. It is time for our nation's middle class to start a "BLUE REVOLUTION"!

This book is written out of the frustration of a common citizen unable to reach our elected officials with better solutions. It seems that the bureaucracy of government is closed to ideas or solutions unless they are born within their own circles or in the minds of consultants who charge huge sums of money. Any forms of communication that ordinary citizens attempt to use to reach these individuals are totally ignored.

Writing to these officials is the biggest waste of time in your life. I hope that some citizens or officials across our nation might find valuable solutions here that will guide our nation and communities into a better future. I hope to prove that ordinary citizens can make valuable contributions to society and government. We need to be heard!

"To my country, 'tis of thee, I leave to thee".

CONTENTS

Introduction

I have been analyzing the problems of our communities, our nation, and the world for over a decade. I am not a writer, and I have no education in the field. However, I have had the perception of predicting events, and I only wish that I had stepped forward and brought those predictions to the attention of America.

Having had visions of 9/11 a few years prior to the event, and having realized that unless you are rich and powerful, you cannot get the attention of any government official, I decided that one day I would write a book about my prediction and warn America of the impending attack. Needless to say, I procrastinated too long.

I promise that *Let the Eagle Soar Again* has something for everybody. You will hate parts, and you will love other parts. I try to observe the world and its ugly history as if I came from another world, with complete neutrality, and attempt to correct failures and offer solutions for mankind's direction in pursuit of a better future for all.

The world and our society are evolving so rapidly that we seldom have time to sit back and study the lessons of our failures and successes and put them all into perspective so that we might avoid the catastrophic failures of the past and the unimaginable problems of the future.

War will never achieve its goals as it has in the past. The enemy is not clearly defined as in the past. Often, the enemy is not a nation that can be brought to its knees. The enemy often hides behind the skirts of women and children. The enemy is most often not the citizenry of any nation.

Religion plays far too great a role in societies throughout the world. Many religions forbid birth control, and apparently they are okay with millions of starving and suffering children (and parents too). Far too many nations do not have the natural resources or industrial resources to support their people. The millions of prayers do not stop these depravities.

We may never before have encountered the tremendous problems society now faces with the advent of mind-altering drugs and the unimaginable network of crime that destroys society and corrupts nations, resulting in the heartbreak of senseless and needless crimes.

I will offer a far more in-depth perspective and more thorough solutions if I complete my next book. For now, society has enough to swallow and sort out.

Therefore, I have decided to put my ideas, solutions, and perspectives into a book. I feel compelled to offer America and the world these solutions before I leave this world. With the serious health problems I have faced, I have been unbelievably stressed, and I am relieved that I have finally achieved this goal. I firmly believe we should all make any contribution to mankind and the world that will improve society and build a better future. I only hope I will achieve that goal with these offerings.

Since there is so much to swallow and there are so many areas of concern, my best hope is that these issues will create public discussion and open debate on all the many points touched upon here. I hope the book might be a valuable addition to the curriculum and starting point for debate for high school and college students facing this complicated new world. I doubt I will be able to change the minds of people who are deeply entrenched in their ideologies and unwilling to open their minds to better and more logical approaches. I believe that mankind can find better methods to coexist in this ever more dangerous world than the troubling direction that we are evolving toward.

Mankind is always striving to perfect the world and society. This is simply my offering toward that goal. You will need to put aside your ideology and open your mind to a picture of the future direction of mankind and how we may learn to coexist and achieve the ultimate goal for humanity.

The publisher has pointed out that I make no reference to research on the issues. I am here to say that all the issues are common knowledge for anybody who stays abreast of the news concerning government, world affairs, community affairs, and politics.

I have gathered my perspective and solutions from studying Associated Press reports and television news stories.

Author's note to editor and readers: I believe that all spaces between sentences should be double spaced. Exclamation marks should be spaced and separated from any word. The exclamation mark applies to the sentence and is not part of the last word in the sentence. It sometimes becomes confusing, especially when a last word ends with 2 1's. Quotation marks should surround a phrase and not come after a period. Whoever makes these rules should exercise a little common sense and make reading a lot easier.

Chapter 1

9/11 and Terrorism

As I start this book, I almost feel that I need to apologize to America. I was always too busy to focus on what I felt was an impending 9/11 type of attack on America. I doubt that I could have gotten through the bureaucracy to alert the powers that be. Of course, I also realize no matter what advice or premonition I or any other common citizen might have, it would be absolutely impossible to get the attention of any of our government officials. If you knew that city hall or the White House were going to be blown up tomorrow, you would most likely get a canned response long after the ashes had settled.

I was actually in a similar situation a few years before 9/11. I had wanted to write a book describing the danger America faced as a result of our foreign policy and past events. I examined past attacks on America and American concerns throughout the world. There was a clear pattern of terrorists hell-bent on inflicting the most damage and terror possible on America.

Therefore, I put myself in their position, imagining how I might deal the severest blow to America imaginable. I thought the worst that could be done would be to crash airliners into the Pentagon, the White House, and Capitol Hill when Congress was in session. I did not, however, imag-

4

ine the World Trade Center, because it had no strategic value in disabling our government. To inflict the most damage and chaos on America, the federal government and military command center would need to be wiped out. If the two hijacked airliners attacking the World Trade Center towers and the one that went down in Pennsylvania had instead been directed at Capitol Hill, the White House, and the Pentagon, we would have had a very serious problem on our hands.

So let's put this into perspective. If 9/11 was considered a war, the terrorists won and America lost. We failed to prevent an attack on America. For the enemy, it was almost ingenious ! I said *almost* ingenious. If they had directed the attack exclusively on Capitol Hill, the Pentagon, and the White House, we would have had absolute chaos. We would have had no central government left and no central command center. The terrorists had no organized military with which to invade America when we were unable to organize our forces to respond. This, fortunately for us, is how terrorism works. They simply make random attacks that will inflict the most havoc, fear, and terror upon a nation. However, if a superpower were to attack, they would likely choose to take out our government and command center first. So there are serious lessons to be learned from 9/11.

If the White House, the Pentagon, and our Congress were moved to a remote area of the United States, such as Arizona or Nevada, hundreds of miles inland, it would be nearly impossible for them to be subjected to a surprise attack like Pearl Harbor was in World War II. This new center would be a community where nobody but government officials and military commanders would live, completely surrounded by the largest and most strategic military complex in the world. There would be no crazies walking up to the Capitol or the White House with weapons. There would be no powerful semi trucks loaded with explosives crashing the gates.

That is exactly why I felt I needed to write a book prior to 9/11 explaining the danger our nation faced by having both our central government and military command center right in the middle of one of the most populated areas of the United States.

Our genius experts are supposed to be paid to put their brains into the minds of enemies and preconceive all these scenarios. I saw these scenarios years before 9/11, but I am just a common citizen who cannot reach government officials. I will guarantee that terrorists are working on a much more devastating plan and unbelievable weaponry to use down the road. It may be years away, but we damn well know that 9/11 gave millions of terrorists encouragement to revel in the possibilities of finding another weakness in our defenses and dealing another mighty blow to America. They might be kicking themselves for not concentrating more on Washington DC instead of New York.

Meanwhile, we should appoint a Western Command Center that would consist of military officers stationed in the western United States and a small contingent of western Governors who would take over national leadership in the event of an attack on Washington DC.

Here is another scenario that our nation should be on alert for. The terrorists could purchase a fleet of used garbage trucks or concrete trucks that a municipality or a concrete company auctions off. The pretense might be that they intend to renovate and resell them. They would then take the trucks to a warehouse and paint them to match the newer trucks, including logos of, say, New York City or a local concrete company. Then they would set up a false fertilizer distributorship and purchase hundreds of tons of fertilizer to fill them up along with explosive detonators.

On a given day, they would hit the streets early in the morning, pull up to their targets, park, and leave their trucks, pretending to be seeking instructions for delivery location. The rest you can leave to your imagination.

—⁓—

Why are citizens so opposed to imaging technologies or strip searches at airports? You go through even more intimate and revealing exposure at your doctor's office or a hospital. When you are in surgery, you most often are totally exposed to many eyes, both male and female. The examiner at the airport does not see your face, only the imaging. Grow up, people ! And for those who follow religious doctrines forbidding such exposure, don't fly ! If you go to a football game, you either agree to a search, or you don't get in.

Recently, our intelligence personnel have discovered terrorist plans to check into our hotels on each level. Then they plan to start fires on each level. It likely will become necessary to inspect luggage as you check into hotels.

As a result of the so-called crotch bomber, our government has decided to install full-body scanners at major airports throughout the world. This is going to cost billions of dollars, and I doubt it will result in screening out potential terrorist attacks. I have a few potential scenarios our government may wish to be aware of in regard to future attacks.

This may not be a scenario some may be comfortable with, but it is a reality we must face. There is no way to present it without describing it in detail.

The sex toy industry manufactures artificial penises so real that the naked eye would have trouble distinguishing the real thing from the manufactured device. They come in a variety of sizes, including models that mimic extraordinarily large penises. Who or which scanning technician is to determine how large a penis should be or how large testicles should be? Many of these devices actually have a very natural feel to them.

Regardless, most of these are capable of packing enough explosives to destroy an airliner. They would not be detectable to the naked eye or a scanner. Many of these devices come in models equipped with battery power, enough to ignite any such device. If body scanners are designed to read body temperatures and body parts, the devices could be capable of thermal temperatures set to ordinary body temperatures via battery power.

So as you can imagine, body scanners are not the total solution to preventing terrorist attacks aboard airliners. The same scenarios could exist for female suicide bombers. Such devises could be inserted into body cavities or false breasts. I have absolutely no solution for these scenarios, and I doubt that our security officials could detect these potential bombs without very intimate searches of most passengers. It may require very sophisticated lie-detection equipment. It is very much a reality that we must be aware of in the future.

Another security scenario we should consider is the following. One day a terrorist may steal a vehicle belonging to a government official while he or she is traveling or duplicate one with identical license, permits, and so on, along with security identification. The terrorist may have a make-over or disguise that closely resembles that official. That vehicle could be loaded to the hilt with explosives and destined for Capitol Hill or another strategic destination. Get the picture ?

What amount of security can prevent a semi loaded with explosives traveling at a high rate of speed from crashing the gates of the White House or Capitol Hill ? I do have a solution for this, which I will offer in detail in a later chapter.

This brings me to the urgency of writing this book now. Due to politics and the illusion that we can now leave Iraq and everything will be fine, I am forced to paint a picture of the reality. We broke it, and now we own it. Many military experts warned us in advance about a pre-emptive attack on Iraq. They warned us about how divided that nation was and the dangers of invading. Our president ignored that advice. He was hell bent on taking out Saddam Hussein, likely because his father had been criticized often for not doing so. As it turns out, *(you may be too young to know that there was a television show called "Father Knows Best" in the 1950's or ".* He knew there would be grave danger in knocking out the central government.

We can only blame ourselves as Americans; we should have known better than to elect this guy who had proven over and over his lack of intel-ligence and knowledge of world affairs. There are enough people out there who vote without having a clue as to the policies of the people they vote for. They simply vote for the best looking and most charming candidate. George Bush's grasp of the Spanish language won over millions of Latinos. That in itself made enough of a difference to win a majority.

You might believe at this point that I have it in for Republicans. Ac-tually, I consider myself an independent and a political moderate. I had much respect for President George H. W. Bush and was shocked that he was not re-elected. He had great wisdom, which his son did not inherit. We owe the Free World an apology for electing an incompetent president. This should serve as a warning to future generations of the dangers in electing warmongers and incompetent leadership.

The Republicans are right about one thing. We will be in Iraq for the next hundred years in some manner. For now, there is one thing that is very clear. We are going to need the help of the entire free world in order to maintain stability in the Middle East. With our treasury going bankrupt, we can no longer afford to go it alone.

President Bush should apologize to our allies for making a huge mistake in thinking we could build a democracy in Iraq. We had very good intentions, but time has proved that it will not work. As soon as we leave, full-scale civil war breaks out. It does not get headlines; however, in the back pages of most newspapers nearly every week, there are articles of continued suicide attacks in Iraq resulting in scores of civilian deaths. A small percentage of Americans read their daily newspapers in their entirety every day. If they do not, they are not aware of the magnitude of failure in Iraq.

When I hear the talking heads stating how well things are going in Iraq, I wonder if they and members of Congress get daily reports on the numbers of suicide attacks and the numbers of deaths occurring almost daily.

The only form of government that has achieved stability in Iraq is a totalitarian dictatorship. That is what keeps order in most of the Arab nations. Iraq was much better off with Saddam in power. It takes an iron fist to keep order in such a divided country. People talk about how abusive he was and how he gassed thousands of Kurds. Well, since the United States invaded Iraq, there have been tens of thousands of citizens killed or maimed, and the killing never stops. The worst part of this reality is that most of the Iraqis hate us more and more every day, because they realize that without our invasion and presence, those hundreds of thousands of loved ones would be alive and doing well.

Iraq was actually closer to being a democracy under Saddam than most other Arab nations. They had more freedoms, especially the women. They were not forced to wear burqas, and they attended colleges and had many of the same freedoms as men. Citizens were not forced to abide by the strict teachings and doctrine of the Muslim religion.

The Sunnis were the people who took a stand against the very strict theocracy of the Shiites, which originated in Iran. They went to war against Iran to prevent their country from being taken over by that theocracy, and the United States became an ally of Iraq. We gave them hundreds of millions of dollars worth of weapons to help ward off Iran. Those weapons were eventually used against Kuwait and the United States in the 1992 Persian Gulf War.

The lesson we should have learned is that we should stop providing weapons to other nations. Events down the road may force a change of attitude toward America, or a change of leadership could turn those weapons against an America-friendly nation or against America itself. We should instead offer protection to those nations if an enemy attacks them.

Now, I wish to make it perfectly clear that I was opposed to this war from the start. I actually got into trouble with the Secret Service for trying to stop the war. I wrote letters to numerous government officials and major newspapers outlining a plan to give Saddam Hussein forty-eight hours to leave Iraq. In that letter, I stated my frustration as a common citizen unable to reach our president or representatives under any circumstances. Most correspondences go into a file of thousands, and staff members read them and choose a canned response letter from a computerized database. Most responses come months later, followed by solicitations for donations to the politician's election fund. It is absolutely impossible to get a representative's personal attention unless you shoot up the White House. That statement brought the Secret Service to my door. It seems that a so-called friend that I had met through talk radio and begun e-mailing daily about local and world politics decided to inform the Secret Service about the letter I had sent to the media and government officials.

Another time, I was downtown protesting the Iraq war when President Bush was in town campaigning for his second term. I set up a large sign and flags with a picture of all the soldiers who had died in Iraq that had been printed in the local newspaper on Memorial Day. It was only a few hundred at that time. Included on that memorial was a statement that Iraq was 70 percent Shiite, the same as Iran. You cannot turn a nation that is 70 percent Shiite Muslim into a democracy. They now have a democracy; however, it is a corrupt democracy. They also have close diplomatic relations with Iran and are trade partners with them. They are now telling

America that they want us out of Iraq. All this after we invested billions of dollars in their infrastructure. What gratitude ! Eventually, they will be Iran the second. Clearly we have created more hatred than good will.

———

Now I will describe what could happen in future years. Total civil war breaks out. Those nations smuggling weapons into Iraq to feed the insurgency go full bore with weapons never imagined. When Iran sends troops and weapons after the Sunnis, Saudi Arabia responds. Then other countries jump in. Soon you have full-scale war throughout the Middle East. Each hits the others where it hurts the most—the oil refineries. There will be little or no oil flowing from the Middle East.

How will this affect America? There will only be enough oil for industry, government services, and commerce. Home heating oil will be rationed. There will be limited gas for automobiles. You will be forced to use public transportation, which will not be able to handle the demand. This will only serve a small percentage of the need, so many of you will be walking or biking to work. Obviously, the economy will go completely to hell. Other nations that depend on our economy will also be affected. Soon the whole world will be in chaos, and an economic depression never imagined will occur.

———

Al Qaida and the Taliban have us right where they want us. They forced us to kill their people, and that is the best recruiting tool for building their network.

We are stuck between a rock and a hard place. We can only blame ourselves for electing a president who lacked the integrity to lead our nation. Personally, I blame the Republican Party for passing over many intelligent and qualified people in order to nominate the handsome and charming individual without integrity or knowledge of history, diplomacy, and world affairs. The problem is they put all their eggs in one basket years before the election. Hundreds of millions of dollars were invested in George W. Bush before anything was known about him and how he could embarrass Republicans in serious debate. He had name recognition, charm, good looks, and charisma. And that's about it.

I admire President Obama and his determination to get us out of this mess. I admire his commitment to diplomacy rather than the saber rattling of past administrations. However, time will prove to both him and Iraq that our presence as a peace-keeping force will be necessary until these nations and ethnic opponents learn to live in peace with each other, which may never happen. The Taliban and Al Qaida love to keep us in Iraq and Afghanistan as targets because it is very difficult to bring their terror to our homeland.

I believe that it is impossible to stabilize the Middle East. It is likely that we would be better off just to let these nations fight it out until they realize that they have to form a union of democratic nations and stand together against aggression and terrorism. I am afraid that is the only hope for those nations if they wish to avoid a nuclear war in the future.

In the mean time, the United States should focus on domestic defense, intelligence, and strategic strikes with drones against Al Qaida camps. President Bush stated shortly after 9/11 that we will go everywhere and anywhere to destroy terrorists. We should not need any nation's permission to make strikes against terrorists. That is the only way you can fight terrorism. Superb intelligence is what has prevented further terrorist strikes against America since 9/11.

This boondoggle in Iraq leads me to the conclusion that there needs to be a constitutional amendment stating that in order to run for president, you need to have served in the United States Senate for at least one term. Being a governor is the same as being the CEO of a business or corporation. Federal government is a totally different field of expertise. You learn nothing of world affairs by being the CEO of state business.

The world has become far too complex to jump into the most responsible job in the world without having spent years of experience dealing with these complexities. The Senate is the only place you can gain that inside knowledge and experience. This is the place where you can prove your leadership skills and knowledge. Being the CEO of state business is no proving-ground for being the commander-in-chief of the world's strongest and most lethal military or making decisions about international diplomacy or world economic matters. Only serving in Congress can give an individual experience and insight into these matters. Let us please, for the sake of our nation, not make this mistake again. The Iraq war has destroyed our economy and left over four thousand of our troops dead and tens of thousands more seriously maimed.

Realizing the tremendous mistake our nation made in attacking Iraq, I am now examining whether we will, in the long term, benefit from our war in Afghanistan. As of the writing of this book, we are making great strides against the Taliban in Afghanistan. However, we must acknowledge why millions of Muslims hate America and face the reality that their hatred will never go away. Will Afghanistan approve of us continuing to occupy their nation? Not likely. More than likely, the Taliban will rise again, because they have the backing of millions of Muslims simply because they hate Americans.

I'm afraid our quest for revenge for 9/11 may have been misguided and may perhaps have created more damage to the image of America. Hundreds of thousands of Iraqis are dead, leaving hundreds of thousands of grieving relatives and friends. Probably tens of thousands of Afghanistan citizens have been killed, resulting in the same kind of grieving and despair. How much good will have all those lives cost us ?

We have also lost over eight thousand American lives, and many thousand more veterans have been seriously maimed, both physically and psychologically. We have been forced to hire millions of security guards throughout our nation. We have to guard every government facility, public building, arena, airport, port of entry, dam, and power plant, along with numerous other facilities. We have been forced to invest in very expensive technologies and equipment to protect all these facilities and citizens. We have been forced to create a new and very expensive branch of government—the Department of Homeland Security—and hire tens of thousands of intelligence officials.

All this protection is costing us billions of dollars and great inconveniences in our lives. All this expense has caused a tremendous hit to our economy. And we have many citizens complaining of high taxes and the phenomenal escalation of our national debt. There is more than one way to wage war in this day and age. One way is to destroy the economy of a nation. All this for our well-intentioned desire to build a democracy and ally in the middle of a billion Muslims. Should we send the bill to Israel ? I don't believe all the democracies in the world can pay this perpetual bill. Many are forced to spend billions themselves in security for being our ally. Are there lessons to be learned ?

In my opinion, we would be far better off focusing on guarding our homeland through more and better inspection of cargo ships. Then, of course, we need more and continued intelligence on citizens attempting terrorism from within our homeland. So far, I believe that our intelligence agencies have done a remarkable job in this area. Realize, though, that this is very expensive, and there will always be terrorists because of the theocracy of Muslims. They will always believe that any nation or people that does not share their religious beliefs and laws is evil, and it is their directive to wipe out the evil forces of the world.

Chapter 2

Freedom Pact

One lesson that all the world clearly understands by now is that money is the root of all evil. If we are going to continue arming and assisting other nations, there will always be a market for weapons among those nations' enemies. So how can we ever expect to get a handle on nuclear proliferation? How about stopping the arming of other nations and putting the burden of dangerous and threatening nations on the United Nations or NATO? It is in their best interests to take a stand.

Actually, this is leading me into the main purpose of writing this book. The world is getting far too dangerous to continue the business as usual that the world powers have exhibited since World War II. The world keeps watching as new, more dangerous and more threatening powers emerge in the world. We have China, which is quickly becoming the economic power of the world. Economic power equates to more education, technology, research, etc. All of this does not just apply to commerce superiority. It applies to superior weaponry and intelligence in combat. This is how the United States became the only superpower in the world.

I actually see no reason why China would become a threat to the world unless the United States aggravates the situation by threatening China over Taiwan. I have seen no problems following China's takeover of Hong Kong, so why would it be any different if Taiwan were absorbed into China? Actually, China no longer needs Taiwan. Their economy is flying high. Democracy is on its way to China, ushered in by capitalism and greater economic times. That capitalism was learned from Hong Kong, so why would Taiwan be in any danger?

The lesson to be learned by America is that the best way and perhaps the only way for democracy to develop when it is born within a nation. Show a nation how to get out of poverty and get its economy rolling. Teach a nation how to check corruption internally, and its citizens will be inspired to work harder. We should try every method of influencing these nations or educating them about the benefits of free enterprise and democracy.

Of course, America cannot even get a handle on corruption. We have to admit to our own struggles and deficiencies. Financial empires afford the best legal representation, and the government struggles to compete with high-priced corporate lawyers. This situation is almost becoming obscene in America, because the government is not able to keep pace with the high-powered lawyers millions of dollars can buy. Money talks, and he who has the money buys justice and elections. We will revisit this problem in another chapter.

Getting back to the greater subject of this book: I have to put the future of the world into perspective. Too many nations have fought and sacrificed many lives to give a good percentage of the world the freedom mankind craves. If the United States had not stepped up and sacrificed so many lives in World War II, there would be no free nations of the world. Adolf Hitler and the Third Reich would have controlled the entire world, and there would have been no opposition. They would have continued to annihilate enemies who opposed them.

America has reached a point where we cannot financially bear the burden of being the world's police and world's only superpower as we have in the past. There are far too many conflicts and threats to world peace. Of course, if we had not elected a charming and handsome idiot as president, we would not be in such a precarious and impossible situation.

We likely could have put a hundred thousand troops into the mountains of Afghanistan and wiped out the Taliban entirely. Then we could have concentrated on the obscene atrocities and human suffering in Africa. Hundreds of thousands of defenseless people are being annihilated in those countries, and the world just ignores it all. Of course, those people are black, so it apparently does not matter. If they had lots of oil, their lives might be more important to the world. I am so ashamed of mankind. I almost lose any desire to live in this ugly world. It is so sickening that it provides little hope for the existence of mankind or any reason why mankind should exist. What keeps me going is the small percentage of people who truly care for the welfare of all human beings.

I'm talking about the people that fight every day for the poor and unfortunate who are the victims of the wicked dictatorships and warring factions throughout the world: the doctors, the scientists, the agriculture experts, the teachers, and the missionaries.

Every nation in the world that enjoys the freedoms of a legitimate democracy owes its democracy to the sacrifices of American soldiers. The way democracies have risen and spread throughout the world in the past seventy years made it seem as though the entire world would soon be free, and we would be on a course for world peace. I thought this was the purpose and mission of the United Nations. Instead, the UN has become a joke. It has given powers to rogue nations to stymie the efforts of free and democratic nations trying to pursue world peace through diplomacy. There is no longer any bite or pressure to enforce the United Nations' original mission. Any nation not a legitimate democracy does not belong on the Security Council. What a farce!

This world is becoming far too dangerous for this nonsense to continue. Mankind is flirting with nuclear war and Armageddon. When such a huge portion of the world's people believes that democracies are evil empires and is willing to seek martyrdom, why would those people hesitate to destroy the world? They believe they are doing God's work. Couple those beliefs with the obscene hundreds of billions of dollars these nations are making from oil, and you have a recipe for disaster. Is the free world going to sit on its hands and wait until all that money purchases the most devastating weapons money can buy?

This is why I am proposing a pact of all free and legitimate democracies of the world. The mission of the Freedom Pact would be to join together to preserve, protect, and propagate freedom throughout the world. These nations would have a combined military and intelligence agency. Each nation would contribute on a per capita basis, because freedom is not free.

The combined effort of all these nations would create the largest and most powerful military in the world. This organization would identify the most dangerous rogue dictatorship in the world. It would then negotiate and try every diplomatic effort available to get that government to reform. It would then try every sanction, embargo, and blockade. It would then resort to assassination of the leadership. If that were unsuccessful, it would demand the surrender or exile of the country's top-level leadership. If the leadership failed to cooperate with that demand, then all their military installations would be targeted. I cannot imagine that it would be necessary to go as far as any of these options. However, if all of these efforts failed, the nation would be annihilated, and it would serve as a lesson to other vile dictatorships and rogue nations throughout history.

Now you say, "What about all the thousands of innocent people who would die?" Is it better that one nation be extinguished from the world than that all of mankind be annihilated? Is it better that the world be free and that we finally achieve world peace than that we all live under a vile dictatorship or totalitarianism? We are at a point in history when we must make a stand, or the window of opportunity will pass us by. There won't be many historians around after a nuclear war.

Throughout history, the fear of death always has been a deterrent and consequence of war. Now we have a huge group of people who are willing to blow themselves up in order to take out their enemies. How can that philosophy not translate to a billion people willing to wipe out humanity in order to please their God and get their seventy-two virgins? When so many people live in poverty and hopelessness, how can they not be captivated by such a fantasy?

Incidently; why is it that the non-Muslim nations and religions never address the absurdity of the Islam promise of seventy-two virgins. Shouldn't we be focusing on the logic of such a promise from God. First of all, there is the commandment of "Thou shall not kill". Then what is the reward for women? Would God just ignore the needs of the mothers of mankind? Where would these seventy-two virgins come from? How could a man handle that number of woman, when common sense says that most men cannot pleasure even two women? What happens to your wife while you are in camp with your seventy-two virgins? Finally, if God created mankind, why would he advocate having one group of people kill off the other group? The Commandment states: "Love thy neighbor as thyself".

Why does the media not sit down with these clerics and address these issues?

Most of the billion Arabs have little or no sports or entertainment in their lives to detract from the ordinary stress and pressures of daily life. There is a natural desire for mankind to enjoy winning in life and a desire for victory. In America and many other nations, we have entertainment and competition every day of our lives. We can temporarily escape from the stress and disappointments of daily life. Imagine living in countries where no matter where you go or what you do, you must live with the real possibility of being blown up or witnessing your friends, neighbors, or family dying in your sight. Human nature dictates that you will become irrational and angry and seek revenge. And why not ? That is a human instinct of survival. So while we can look forward to the next ball game or next season, these people look forward to the next attack by their core-ligionists to even the score. This becomes their sport, their emotion, and their victories in life. Is that not sad?

I often wonder whether, if these people had baseball, basketball, football, hockey, tennis, pool tournaments, golf tournaments, skiing, ice skating, Hollywood entertainment, and so on, they might not be less preoccupied with the only competition they live with: killing ! Again I say: Is that not sad? What is even sadder is the fact that we face impossible odds in ever overcoming the tragedies these people live with day in and day out. When you live every day with such hopelessness, you become a victim of the religious messages all religions are forced to offer to comfort their victims of tragedy. Most often, that comfort is taking pride in what your family, friends, or brethren died for. And that only reinforces the idea that it is your responsibility to fight and die as a martyr and serve your God in paradise.

The bottom line is that the world cannot afford to stand by any longer and allow dictatorships and dangerous theocracies to reign. Mankind has too many serious challenges to meet worldwide to be spending billions of dollars every day fighting wars that will ultimately lead to the destruction of mankind. There is no longer a place in the world for warmongering nations threatening world stability.

If we don't stop our continuous arms buildup and learn to settle our differences peacefully, we will be on a path to certain destruction of our world. I have a proposal to change this course outlined in chapter 15.

Chapter 3

Wars in the New World

One thing we are learning in this new world is that the conventional wars of past centuries will not fly in these times. If we had a war between superpowers, it would be devastating to the world. Millions on either side would die, and the environment in much of the world would be destroyed and would no longer sustain life.

So this leaves many warring nations actually fighting wars by supporting and supplying smaller nations. Those nations never realize that they are actually the guinea pigs of the real war between superpowers. It happened in Vietnam, and it's happening in Iraq, Afghanistan, and Israel. Without the support of superpowers and their supply of weapons, these nations would not be able to battle.

Worse these days are the methods of waging war through terrorism. Terrorism is a method of war that attacks innocent civilians and avoids contact with the military of the enemy. It is actually a chicken-shit method of waging war. It seems in this day and age that anything is fair in war.

Some of our enemies supply both sides with weapons and funding in order to draw the United States into battle. Then, when we are drawn in, in the pursuit of the enemy, we often wind up killing innocent civilians. This is the terrorists' plan. If you had loved ones or neighbors killed by a foreign enemy, you and your neighbors would rise up and fight to the death to avenge their deaths. This is the way it works in the terrorist wars. It makes it so simple to recruit warriors willing to give their lives to avenge their loved ones' deaths.

There are many vile dictators who are a threat to world stability or who could cause a world war. They are often hated by their own citizens, yet every effort to overthrow or assassinate them fails. If the dictator and his inner circle could be removed, the nation and its citizens would likely not be an enemy or a threat to other nations. You would in fact be doing the innocent citizenry a huge favor by getting them out from under the suffering of so much oppression.

Therefore, I propose that America invest a great amount of money in the research and development of a weapon that will put a city or an area to sleep for a short period; then covert operatives can go into an area and remove or assassinate these vile dictators. They could then be tried in a world court for their crimes against humanity.

We can no longer allow these types of tyrants to cause so much suffering in this world, creating a threat to democracy and upsetting world stability. I like to think of them as the few bad men—the few tyrants who can cause so much suffering and create so much of a threat to world stability. The freedom-loving nations have to spend a great deal of money and a huge number of lives to preserve and protect the dream and fulfillment of world peace. How much more could the free world do if we could invest the billions of dollars we currently spend on weapons and warfare technology on aiding nations suffering from poverty, disease, starvation, illiteracy, and other ills?

It's unbearable that so much of humanity is held hostage by a few vile dictators. So much suffering. So much money and resources committed to the threats of a few could be redirected to so many humanitarian needs and provide life-saving support.

Are we ever going to become a civilized world? Just when I felt that the world was done with war a few decades ago, there suddenly seemed to be more war and killing than any time in history. The chief reason is that vile dictators who have such a lust for power that they kill any and all that stand in their way rule so many of these warring nations. How long is the world going to stand by and allow civilization to go to hell? If we don't get a handle on these atrocities now, what will happen when all these rogue nations have nuclear weapons at their disposal? It's time for the democracies of the world to stand up and end this bullshit.

I'm afraid that the United States may have made a huge mistake when we adopted a policy decades ago never to assassinate a foreign leader. It seems that it's better to allow the vile dictators to live and allow thousands to be massacred. The United Nations or NATO nations should damn well adopt a policy of removing vile dictators who cause so much oppression to their citizens and who become a major threat to world stability. Why in the hell should millions of people suffer under so much oppression? Why should we stand by and allow a handful of people to create so much instability, danger, and chaos? We could save hundreds of millions of people living with so much suffering and oppression. The whole course of history and humanity is altered by so few. Why can't we extinguish them? I'll bet that it would only take one or two assassinations before the rest got a clear message of intolerance. If we have to, we can always hire a private security organization to do the job.

Above I outlined the need to remove vile dictators through nonviolent means. However, if these methods fail, the free world has to resort to more aggressive means. We cannot stand by and continue to demand certain nations abandon their ambitions for nuclear weapons while they continue to ignore the majority of the world's demands.

We have determined in the past that further proliferation of nuclear weapons would be a threat to the existence of mankind. A supermajority of nations has formed a pact prohibiting the proliferation of these weapons. Yet all these nations do is criticize those in violation or threaten sanctions against them. What is the free world waiting for? Will they wait until these rogue states have the weapons to engage in a nuclear war?

I fail to understand why NATO nations do not make a strike on facilities for developing nuclear weapons. If it starts a war, it is far better to engage an enemy with conventional weapons than wait for an engagement with nuclear weapons. Shit or get off the pot ! It's simple logic ! Will we wait until all NATO nations are attacked with nuclear bombs? What was the purpose of forming the International Atomic Bomb Commission? Is it just a wishful thinking organization? Is the United Nations only a paper tiger?

Chapter 4

Big Government

For years I have been listening to a huge segment of society complain about big government and high taxes. I too wish we didn't have to pay so many taxes and employ so damn many government officials. I would guess most of us wish for that. So I have to wonder about people who keep complaining about big government. It's simply because there are so many crooks in our society that government cannot begin to keep up with them. So I always wonder whether citizens that complain are in fact crooks themselves.

However, what time has proven is that it seems cheating and skirting the rules for financial gain is human nature. Ethics seem to be becoming a rarity in society. Even government officials who you would expect to employ strict ethics seem to be corrupt as hell, so many of them cannot seem to resist the temptation to sell their souls to the devil for financial gain and political power.

Why is it that we only discover their malfeasance when they are considered for promotion or as a candidate for higher office? It seems that all the unethical actions and corruption go on as usual business until society has a reason to examine their personal dealings or a red flag goes up for some reason. It makes one wonder how many executives and government officials' misconduct is never uncovered.

We have the tremendous expense of cleaning up the environment we have unknowingly contaminated for centuries. The more science evolves, the more science discovers the source of previously unknown causes of disease and death. This will likely go on forever, since we keep introducing new chemicals and materials into our lives.

We have new technologies evolving that give criminals methods of spying on private citizens, business interests, and intellectual property. This gets more expensive all the time, as government has to investigate, regulate, and prosecute these legal issues. It's a never-ending battle.

Of course, nothing has cost more than 9/11. We have the tremendous expense of the wars in Iraq and Afghanistan, the most expensive wars in U.S. history. We have the gigantic expense of millions of additional security personnel guarding all airports, seaports, railroads, and borders. We have the huge expense of guarding all public arenas, dams, power plants, courthouses, and all government buildings. We have the tremendous numbers of covert and intelligence operations within our nation and throughout the world. I would guess that the number of those personnel might have increased a hundred fold since 9/11.

With all the tremendous expenses listed above, we have not even considered the billions spent on technology to enable our professionals to perform their jobs and stay one step ahead of the terrorists. We have not even considered the necessity of developing better and stronger military vehicles to withstand the new methodology of our enemies' weaponry. These vehicles are coming off the assembly line with unimaginable price tags. This is partly due to the lack of competition in manufacturing military vehicles and weapons.

Of course, there is also the issue of dealing with the overpopulation of our metropolitan areas: transportation problems, environmental problems, crime problems, employment problems, health problems, police problems, water problems, energy problems, and social problems. With each year, these problems continue to multiply.

One of the biggest and almost cost-prohibitive challenges is building roads, bridges, and public transportation to keep traffic moving. Building roads in rural areas and new development is very expensive. However, the burden these additional millions of people put on the greater metro area and urban core roadsis unbelievable. Most of those areas are solid with development, and the property values are extreme. The costs of widening bridges or building new ones are astronomical. Widening roads is mostly cost prohibitive. Constructing new roads and highways creates problems for handling runoff.

Even building light rail or monorail is an extreme expense due to many of the reasons listed above. You have to believe that at some point the overcrowding of metro areas must stop. Otherwise, the cities will become nonfunctional.

I have a solution to present that might be worthy of study. There are many thousands of small townships drying up that were former farming, ranching, mining, and forestry communities. It's time to start bringing life back to those communities and take the growth burden off the overgrown metropolitan areas.

I recommend that these communities not be located adjacent to interstate highways so they do not add additional traffic burdens to those highways. Among the criteria would be an abundant supply of water. Once a community is identified, the planning and engineering would start.

The state government would offer incentives for a variety of industries to move there or open a branch office. There would be careful study to plan for all the services essential for a community to be independent. There could be tax incentives for medical services, grocers, hardware, automobile dealerships, department stores, etc. In other words, it would be a well-planned community geared for growth. Residential neighborhoods could be planned to provide commutes to work by foot or bicycle.

People all over the nation who are sick of the congestion, long commutes, pollution, and crime of big cities would find these communities very appealing. These communities would offer more family time and community activity. Moving to such a community would add hundreds of hours per year to your recreation and leisure life. It would save you thousands of dollars per year in fuel and auto maintenance. The money you saved could make for great vacations or saving for retirement—in other words, a better life and a more economical life for all.

There is absolutely no reason why major metropolitan areas of our nation need to grow beyond their means into a sea of humanity that is not functional. Hundreds of communities could be developed into family-oriented communities offering society a much better lifestyle.

By the way, I would not limit the selection process to those dying townships referred to earlier. In some states, the best location might be a completely undeveloped area that offers better sites for development with better natural resources. Building a city may in some cases be more successful and inexpensive than rebuilding smaller communities. Some sites may offer much better recreational opportunities.

The main reason why these rural communities can be successful is that business in this modern world is no longer dependent on location. Many can set up business anywhere in the nation. All they need is the infrastructure and skilled employees. There are hundreds of industries, technologies, and commercial activities that can locate anywhere they choose as long as there are employees trained in their specialty. The skilled employees can easily be recruited from all over the nation from a gigantic pool of those seeking a more livable lifestyle and seeking to escape the Zoo.

I have read of people who actually live on a mountain top and run a successful business around the world from that rural location. So the bottom line is that commerce has changed with time. In past times, business and industry were forced to locate in major metropolitan areas for a variety of reasons. Some had to be located in an area of natural resources. Some had to be located near major seaports, airports, or rail centers. Some required locating near educational institutions specializing in their fields of industry. Some were located in the center of oil or mining industries. Some were located in agricultural centers.

Building well-planned communities away from metropolitan areas is a common-sense solution to give millions of citizens a better quality of life. All it takes is strategic planning, cooperation, and the support of government. It is a hell of a lot cheaper than trying to cram metropolitan areas with more growth and the impossible social problems that ensue.

—◆—

Now I wish to bring up another serious subject. Many states are currently proposing that they pass legislation that will ignore federal law and allow them to secede from the union. These are states that are refusing to adhere to the law, democracy, and majority rule. Therefore, I propose that we implement an amendment to the Constitution that no state can secede from the United States of America. United we stand and divided we fall. For all of those dissidents, I offer this solution. Learn to live with the concept that the majority rules, and if you cannot adhere to those principles, then find yourself a better nation. If you cannot understand why the cost of government continues to grow (for your protection and the reasons listed above), then you are too ignorant to live in a modern society

Chapter 5

National Heroes and Holidays

This generation has a puzzling definition of who our national heroes really are. I would like to ask Americans just who is most valuable to our nation. What exactly does a sports superstar or Academy Award–winning movie star add to our society? Bravado, I presume.

In the mean time, we have soldiers dying practically every day defending our freedom. We play our national anthem before most athletic events. Wouldn't it be appropriate to announce and honor those fallen soldiers prior to our national anthem? The same could be done for our guardian police and fire fighters who die protecting our lives. Our local communities and news media do give appropriate time and recognition to these local heroes; however, they are long forgotten after the day's news cycle.

Then we have perhaps the greatest and most valuable heroes we hardly ever hear of. Those are our physicians and medical research scientists. A very great percentage of us are alive as a result of the efforts and ingenuity of those mentioned above. Yet none of us have any idea who we might thank for the labors and discoveries that led to the saving of our lives or the lives of our loved ones.

I don't know who we might blame for our disregard of our greatest and most valuable of heroes. Is it society or the media ? I suppose that if the media put on an Academia Awards program for the most valuable scientists and research medical technicians, it might be the greatest flop in television history. It would break my heart by demonstrating what I believe Americans stand for and value.

I love sports; however, I have a greater appreciation for those who make incredible discoveries that save lives, end suffering, and provide hope for those who face deadly disease. If I had to choose between viewing a Super Bowl or an awards ceremony for the many who give hope to millions of suffering people, I certainly would know where my priorities lie. When the ball game is over, it is over ! While we are watching sporting events, thousands of doctors are saving lives worldwide because of the conviction and dedication of doctors and medical research technicians.

There are so many individuals and organizations in our nation and our world that deserve a moment in our lives to recognize and honor their achievements. Can we not commit one week a year in our lives to get out of our tabloid mentality and honor those who give us life and better lives? Those superstar athletes and movie stars deserve recognition for their individual achievements. However, when the lives of your loved ones are saved, who do you value the most?

Should there not be a memorial plaque in each community honoring every individual that has either died for our freedom or provided great achievements for mankind? Every community has its sports hall of fame. Why not a humanity hall of fame?

Our nation has certain national holidays for the purpose of celebrating our independence and memorializing and honoring our veterans. Yet when you go to the ceremonies honoring soldiers who died for our freedom, most of the citizens who attend are relatives of fallen soldiers or veterans who live to honor their fallen comrades. How very shameful for our nation.

These holidays have become nothing more than a paid day off work and reason to socialize. Lots of picnics and barbecues are held at the expense of fallen soldiers. These and Presidents' Day are nothing more than a great opportunity for retailers to have a grand sale.

Who are the greatest recipients of these holidays? Government workers, of course ! While many industries cannot afford these paid holidays, all government employees and elected officials get this fringe benefit. However, eventually all industries gravitate to these fringes.

So wouldn't it be appropriate for Congress to extinguish these holidays on the grounds that 99 percent of citizens do not value the intended purpose of these holidays? Are we not capable of honoring our great heroes and fallen soldiers without putting unearned bucks in our pockets and partying for the day? Have we no idea how much damage we do to our national productivity while we are partying?

How about taking the Sunday of that anniversary to demonstrate our appreciation for those people—a true demonstration of appreciation by churches and other organizations at public places? How about if Congress changes those holidays to Sundays without the bonus to paychecks ?

While we are at it, why not change Christmas to the last Sunday in December? We all know that Christ's birthday was not on December 25. There were no calendars in biblical times. That date was chosen to coincide with a holiday of another religion. Would it not be more appropriate to honor Christ's birthday on a Sunday? That's the day of the week that believers were instructed to worship their God and Savior.

It seems that the majority of all industry and commerce shut down for the week between Christmas and New Year's Day. Sometimes that encompasses nearly a week and a half. By designating Christmas as the last Sunday of December, we could confine loss of national productivity to at least less than one week.

As a matter of fact, there is no logical reasoning for any holiday to be specific to a day of the week. If the purpose of a holiday is to honor a person, people, or an event, it matters not when you do it. It only matters that you set aside a day for that acknowledgment. If you wish to have holidays as a stimulus for retail commerce, then you would logically choose to create a three-day weekend. That would provide for short vacation getaways or for people to combine a few more days of leave for a solid week of travel and vacation. Is there anybody who would prefer to have a holiday on Tuesday, Wednesday, or Thursday? Clue to Legislators: What business would criticize you for designating that all holidays fall on or adjacent to weekends? How many voters would throw you out of office for giving them a three-day weekend? How many employers like to have their employees show up for work with hangovers following a Fourth of July that falls on Tuesday, Wednesday, or Thursday? Got Reality? If I were king, there would be no holidays during the work week. We have an economy in the tank with little hope for recovery. The economy and jobs are a hell of a lot more important than paid holidays.

Chapter 6

Government Authority in Economic Meltdown

For many years, we have witnessed a decrease in well-paying jobs in this nation, especially in the manufacturing sector. Unions will not make concessions to save their jobs. Strangely, they would rather see their plants close down and their jobs go overseas. I will never understand the logic and reasoning behind those decisions by union personnel. It seems the years invested in vacation time, pension funds, health care, and so on should be cause for strong consideration and sacrifice.

So what should government do? Just sit by and allow our nation to decline to third-world status? We elect government officials to make intelligent decisions in the best interests of the nation, regardless of public opinion. If we were all so informed and intelligent, we could all vote every day on all legislation. That, by the way, is how a true democracy works. Instead we elect officials to study these issues at length, and they make the difficult decisions.

Therefore, I propose that the president and Congress be granted the authority to suspend all national holidays in severe economic times. In these times, we must increase the productivity of our nation in order to compete in the world market. We must put our employers on sound financial ground if we expect them to survive.

I would also propose that our president propose a voluntary work day on a Saturday when all patriotic citizens could voluntarily go to work without pay. That would give all businesses a gigantic boost financially. It would also serve to create national unity. Wouldn't it be great to share such a noble and patriotic day with all our fellow citizens? We would be able to recapture the spirit of America and the sacrifices that brought our nation through World War II.

Retired citizens might register to offer a young, low-income couple a week of baby sitting or child care to offset that expense in their budget. They might plant a small garden in their backyards to provide low-income citizens with fresh vegetables and fruits. Others might volunteer at hospitals or clinics to help bring down extreme health care costs.

So as you can see, there are ways we can save our nation and the world from absolute economic collapse. If you have been planning a home improvement, this is the time to step up and get somebody working again. It would likely be a good investment in the most major investment of your life. If you have considered purchasing a new vehicle, now is the time to do it. Don't just spend foolishly. Spend intelligently!

Of all the services local governments provide, parks are probably the one service citizens can do without in times of economic emergencies. This is where a community's citizenry can step up and demonstrate their community spirit. If they all committed one hour a month, they could probably maintain their parks better than the parks department.

Now some municipalities have a voter-approved referendum that sets aside a set percentage of tax revenue toward their parks department. That may have been a good thing in the past; however, times have changed. Local governments may need to put another referendum up to the voters entitling their local governments to drop that requirement in times of economic disaster.

When government revenues are so depleted they can no longer provide basic services, we should not allow the citizens to vote on raising taxes, for the majority of citizens would rather see their communities go to hell than pay a little higher tax. Citizens rarely vote to raise taxes regardless of circumstances; they will almost always vote to dissolve a tax, even if it winds up costing them in safety and the betterment of their community.

This is why we have a republic rather than a democracy. The majority of citizens do not have the time to study the intricacies of our society at length. That is why we hire representatives to study and make the difficult decisions to provide essential services.

Most government bodies have the authority to raise taxes or implement new taxes in severe economic situations. Their responsibility is to manage government and taxing authorities to a level that allows them to provide basic safety and security for their community or state. To ignore those responsibilities is absolute incompetence. However, they also have to have the revenue to pay for those services.

The greatest cost of government is wages, benefits, retirement funds, and associated costs. Governments are by far the largest employers. Somehow most of these employees seem to think that they are immune to making sacrifices when the economy is in the tank and governments are facing bankruptcies. They would rather lose their jobs than make concessions. They seem to be totally oblivious to the dire situation of the economy.

Many retirement plans are obscene by private sector standards. Then we have double dipping, which happens when retires go back to work and continue to build their retirement benefits without making contributions. Many wind up making more in retirement than they made when they were working. So they deprive others of employment who would be making contributions to the retirement fund and decreasing the unemployment ranks.

Then we have elected officials who draw obscene pensions for the small number of years they spend doing their jobs. Those pensions should be based on a percentage of years on the job based on a standard forty-year service.

Furthermore, I don't understand why many pensions are based on a twenty-to-twenty-five-year period of service. Most people work forty to forty-five years in their careers. The bottom line is that our nation can no afford a big government that provides its workers so much pay and so many benefits in an economy that is in the tank. Too many retirees are being paid retirement benefits that leave little to fund existing services. The greatest problem here is that the stock market tanked, deleting the investment funds, and government is forced to fully fund those retirement benefits. If they are expected to provide government services, they will have no choice but to raise taxes and cut pay and benefits. It's simple logic.

Chapter 7

Economic Collapse Destined
(Written In 2010)

What ever happened to George W. Bush's huge tax cuts for wealthy Americans that were supposed to stimulate the economy, create investments in the economy, and create millions of jobs for America? Well, it appears that without those extra taxes, our government is now bankrupt, the investments have gone overseas, and unemployment is historically high.

It's quite clear that if government loses hundreds of billions of dollars in revenue, it is not going to be able to pay the bills. The government is forced to put the cost of services on a credit card that eventually has limits due to the continuous compounding of interest.

I'm sure that the Republican strategy of refusing to raise taxes to pay for past-due bills is for the purpose of destroying our economy and credit line. Then they can blame it on President Obama (who they despise) and get him out of office. They certainly do not give him credit for saving the banks and the rest of the financial industry. They do not give him credit for increasing the number of soldiers in Afghanistan and cleaning out the Taliban and Al Qaida, which was the Republican agenda. They don't give him credit for investing hundreds of billions of dollars in construction projects. We likely would have been much worse off without that stimulus.

Proud to be an American? We have no reason to be proud! What was once the greatest nation in the history of the world has deteriorated into a shameful, struggling nation. Our federal government is bankrupt. China owns America. It doesn't matter which nation owns our debt, whether it is China, Saudi Arabia, or the Netherlands. We should be ashamed of ourselves as a nation that can't stand on its own feet financially.

First of all, when a nation is facing war, that is not the time for a huge federal income tax cut, the largest tax cut in history. It is time for a tax increase that will finance the hundreds of billions needed to pay for that war. If the citizenry balks about the price, then those citizens have no regard for their own security and freedom or the lives and limbs lost as a result.

There are numerous reasons why our nation has sunk to such a low level, and I will outline those in this chapter. First of all, trying to be the world police is finally catching up to us financially. There have been too many years of fighting two different wars that cannot be won, one of which we had no business starting.

Another issue is that terror threatens the entire world. We clearly are not getting the help we should from our allies. We gave all those nations their freedom from oppressive regimes (remember Hitler and the Nazi regime that attempted to take over the world?) and they apparently don't feel that they need to help the United States when we desperately need help. We simply cannot continue to invest hundreds of billions in technology and arms and carry on these expensive wars perpetually. There will be no end to the war on terror.

I recall the decades when OPEC met periodically to discuss whether they would increase or decrease their production of oil and what prices they would set. They carefully analyzed how their decisions would affect the world economy. Why those nations have changed their strategy is beyond me. Those OPEC nations make such obscene amounts of money that they don't know what to do with it. Meanwhile, they drive the world's economy into the toilet.

Then you have the oil stocks and futures that are most responsible for raping the public and industry. Anything that can destroy the world economy should be illegal and certainly should not be in the hands of gamblers.

You cannot double the price of fuel in a year or two and expect that it will not destroy the economy. Every facet of the economy is affected by the price of fuel. I knew when oil prices were escalating that the economy could not sustain such a great expense and that eventually the economy would go to hell. It's just simple mathematics.

I propose that the government purchase huge amounts of petroleum directly from the nations that pump it, thus avoiding the speculators. If they can purchase oil for our strategic petroleum reserve, then why not to stabilize the market? First, our government officials have to get out of bed with the corporate oil executives. Our federal government can then sell it to all government agencies for use in their vehicles. If this helps stabilize the market, then they could make even greater purchases and sell to distributors and retailers. We should do everything to stop the stock market from destroying our economy for the sake of individual greed. Besides, many Middle Eastern nations, such as Iraq, Kuwait, and Saudi Arabia, owe us big time for defending them from Saddam Hussein. The least they should do is sell their oil to the U.S. government at wholesale prices. If I had my way, our federal government would purchase, control, regulate, and distribute all petroleum and natural gas. It is simply too vital a resource for our nation's economy to be in the hands of gamblers and speculators. They hold it for ransom, blackmail, and extortion. You name it, they find a way to screw over the public.

—⁂—

Our education system has failed to the point where our corporations have to either import educated people or send their businesses overseas for technological expertise. While our schools are facing the most severe budget deficits in history, there is no touching the sacred cow of sports and extracurricular activities. They spend millions of dollars for infrastructure, transportation, maintenance, personnel, and so on. Meanwhile, the school administration is forced to cut classes, increase class size, and lay off personnel.

We spoil our brats with so many toys, games, devices, and everything else that their little hearts desire that there is little interest in getting an education. There appears to be more emphasis on athletic activities and extracurricular activities than scholastic achievement. The majority grow up expecting to play and socialize throughout their lives. When the reality sets in, they seek out artificial happiness in drugs or alcohol. The illegal drug market feeds the growth of gangs, drug cartels, and all the ensuing crime overwhelming our justice system and prisons.

I wonder just how long Americans thought we could be a self-sustaining nation while purchasing most of our goods from foreign countries? How do we figure we can supply our citizens with jobs when most of the manufacturing jobs have gone overseas? Is there any wonder that our unemployment numbers continue to rise? I've been astounded for decades by the fact that employees of American auto manufacturers can drive into the gates of their plants driving foreign-manufactured vehicles. For shame !

I recall that when I was a young man working for a grocery warehouse, we would not be caught dead shopping in a competitor's grocery store. This is exactly why America is failing. We have no allegiance to each other as Americans.

Another huge factor in the jobs market is automation. We have known for many decades that automation was going to destroy our work force. I never would have imagined, for instance, that automation would take away warehouse jobs. Yet we now have fully automated warehouses that have taken away hundreds of jobs in a single warehouse. This is just one example among thousands.

Our corporate boards and leaders have little concern for America; they only care about the almighty dollar. Those extra dollars that they can generate by moving their factories overseas are far more important than whether American citizens have jobs. Their selfishness seems to be a point of pride or a feather in their hats. Boy are they proud to be Americans.

—᷍w᷍—

I recently saw a report on *60 Minutes* about how thousands of American corporations are moving their corporate offices overseas to Ireland and Switzerland in order not to have to pay corporate taxes in the United States. In reality, their corporate offices are not in those foreign nations. They either have a small shell of an office or just a post office box. They simply register their corporation there, and that nation becomes the taxing authority. They pay corporate taxes at just a fraction of what they would pay in the United States. They have cost the United States nearly 1.5 trillion dollars in federal income tax per year. That is just about the federal deficit yearly. Is there any wonder that our nation is going bankrupt and the national debt is soaring beyond comprehension?

Our elected officials are claiming that there is nothing they can do about these atrocities. Actually there is—if they would get out of bed with the corporations. The federal government is the taxing authority for our nation. If these rotten corporations are going to play dirty, then our legislators can play dirty as well. They just have to change the tax structure to tax a corporation's sales in the United States and abroad. Many states tax businesses on their gross revenues regardless of their profits. This would be justice to all of the rest of the taxpayers. We cannot provide government services in this nation if all our corporations are not contributing. Our corporations are what built a strong America. Now their greed and tax evasion is destroying America.

Of course you could say that nearly all Americans are to blame. Most of us have absolutely no concern whether the products we purchase are made in America and provide Americans with jobs. Then we wonder why our economy has gone to hell, why more and more people are without jobs, why our state and local governments can no longer generate sufficient revenue to provide essential services for their citizenry.

There is also a huge amount of corruption and negligence in our financial markets. Even after hundreds of billions of dollars of losses and the near destruction of our financial systems, there are those who are still opposed to regulations and oversight. I guess they are opposed to legal and ethical standards in the business, banking, investment, and corporate worlds. Just let the corruption continue until nobody will have any confidence in investing their money in anything but gold.

There are stock market investors whose portfolios are based mainly on foreign markets. Many of those are doing well and could not care less that America's economy is tanking. So here we have Americans who are selfish and greedy and could give a damn about the plight of jobless Americans. The stock market can do very well based on overseas investment while more and more Americans are jobless and losing their homes, health insurance, and life savings.

America is standing by, waiting for the economy to turn around as it has in other times in history. I see no reason why it will. I believe that the worst is yet to come. Right now, nearly every state and local government is facing historic deficits. They will be laying off perhaps millions of employees, cutting purchases of equipment, supplies, construction, health insurance, retirement investments, and so on. All of these will have a huge ripple effect throughout society. Those employees will lose their homes, further damaging the housing market. Their purchasing power will be reduced to near zero. College graduates will not find jobs, and most will default on their loans. (I wrote about this scenario over a year ago, and now our employment numbers are plunging once again.)

The government is the largest employer in the nation. Those severe cuts and layoffs are yet to come this coming fiscal year. This inevitable scenario is scary as hell to me and should be to all Americans. Yet government employees and their obscene benefits have risen to a level that it is impossible for taxpayers to sustain their services. Many of these employees refuse to make any concessions in regard to their pay, health insurance, or retirement benefits. They apparently would rather lose their jobs than make any concessions.

Many retire at an early age and then go back to work and continue to build their pensions through further taxpayer contributions. Many of them wind up getting paid more in retirement than they did while working. It's referred to as "double dipping". Meanwhile, we have millions of people out of work, homeless, and hungry. It's time for these people to work up to the legal retirement age for Social Security like the rest of us working stiffs. We simply cannot afford to give these people a life of luxury any longer.

Another factor to consider is that even the citizens who survive these worst of times are going to be very conservative in their purchasing habits. Our elders who survived the great depression became very conservative and scrupulous for the rest of their lives. They learned the value of saving for rainy days and never purchased merchandise unless it was essential to their lives. They bought homes they could afford, not brand-new dream homes. Americans of the present generation will always remember the fear and suffering they encountered in this severe recession. There will never again be the reckless and wild spending that drove the economy for the past few decades.

So as you can clearly see, the economy cannot possibly ever gain the traction that it enjoyed for the past few decades as long as the memory of this recession lives on in the minds of Americans. Considering all the factors listed above, any reasonable and logical analysis would indicate that there is little hope for anything but doom and much worse times for America.

The last thing in the world I wish to be is a prophet of doom. If I did not have clear and practical solutions to avert this disaster, I would not be writing this book. The next chapter will outline the only solutions that will put America back on its feet and let America soar like an eagle again.

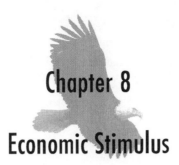

Chapter 8

Economic Stimulus

So far, every method that government has used to stimulate the economy has failed. Each party seems to think that if they get in power, they will wave a wand and the economy will magically recover. The Bush-era tax cuts did nothing but drive our national debt to astronomical levels never before imaginable. Actually, both parties are responsible for the lack of oversight of the financial markets and the mortgage industry, which did the most damage to the economy. Even after hundreds of billions of dollars of damage, there are still bureaucrats calling for deregulation and less oversight.

In the future, if the federal government is honestly intent on stimulating the economy by spending billions of dollars in loans that taxpayers will have to pay back with heavy interest, they should consider the proposal outlined below. Most of the stimulus dollars have been an absolute failure. In the future, they should consider printing special-issue hundred-dollar bills redeemable only at retail stores (no alcohol) or to hire the services of contractors and service industries or to buy American industry stocks. Those currency serial numbers should be recorded at the proprietor's bank in order to track their effectiveness.

In order to prevent mail theft, the recipients of these special bills should be mailed certificates for a designated amount of dollars redeemable at any bank or credit union with proper identification. The bank would then issue the special-issue bills to the recipient. This will force every dollar of stimulus directly into the American economy by requiring every citizen to spend the money on things like vehicles, clothing, food, home improvement, repairs, or investing in the stock market.

The manner in which hundreds of billions of dollars were wasted on foolish ideas in an attempt to stimulate the economy is unbelievable. When times are tough, people do not spend. They save ! Others waste it on liquor or drugs. Most will pay bills if they are heavily in debt, just as many pay bills with their income tax refunds. Little of this benefits or stimulates the economy, doing a grievous disservice to the citizenry responsible for this huge debt. It is the equivalent of burning a huge percentage of the stimulus money.

The stimulus package should have gone toward infrastructure jobs, retail purchases, research, and developing technologies. Not a dollar should have gone to education unless it was for the purpose of building schools or manufacturing needed equipment for schools and universities. Instead, hundred of billions have gone to states in support of colleges and universities. It is up to the citizens of each state to contribute to or finance the education of their students. Contributing dollars toward education is the same as paying overdue bills for the state. It clearly shows that many states underfund their education systems. There is no stimulus with those dollars, just debt relief.

Furthermore, we don't need more highly educated workers. There are already far too many out of work. We may need millions more trained or educated in the medical field if our nation adopts national health care. Another area suffering in the job market is engineering. Grants to encourage this field of education are imperative.

I will repeat again it is not the responsibility of the federal government to shore up the deficits of local and state governments either over-spending or under-funded. This is specifically why we have local and state taxing authorities to fund the societal needs of their states and communities. Stimulus funds do not stimulate an economy by bailing out strapped governments. It is up to the voters of a state or community to tax themselves according to their basic needs.

We should also create a special investment category with tax breaks for new technologies and products developed by companies that create new manufacturing jobs for Americans only. If they move any part of their manufacturing overseas in the future, they would then be penalized and required to pay back the taxes from which they were exempted.

Our nation's worst infrastructure crisis is the deterioration of thousands of bridges. Remember the bridge in Minneapolis that collapsed and left several people dead? Shortly afterward, it was revealed that thousands of bridges in this nation are deteriorating and in desperate need of rebuilding. Not only would rebuilding them create much-needed jobs in every community, but the taxpayers also would get a lot of bang for their buck—something to show for the phenomenal debt and interest to be paid in the future and perhaps eternally. So training in construction would be a better education investment.

Imagine spending hundreds of billions to stimulate the economy, creating jobs, generating taxes, and rebuilding bridges that would have to be closed if not rebuilt. Perhaps they will have to be closed before the public understands their value to society.

Another part of our infrastructure in desperate need of rebuilding is our natural gas pipelines. There have been several explosions and failures in this infrastructure in the past few years, causing numerous deaths. It has been reported that much of this infrastructure throughout the nation is deteriorating and in dire need of rebuildi:.g. This would be a good investment in infrastructure and jobs.

It is the American taxpayer's risk and debt. We should have a right to ensure our debt is a wise investment that will pay dividends for America and our future. We have to prove that our government can make wiser investments than the foolish bankers, stockbrokers, and mortgage industry.

Another issue government seems blind to is the hundreds of billions of dollars of revenue deficits all states are dealing with. I know the economy is suffering; however, when did these states determine that the loss of state sales tax through internet sales was going to catch up to them and create a huge deficit in their budgets? Duh !

What's even more amazing is that local merchants have not raised hell from the beginning. How long did they think they could compete with tax-free retail? Is it any wonder so many small entrepreneurs and local businesses have bit the dust? It is disgusting to see hundreds of shopping centers and thousands of retail stores closing due to online retailers like Amazon. Millions of jobs are lost, and local governments are bankrupt due to the loss of property taxes and sales taxes. Meanwhile, stock market investors get richer if they invest in online retailers. If I were king, all online retailers would be banned with the exception of companies that sell products that cannot be sold from a physical retail store.

All citizens and all communities should be very alarmed by this trend. Are we going to let our communities rot, leaving our citizens without jobs and our local governments going broke for lack of revenue? Are we going to allow all these vacant shopping centers to become graffiti-covered eyesores overgrown with weeds and cluttered with litter?

It is totally unfair to a state that has a retail sales tax for an adjacent state to have no such tax or a much smaller one. Thousands of citizens a day drive across the state lines to make purchases in another state. Additionally, it wastes fuel, adds to traffic congestion, and increases pollution.

Some states do not have retail sales tax. So the only practical solution is to have a national retail sales tax to replace state retail sales taxes. I propose that the tax rate be based on the average tax rate of all states that do have a state sales tax. The state where the products are manufactured or shipped from would split the tax revenue with the state that the product is sold to.

The local bank where the sales revenue is deposited would simply send the tax revenue to the state of origin and the local state. Of course, each state would pay a fee to those banks equivalent to what the costs are for tax collection and accounting per dollar. Or perhaps each state can utilize its own accounting personnel over a secure network, such as that used by financial institutions to transfer funds from one to another.

I also suggest that foreign sales be taxed by the same method. Additionally, I suggest that all interstate and foreign purchases be required to have their transactions run through a secured credit card network tied to a local bank or branch that can monitor and deduct tax revenues.

Mailing cash, checks, or money orders for retail sales would become illegal unless a tax certificate was purchased at a bank and a copy was included in the mailing.

All this seems very complicated. It would be simple just to implement a national sales tax. Abolish all state sales tax. The federal sales tax would be calculated by averaging all the sales taxes of states that have sales taxes. That way, all states will be equal, and it will stop the running across the border to make retail purchases. No state will be deprived of sales tax revenue or retail sales. Local retailers will not lose business to internet and mail-order businesses based on customers trying to avoid sales tax.

It's all about equality and fairness for all retailers. Each state would reap economic benefits and earn tax revenues to support its government services.

Most important of all is that all these taxes would go back to the communities where the sales originated. Interstate sales tax would be split evenly between the selling state and the recipient state. Internet and foreign nation sales would be split in the same manner. Is this method too logical, simplified, and fair for all?

By the way, shouldn't all government purchases and contracts be equally distributed among all states on a per capita basis? This could bring jobs to economically depressed states. Major military suppliers should be awarded contracts based on their locations and ability to locate to communities that are the most economically deprived. Some states would probably meet their quotas based on the number or size of military facilities within their states. Others would meet their quotas on the basis of IRS or Social Security offices and still others on the basis of military equipment manufacturing.

It would certainly be interesting to make a comparison of these economic drivers throughout the states. We need to find balance in federal employment while focusing on states with the worst unemployment.

With the recent crisis in the Middle East, our government would be wise to ban the manufacture and sale of internal combustion engines as the sole source of power in passenger vehicles in ten years. If the government can ban incandescent light bulbs, then why not internal combustion engines in passenger vehicles? Then we can quit worrying about defending the nations that supply our petroleum. This will save us hundreds of billions of dollars a year.

Then the federal government should give grants and low-interest loans to manufacturers of hybrid and battery-powered automobiles manufactured in the United States. Grants should also go to industries that manufacture charging systems and build charging stations at gas stations, shopping centers, and places of employment.

This can reduce greenhouse gases, spur economic development, provide millions of jobs, and end our dependence on foreign oil. Without our dependence on foreign oil, we can stop spending hundreds of billions of dollars on wars and nation building in the Middle East. Then we might be able to afford health care for all Americans. When will our federal government act on the inevitable crisis? When gas gets to be ten dollars a gallon?

There can be provisions for commercial vehicles and special license plates for business people that travel long distances. There can also be exceptions for people who live in rural areas or who must commute farther than current electric-powered vehicles can travel. In these situations, hybrid vehicles can be used.

We really need to conserve our remaining domestic petroleum for industry, heavy-duty trucks, and manufacturing. Petroleum in not an infinite resource. With the rapid economic growth of nations like China and India, the world's petroleum reserves soon will be depleted. There will be no legal recourse to prevent our domestic producers from selling to foreign nations when the price is right. This issue is ripe for future consideration and perhaps legislation to address this inevitable dilemma for our nation.

Everybody complains about the obscene salaries that corporations pay to their CEOs and top management. Government cannot regulate salaries and bonuses; however, there is something it can do. It can tax the hell out of obscene payouts. Nobody needs the hundreds of millions of dollars per year that so many get paid.

Chapter 9

Let the Eagle Soar Again

As I stated in the previous chapter, I see no evidence that America will recover from this recession rather than continuing to decline. Our economy was a *false economy* driven by reckless spending and unmanageable credit card debt.

I only see one possibility that can prevent a further catastrophic collapse of America's economy. That is if American citizens are willing to commit to it unanimously. There are certain problems in society that government cannot control and fix. There are problems that only the people can fix. Like Smokey the Bear used to say, "Only You Can Prevent Forest Fires". I say to you Americans (all of you) that only you can turn the economy around and prevent this country from becoming a third-world nation.

You've all heard about the concept for decades. It has only become a point of pride for a small minority of Americans. Millions of citizens proclaim that it is impossible to fulfill the commitment, because it is nearly impossible to find products made in America. Well, that is simply because we are not willing to stand our line, stop buying foreign products, and insist on American-manufactured products.

There has never been a greater need in history for Americans to collectively pull together and make a strong commitment to buying American products. There was a time in America's history during World War II when Americans pulled together and made extreme sacrifices in order to save the free world. Not every American was in a position to contribute, but those who could did. Now, all Americans, regardless of their positions in life, are capable of preventing the economic collapse of America and perhaps even the collapse of the global economy.

The United States government cannot adopt any such policies, nor should it be expected to. That would be very dangerous to international relations. However, we as citizens of America can collectively pull together and make a strong commitment to purchasing all the American-made products that are offered. Wouldn't this create fantastic unity and pride among all Americans?

We have come to expect government officials to solve all our economic and social problems. All government can do is throw more of our tax dollars at the dilemma and put it on a charge card for future generations to deal with. Well, I'm here to state that government cannot solve all of our problems. There are some problems that only American citizens can solve, and this is one of them. I guarantee you that if Americans stand together with this endeavor, the economy will thrive like never before in history. With a thriving economy, there are numerous other social ills that can be healed. The greatest gain would be the elimination of the national debt and the atrocious interest that Americans pay. We can do incredible things in this nation if we are not dumping the majority of our tax dollars into an endless pit of obscene interest and debt and failed stimulus packages.

We will be absolutely dependent on high-profile and popular Americans in order to be successful with this critical endeavor. I'm talking about athletes, artists, actors, actresses, talk show hosts, news commentators, corporate executives, and candidates for public office along with everybody else who has the public's attention.

Just as many government officials end their speeches or public appearances with the phrase "God bless America", all influential citizens should say, "Let the eagle soar again—buy American" !

The best place that America can start this mission is with the purchase of American-made automobiles. We should not care if the vehicle is a foreign brand, such as Toyota, Nissan, Volkswagen, or Hyundai. It should only matter that the vehicle is manufactured in America so that its construction provides Americans with jobs. There should be a certification emblem on all vehicles manufactured in America. This insignia would likely become a source of pride for Americans. I hope that artists can design such an insignia that all American manufactured vehicles can display, and there should be a similar insignia on all clothing, appliances, and other manufactured goods. A licensing fee would pay for the continuing promotion of the program.

Not only do we need to purchase American-manufactured products, but all the parts for those products must be manufactured in America. This will put tens of millions more Americans to work.

This movement could be an easy transition for all foreign manufacturers. There are scores of closed auto plants throughout America. So the foreign companies do not need to build new factories. All they need to do is lease and adapt those factories. But Americans have to prove that they will only purchase vehicles manufactured in America. The rest will all fall into place.

All current American manufacturers will need to put on a huge advertising campaign promoting the theme of supporting American jobs and building a strong American economy and future.

These methods can be extended to many other products manufactured in America. Let's use Nike as an example. I would guess that most if not all their shoes, equipment, and apparel are manufactured overseas. So they could experiment with manufacturing a specific line of products that bears an insignia proving those items to be made in America. If Americans stand together and prove to Nike that they will support the American products even if they cost more, we could prove that there is a strong market for such products.

Imagine retailers having sales for all American-made products and handing out discount coupons for American-made products as you enter their stores.

Now I'm going to prove how buying American-made products, even if they may be more expensive, would be beneficial to every American's pocketbook and future. If the economy never recovers, more and more people will continue to lose jobs. The stock market will tank, and pension funds will dry up. Crime will be rampant, and there will be drastic cutbacks in all government services. There will not be enough government funds to employ enough police for adequate protection.

There will be homeless and hungry people everywhere. There will be children suffering. Since Americans don't let their citizens go hungry, especially people with children, all the expense of keeping these households going, whether via taxes or donations, will fall upon those who are working.

We all know of the sacrifices of the Greatest Generation during World War II. When America faced the greatest threat to our freedom and democracy in our history, all Americans stepped forward and contributed. Current generations of Americans must now make sacrifices and covenants that we will all stand together and put America on track to be stronger economically than ever imagined.

So if we are capable of creating a healthy, thriving economy instead of succumbing to the above scenarios, won't we all be better off? Won't our investments, pensions, environment, and the future for our children and grandchildren be much better with a healthy and thriving economy ?

When all capable workers are employed, paying taxes, and contributing to Social Security and Medicare, the economy soars, and the future is bright for retirees as well as for our youth. More money will be available for research and education, which will put America on top in the technology world, and the stock market will soar. Then, of course, there is the factor and expense of social problems and crime. Would we rather pay billions more for more prisons, justice expenses, welfare for families, subsidizing food banks, health expenses, and a whole host of other social expenses that are essential when the economy is tanking?

There is no way that our economy can fail with a strong commitment by Americans as outlined above. Our foreign trade partners will not be that upset if we do not buy all their products during this recovery. They will understand that having a healthy American economy is essential to having a healthy world economy. They know that it is absolutely fundamental that America recovers economically if there is to be any hope for a world recovery.

Can we remember the years a decade or two ago when there were Help Wanted signs out all over town? We can get back there and beyond if we stand together and make a united commitment. We are the *United* States of America !

A catastrophic collapse of America's economy would be a threat to world stability, freedom, and democracy. The free world thoroughly understands these issues. The free world is absolutely dependant on an economically strong America for their own security and survival.

Another thing that is fundamental to America's recovery is that our government must invest heavily in alternative energy both for electricity generation and vehicle power.

If our federal government were wise, they would ban the internal combustion engine for passenger vehicles ten years from now. They could justify the ban on two different grounds. One is that the emissions and pollutants are hazardous to the health of citizens. As the population continues to grow, these problems are going to multiply The other is that fuel consumption is a national security issue; continuing to purchase oil from nations that support terrorism is not in the best interests of the United States. Were not nine of the twelve 9/11 terrorists from Saudi Arabia? We continue to increase the wealth of these Muslim nations, and they continue to build their arsenals and support terrorism with that wealth.

Terrorists and the financial support for terrorists originate from throughout the Arab and Muslim nations. We must quit aiding our destroyers. Perhaps at some point they will discover that investing in their own nations and people instead of in weapons and terrorism will make them much better off.

Personally, I have been back and forth on the issue of buying American. I have never been able to purchase a foreign-manufactured vehicle. At times in my life, I have almost felt that it would be sacrilegious to do so. Then, when America's economy was soaring, I looked at the situation a bit differently. I thought that if the products we purchased provided food and shelter for impoverished families overseas, those might be dollars well spent for the sake of humanity.

However, now I must look at this situation in a very different context. If America fails, the eternal hope for world peace and stability will never materialize. Billions may suffer as a result. A strong and thriving America will continue mankind's pursuit of peace, freedom, and equality for all of mankind. There simply is nothing of greater importance in the history of the world than mankind's quest and America's quest for world peace, freedom, and true democracy.

The stock market may stabilize, because most of the stock market is based hugely on foreign sales and foreign manufacturing. That will not do much for millions of middle-class Americans who need jobs.

I recall the message that Smokey the Bear has professed for decades: "Only you can prevent forest fires" ! Well, my fellow Americans, only you can save the economy of America ! Your government cannot do this ! Let's prove that our government cannot do what unified citizens can and that they cannot stop us from standing together and building the strongest economy in American history ! It's time to quit relying on bureaucrats, banks, and corporations and prove we are stronger than any of them and that we can solve more social problems than government officials can. On our government officials' watch, the economy of America has been destroyed. It's time for Americans to take back their country.

I'm sure that we are all familiar with the song "New York, New York". The lyrics say, "It's up to you, New York" ! We should borrow that phrase and adapt it to say, "It's up to you, America" ! The ball is in your court, Americans ! Shall we sink or swim?

We can pledge our allegiance to our flag and the United States of America everyday of our lives. However, this is nothing more than an empty gesture. Actions speak louder than words. Now is the time in our nation's history when our country needs our actions and commitment to save our nation from third-world status.

Can we call on some of our great patriotic songwriters to write an anthem for this mission? I guarantee you that if Americans stand together in this endeavor, we will not fail, and we will enjoy the greatest and strongest economy in history. If Americans fail to stand together in this endeavor, we will then deserve our destiny as a third-world nation ! The ball is in your court, America !

Let the eagle soar again ... Buy American !

Chapter 10

Blue-Collar Power

I have watched the inception of credit unions in America and their rise to power in the banking and finance world. Decades ago, government tried to do everything possible to prevent their growth and protect the investment bankers. It is amazing to watch them grow and gain power in the financial world. And they belong to the members. The profits go right back to members instead of some fat-cat investor. This is one of the greatest developments in America to narrow the gap between the rich and poor. However, they have only scratched the surface of their potential.

My first recommendation is that all credit unions combine and unify into one giant institution. The only reason there are so many different credit unions is because of the restrictions placed upon them by government in the early years. They restricted credit union membership so that each credit union could only serve a particular industry or craft in a restricted area. Now almost any working employee or small–business entrepreneur can join any credit union. So there is no practical reason for all these credit unions to exist independently. They can all unify into one giant universal financial institution.

In the business world, we know there is strength in numbers. This is why so many companies swallow up others as they expand their territory.

Each of these credit unions has to have officers, managers, staff and numerous specialists to operate. They also have to have numerous convenient locations throughout their territory. Some credit unions are far more successful than others and offer better rates, services, security, and other benefits. Some have better management and some are larger and more powerful.

So if you eliminate the duplicity of central management and staffing of all these different credit unions in a region and select the best professionals from the most successful operations, you will have a winning ticket. Then, if you eliminate numerous branches serving the same neighborhoods, you will eliminate huge expenses and overhead. You can imagine how much more efficient and profitable credit unions could become with such integration.

Can you imagine how fast Congress, financial institutions, and lobbyists would scramble to put and end to this threat? And this is just the beginning of how powerful blue-collar working Americans can become. Sure, all of those institutions will scramble to pass laws prohibiting this. However, they will be cutting their own throat, because blue-collar working Americans represent the strongest voting bloc in America.

Once American workers form the strongest and most powerful financial institution in the nation, we can start branching out into numerous other areas of commerce. Allow me to give an example. Have you noticed how fast Costco rose from being a startup in Washington to being one of the largest and most powerful retailers in the nation? I would guess they accomplished that in approximately twenty-five years.

Now imagine if a national powerhouse credit union decided to start up a retail operation designed on the Costco model in a test-market area. I chose Costco as an example because they are the most perfect illustration of how successful a corporation can become and at the same time provide decent pay and benefits to its employees, unlike Wal-Mart !

If the American workforce sticks together and makes a commitment to supporting this enterprise, it will kick Wal-Mart's ass, as well as that of Costco, Home Depot, and every other massive retailer. The workers of America will own them all. It would become the greatest co-op ever imaginable.

The Walton family would no longer dominate America's most-wealthy-billionaire's list. The billions of dollars all those family members possess through no effort of their own are obscene. Talk about being born with a silver spoon in your mouth ! I don't know how they live with themselves while so many of their employees struggle with low pay and without health insurance. If this united enterprise thrives, as I know it could, all those billions of dollars of profit will go back to their members in the form of a much better lifestyle for all.

I am proposing a name for this united credit union force. It comes from my own credit union of approximately forty years. It was formerly called the Spokane Railroad Credit Union. When government relaxed the rules and regulations for membership, it soon became the largest and most successful credit union in the Spokane area. Later they adopted the name Numerica. I don't know the how the name came to be chosen; however, it is very unique and all encompassing. To me it also signifies "numbers of Americans," an infinite number of Americans who could become the unified force of a financial empire for Americans, or even a new America dedicated to the unity of all working Americans and their commitment to standing together and thriving—the ultimate co-operative.

One provision I would strongly advise Numerica to adopt in the formation of this organization is that employees should not be allowed to form unions. Unions have made it impossible to get rid of lazy and unproductive employees. Instead, a creed should be formed to ensure that all honest and hardworking employees would be paid a living wage and treated fairly. If an employee of any of these Numerica industries and ventures were found to be incompetent or unwilling to perform his or her job based on average production and performance, he or she would be placed on probation and given an opportunity to bring his or her job performance up to average expectations.

Every hardworking American has an expectation that his or her co-workers perform their work up to average standards. Just as with successful sports teams, everybody is expected to pull his or her weight and contribute to the success of the team. I emphasize this provision very firmly due to the dilemma in America of lousy teachers in our education system and society's inability to get rid of them.

All credit union members would be encouraged to support the enterprise with a long-term goal and benefit to come. All that would have to happen is for all members to commit to supporting a venture they would own stock in, and this unified force would kick ass and put Costco out of business in that test market. If the credit union demonstrated its power in a few areas, Numerica would soon own Costco, Wal-Mart, and other major retailers. Those companies' investors would be glad to sell before their stock became worthless.

Well, this would only be the beginning for Numerica. As they grow their assets just like so many banks and financial institutions do, they would diversify into mortgage, insurance, industrial investments, pharmaceuticals, health care, retirement funds, and so on. Imagine the nonprofit health insurance empire that could be built if we could take the profit out of medical care. The sky would be the limit.

Imagine all hardworking and dedicated employees owning shares in employee-owned and supported industries without having the wealthy fat cats benefit from every dollar workers spend. Imagine how much better and more affordable life would be if the profiteers were not gouging citizens at every opportunity.

Our products and services would be reliable, honest, and safe. There would be no more purchasing phony products and incompetent services. Our stocks would be sound, because we would all support these industries and insist on ethical professionals with the greatest integrity.

Imagine having a strong financial institution that cares for the dilemmas so many face in building a life and assets. If you have a mortgage through a bank or financial institution and your employment is eliminated due to layoffs, downsizing, bankruptcy, buyouts, or some other factor beyond your control, the bank or financial institution does not care about your situation. If you have a major medical problem or disability, the banks don't care. An institution like Numerica could carry you for a period of time, downsize your housing or vehicle, and restore your credit when you got back on your feet.

No hardworking American would have his or her credit destroyed due to layoffs or medical issues. Americans may have to adjust their life-styles due to these unfortunate circumstances, but their credit will not be destroyed. They will not be blackballed from obtaining credit once they have restored their incomes and overcome their setbacks.

In the mean time, another member who might be ready to upgrade could take over the home or vehicle you could no longer afford. In other words, the organization would take care of its own and keep all the profits, property, and assets within the organization for working people to benefit. If members are loyal to all the member-owned investments or enterprises, they can grow the most powerful financial and investment institution in the world. There would be no corporation that could compete with the power of the people either politically or financially. This could completely reverse the ever-growing gap between the rich and the middle class in America. The people could actually become the corporate power in America.

Imagine that some American inventor came up with a great new technology to solve our reliance on oil and stop the proliferation of pollution in our atmosphere. Numerica could invest in that technology, and members could support the product and return the strong auto manufacturing industry to America. Imagine our corporate executives receiving fair and reasonable compensation for productive and successful leadership instead of the tens of millions of dollars a year corporate executives currently make for failure and the additional tens of millions of dollars they get as they go out the door.

So if American blue-collar citizens wish to see a stronger, thriving, and more successful nation, they can unite and commit to each other to build the greatest financial empire in society imaginable. There is no reason we should be supporting the lifestyle of arrogant billionaires while hardworking Americans continue to struggle more and more every year. We have the power of the people. We just have to learn how to organize and exercise that power and then make a strong commitment to it and to each other !

Chapter 11

Small Business Aid

The government apparently defines a small business as one with fewer than two hundred employees. I have a different definition of a small business. I would consider a small business to be one with from one to ten employees—a mom-and-pop operation or a small group of entrepreneurs.

Apparently three out of four small businesses fail in the first year. If it is so important that small businesses succeed in this nation, then why not give them a reprieve on state and federal taxes in their first two or three years of business? A new business faces insurmountable challenges when it starts up: tremendous advertising and marketing costs, the difficulty of finding and training new employees who can accomplish their goals, discovering errors and making corrections, and a long list of unforeseen circumstances.

Then the new business often has to compete with huge corporate conglomerates. If it is so important that small businesses succeed, why not give them incentives and breaks to assure their success? Some small businesses have turned into huge successful corporations. We need these successes now more than ever.

Those businesses that are larger than the ones I describe above should be classified as medium-sized businesses. If a business has grown to have more than fifty employees, it must be doing well and hardly needs the government's assistance or tax relief. Now, if there is a greater demand for their products, I have no problem with the government giving them a low-interest loan to expand those businesses' operations.

Chapter 12

Elections and Voters' Rights

It always amazes me how offended many voters become when they find they cannot cross party lines to vote for a candidate in a primary election. Apparently, they don't even know what a political party is. A political party is a public organization dedicated to a set ideology that seeks out candidates that best fit and commit to that ideology. The political party is not even required to vote for its candidates. It can select its nominees at meetings of party members. This is pretty much what a caucus is, and some states choose that method.

The parties are also aware of movements by other parties to infiltrate their primaries and vote for the weaker opponent. There are also truly independent voters who don't belong to a party. They become incensed when they cannot participate in a primary. Well, they do not belong to these parties, and it is not their right to participate in a party's selection of a candidate. They get to vote in the general election.

As long as we are on the subject of independents, why is it that there is no Independent Party? I cannot truly support the ideology of either the Democratic Party or the Republican Party. They both have their extremes and mandates I cannot support. In my opinion, political parties are for people who can't reason for themselves and have to put their trust in other people to make decisions that may or may not be in the best interests of all. Informed voters who pay attention to current events, read newspaper reports and editorials, and watch the news channels and debates are the ones truly qualified to vote.

Let me give an example of my own history of voting throughout the first two or three decades of my adult life. I was always captured by the ideology that it was my responsibility as an American citizen to vote. Nobody ever suggested that to be a responsible voter I should study the issues and candidates in order to make responsible decisions. So I voted. I voted for names that sounded good. I voted for women because it was a novelty at the time to see women in public office. I voted for candidates who were handsome and charming or who I had noticed on billboards. For most of the issues, initiatives, referendums, and so on, I would simply read the title, and if it sounded like a good idea, I would vote accordingly. I never read a voter's pamphlet in order to get the briefs of arguments for and against. But I always voted and was damn proud of myself for fulfilling my civic responsibility.

Now I am very ashamed of myself for voting then. I would have been doing my community and my country a favor by leaving these difficult decisions to informed voters. Thank God no issue or race was ever decided on the basis of my vote. However, I am sure many issues and races are decided by an electorate just as uninformed as I was. This is a very unfortunate aspect of democracy. There is absolutely no qualification for voting. As long as you can scribble a mark on a ballot, you can vote. You may not be able even to read a ballot or understand what you are voting for.

I will now bring up one of the most glaring mistakes I've ever seen by voters in my life. In the State of Washington, we had an excise tax on vehicles. This was a progressive tax based on the value of the vehicle. The wealthy paid much larger taxes on their luxury vehicles and on multiple vehicles. It did not stop them from purchasing those expensive vehicles or multiple vehicles.

In Washington, we are plagued with an antitax advocate who has made a lucrative occupation of coming up with one antitax initiative after another practically every year. One thing I have observed of the electorate is that they will always vote for a tax reduction or tax elimination. They never seem to understand the ramifications of doing so.

This excise tax was a tax that provided a huge portion of the revenue the state used for constructing and maintaining roads and public transportation giving relief to clogged highways. This man managed to convince citizens that getting rid of that tax would be great for them. The common people, who were paying a pittance compared to the wealthy, voted overwhelmingly to get rid of that tax. Now we have roads falling apart all over the state, no revenue to construct new roads, and little money to invest in public transportation.

The state legislature, realizing that the electorate was not capable of recognizing a critical emergency with transportation and exercising their legal authority, imposed a nickel-a-gallon gasoline tax in order to address the problem.

You see, this is why our nation is a republic. It requires a tremendous amount of study and insight in order to govern and make critical decisions to provide basic services and security for the public.

Last year, the State of Washington submitted a referendum to the four most congested counties in the Puget Sound area to rebuild a stacked thoroughfare that is in danger of collapsing, especially if a predicted earthquake happens. The referendum also included several road improvements, construction, and public transportation to relieve the severe congestion in the region. Traffic congestion is the public's number one complaint in the area. Yet they overwhelmingly turned down the referendum. The electorate, in effect, continues to stab itself in the back. And they continue to cut their own throats whenever a new tax initiative comes to the ballot.

What I am about to tell you is what no elected official could ever tell the public. It would be political suicide. The majority of the voting public is not capable of making decisions crucial to the economy and its own safety. If I were in a position of power in local government and the taxpayers refused to finance the necessary improvements and maintenance, I would just order the closing of dangerous roads until the improvements were made. After all, government's primary responsibility is to protect the public's safety. When it doesn't, it leaves the government open to charges of negligence and lawsuits.

Wouldn't it be a wonderful life if we didn't have to pay taxes? I'd even be for that—if magic could provide all our services and needs at no expense to the citizenry. So what it comes down to is that you get what you pay for. The majority of taxpayers have no idea how many needs there are in society and how difficult a job it is for legislators to balance the books and meet the most desperate needs and also keep the state in a progressive mode. If people could sit through a legislative session or watch all the public hearings on government and societal needs throughout the year, they might understand the difficult decisions government faces.

There was a time in this nation when the issues we voted on were fairly simple or pretty much black and white. In this day and age, government is forced to deal with so many complex issues that it would be almost a full-time job to keep up with the problems. Many manage to stay informed on issues of special interest only. Very few citizens have the time in their lives to keep abreast of all the complicated issues that government officials deal with. For a few, government and politics is a hobby and a special interest. These people find the time to stay at least somewhat informed on the most critical issues facing society. These are the citizens I wish to do the voting—the informed citizens, certainly not the citizens who are easily influenced by the high-priced political ads that manipulate the uninformed to vote one way or the other based on rhetorical bullshit. Decisions that voters are faced with are critical to society, the nation, and the world.

In later years, I began to look at issues on the ballot when I received my voter's guide and started studying the issues. I was so busy with my life that I was not able to read editorials and letters to the editor during that period. So I read the ballot title and then the argument in favor. I said to myself, "This sounds good" ! Then I read the rest of the arguments, and I came up with the opposite opinion. Sometimes I realized that the issue was very complex and important, so I studied it in depth.

Needless to say, I have learned the value of an informed electorate. It would be comforting to know that if I ever get so busy in my life again I could count on informed citizens to make the wise choices so critical to our society. I doubt that could ever happen, because once you become a political junky, you realize the importance of these decisions to society and the future of mankind, and there is no ignoring the issues.

Having learned these valuable lessons, I must also explain the dilemma ordinary citizens are dealing with. Life is becoming so complex for ordinary families that it is impossible for them to keep up with so many issues, especially for families with children and both parents working. It may be difficult for many even to find time to get to the polls.

Many people would become indignant if you suggested they should not have a right to vote and would take to the streets. There are also those who do nothing but listen to right-wing talk shows that label anyone of other political persuasions as the evil forces of the devil. Once in a while, I can agree with those talk shows, but most of the time, I have to shake my head in bewilderment. I can also find fault and extremism on the left. If a citizen wishes to make informed decisions, he or she must be capable of examining both sides of any issue and understanding the long-term ramifications of those decisions.

So now I will get to the meat and potatoes of this chapter and likely the most controversial issue that government and voters might ever deal with. It may be more controversial than the right to bear arms. I am suggesting that the right to vote in a democracy carries with it a responsibility to be informed on the issues. Voters should be required to take a brief quiz every couple of years to prove they keep up on the issues and have studied the pros and cons of issues. If they do not pass the test, they should be disqualified from voting for the next year. The following year, they can come back and prove they are informed. They might also have to identify different elected officials in their counties and states as well as noting their political affiliation. It could all be multiple-choice so there would be no strain on memory.

This concept is not all that unusual or convoluted. We actually live in a republic, which is not a complete democracy. When our nation was formed and the Constitution was written, there must have been a history that proved that well-educated citizens and professional lawmakers were much more capable of legislating and addressing everyday problems than the general electorate. They realized that legislating required full-time professional attention and legal expertise. I now have much more confidence in our representatives than I do in the electorate (except for their decision to attack Iraq; I'll never understand the logic in that).

We had kicked Saddam's butt in 1992, and the UN weapon inspectors had found no weapons of mass destruction in repeated inspections. All of these dangers and problems we have been dealing with for the past five years were clearly spelled out in advance. The only thing that I can imagine must have persuaded Congress to approve the pre-emptive attack is the fear instilled in Americans by 9/11 and their lust for retaliation along with the fear of not being re-elected if they opposed the attack. That is clearly not the way to serve your constituents with integrity and honor. You have to stand up for your internal instincts, regardless of political pressure. A vote to go to war can set off economic ruin, world conflict, and perhaps a lifetime of responsibility to prevent the conflict from spreading. So I only hope America and the world have learned a valuable lesson as a result of this poor decision.

The most important reason voters must retain control of government is that the pendulum always swings right and left over a period of time. This is very healthy for democracy. Either side will tend to take you too far in one direction. This is where the independent voters become so valuable. They are at the center of the pendulum.

That brings me back again to the issue of why there is not a strong independent and moderate political party in this nation. We have the Republican Party representing the corporate interests of our nation and the warmongers. Of course, they have to align themselves with the Christian right in order to continue to exist. If the Christian right became too powerful, we would be living in a theocracy, and that scares the hell out of too many Americans.

Then we have the left side of the spectrum, which would lead us into total socialism if it got too powerful. However, if you value your life, the environment, and the world you leave to your children and grandchildren, then you must appreciate the left's commitment to fighting for our best interests and the interests of future generations. Somebody has to keep the corporate interests in check, because corporations care only about making obscene profits and not at all about citizens' health and welfare, let alone the world we leave to future generations.

Very few liberal warriors fight for their own interests. You have to appreciate individuals fighting for the environment, the poor, the mentally ill, the elderly, people suffering, animals suffering, children, and the future of mankind. There is no profit in their battles. You might consider them the saints of mankind's future.

Somewhere in the middle, you would expect to find candidates who recognize the value of having a strong military yet are dedicated to diplomacy, candidates who realize the value of industry and commerce yet have a regard for employees' health and welfare, candidates who realize the importance of education to our society and who wish to find the balance between the extremities.

Wouldn't it be great if a leader came along who would not have to sell his soul to adopt the extreme ideology of a party platform but would commit to finding a balance that best served all of society? Well, hopefully the right candidate will appear someday and create a well-needed political change in America.

While we are on this subject, I would like to throw out this suggestion. I believe that with all the complexities in society and the world, the duties of the President of the United States have become too difficult and time-consuming for one individual to handle with the necessary attention. I therefore propose that the duties be split between two elected officials. They would not be on the same ticket but elected independently of one another.

The president would be the commander-in-chief of the military, just as he or she is now. It might be somebody with military expertise; however, the priority would be that this person be the best collaborator and diplomat we could offer to the world. General Colin Powell comes to mind.

The vice-president would preside over the internal affairs of the nation. That individual would likely be a former congressperson or a proven governor who had pulled off impressive successes in his or her state. This individual would have the final say on any legislation enacted by Congress involving the internal affairs of the nation..

I would also suggest that the members of the House of Representatives become the official lobbyists for their states. They would present their ideals and the greatest needs for their districts to the House. If the majority of the House of Representatives approved unanimously, the issue would be passed on to the Senate for approval. Our Senate is composed of the proven leaders in federal government. You have to be a proven leader and legislator to rise to the Senate of the United States. Any common citizen can be elected to the House of Representatives, and often they have little or no competition. Their only requisite is that they can meet with lobbyists and get in bed with them. The more favors they do for them, the more finances they gain for their campaigns. The more finances, the better chance for re-election.

The only exception I would make is to allow journalists to qualify for the highest offices. They spend their entire careers researching and studying the issues at length, much more than most politicians do. There are numerous journalists who would make outstanding leaders of our nation. Let's start paying attention to them and inspire them. Our nation desperately needs their intelligence, integrity, and leadership.

This brings me to the point of promoting an informed and qualified electorate. The founding fathers never could have imagined how corporate interests would control the direction of this nation today. They would be so very ashamed of what this nation has become. It is for sale to the highest bidders. This situation was already bad enough, and now the Supreme Court, by a narrow margin, has given billion-dollar corporations and unions the right to spend as much money on elections as they choose to. Our democracy just went up for sale to the highest bidder. Shame on our Supreme Court justices. They have just destroyed our democracy. The basis for their decision is freedom of speech. The Constitution guarantees individuals freedom of speech, not corporations, and especially not foreign nations !

America has an obligation to perfect democracy and set an example throughout the world to show that democracy is the best form of government, giving hope to all mankind and not just the corporate interests of mankind. Some might say this is not our responsibility. To them I would say that if the world does not unify to strive for democracy and world peace, then whoever has the most money will rule the world. This is not a case of crossing that bridge when we get there; we will be dead before we get to the bridge.

Our democracy has become a complete sham. It is an embarrassment to even refer to it as a democracy. Who are we trying to fool? Much of the world sees through this sham of democracy. America receives more attention than any other nation. Most nations of the world are hopeful that one day they—and perhaps all nations of the world—will be the beacon of hope they once thought us to be.

Our government could be more accurately described as a corporocracy. A corporocracy is a nation totally controlled by corporate interests and their money. This is exactly what we have in America.

Every election season, hundreds of millions of dollars are spent to buy glorified messages and promote beautified candidates both nationally and locally. Where does the electorate imagine these millions of dollars come from? It certainly does not come from hardworking citizens and families. It comes from billion-dollar corporations. Why do they spend that kind of money? Because the investment comes back ten fold or even more than a hundred fold. They realize they can brainwash an uninformed electorate in almost any manner they wish.

One of the most lucrative businesses in politics is the ability to produce beautified and glamorized candidates. Political consultants, strategists, photographers, and writers used to twisting logic have become essential parts of a political campaign—and their methods have been proven to work. If you spend enough money, you can buy any vote or election. These professional people know they can bullshit the uninformed public into feeling good about voting in their favor. It's all about effective marketing, and it matters little what the actual truth is. There are no laws against twisting the truth and exaggerating in political advertising.

Now, if these candidates and special-interest groups had to reach informed voters, they would soon realize that they could not bullshit them in the same way. These people have studied the issues and candidates extensively, and no amount of bullshit will influence their votes. Certified voters would likely watch local and national government channels often and would be so informed on the issues and elected officials that they would be immune to the millions of dollars spent on political ads.

The marketing firms producing these high-priced political ads count on an uninformed electorate. It is absolutely obscene and a disgrace to democracy that they spend millions to brainwash the citizenry and beautify worthless candidates. The worst part of this dilemma is that all candidates have to cater to the special interests and corporate interests in order to be able to compete. Even honest and decent candidates become obliged to these interests. Once you accept their money, you owe them big time.

With a certified electorate, these candidates and special interests could spend or waste all the money they wished; however, it would be in vain. A certified electorate would be immune to million-dollar television ads and fancy brochures.

America no longer has a right to point with pride to our once-proud democracy. It has become blackmail, extortion, corruption, prostitution, espionage, deception, exaggeration, and practically every evil force imaginable. Are we as Americans to be proud of our political system, a political system for sale to the highest bidder?

The Electoral College and Super Delegates

As you can likely surmise from my disapproval of elections determined by uninformed citizens, I have much respect for the electoral college and the system of super delegates. The problem with the electoral college is that it does not represent voters accurately. Where did they come up with the formula that states, for instance, that if one candidate receives 51 percent of a state's vote and the other receives 49 percent, one candidate gets 100 percent of the electoral votes? It would be more democratic if the electoral votes were awarded on the basis of the percentage of citizens' votes that went to each candidate. This would be true democracy, not the stupid system that most states utilize. However, these individuals are appointed to be electors on the basis that they have the integrity and intelligence necessary to determine who is fittest to be the leader of our nation. If they simply represent the public's sentiment, then there is no reason for their position in the election process. They damn well should have a free hand in voting for the candidate of their choice, and their vote should be counted on a national scale.

I have noticed that since the advent of television, the person elected president has usually been the more handsome and charming candidate. It has become more of a popularity contest than we realize. Let's take the election of George Bush as an example. If you watched the debates carefully prior to his election, you know that he fumbled badly and demonstrated his lack of knowledge in many areas. But he was handsome, charming, and humorous. I must admit I can't hate the man. I'd like to have a few beers with him or play a round of golf with him. However, that was before he became a candidate for president. Now I would have to say, "No, thank you. I can never forgive you for the permanent damage that you have done to America and America's image throughout the world"! So much for respecting the office.

This is why super delegates are such a good idea. Their wisdom and experience in government makes them a hell of a lot more qualified than the millions of voters who think government elections are popularity contests. They have no obligation to satisfy the uninformed electorate. Their decisions should be based on their honest assessments of who can be trusted to make the critical decisions the nation may be living with long after we are all dead. Super delegates have much more wisdom and integrity than the electorate. They should have no obligation whatsoever to honor the public's choice.

I believe we have all generally assumed that if one president leads us in a wrong direction, we can make corrective actions by choosing the next president and Congress. The damage that President Bush has done by his pre-emptive attack on Iraq will live with us forever. Most of our would-be allies are saying, "You broke it; you fix it," or, "You can live with your own mistakes," just as a parent should say to a child who makes a mistake. America made a huge mistake in electing the handsome and charming George Bush, and we will likely be paying for that mistake throughout history.

So the bottom line is that the largest segment of swing voters are citizens who do not do the research required for making an intelligent choice.

There is likely a good percentage of voters who don't even know the difference between the Democratic and Republican Parties except that one has a donkey as a mascot and the other has an elephant. I'm sure if you asked them who best represents their positions, they would not have a clue. I have learned through experience that this is very true. And it does not just apply to the poor and unfortunate in society. Far too many people are just uninterested and have no idea how important elections are to their lives. So when I hear the public whining about their choice not being honored by super delegates and the electoral college, I just want to throw up!

I am sure of one thing: politicians and pundits will come racing out of the woodwork to distract from the damage I may have done to their empires by pointing out how insulting I have been to the citizenry. That's all right! I would expect no less when their lucrative business practices are in danger of being exposed. I get my greatest chuckles when politicians state that voters are smarter than the media gives them credit for. Of course, that is only stated by pundits and politicians when the public votes in favor of their agendas. Often, this is when citizens turn down a tax or regulation that, although they may not realize it, would be in their own best interests and the best interests of society as a whole.

Voters, in general, do not like being regulated. If it were not for regulations, we would all be dead. That is why intelligent legislators are so valuable to society, provided they have not been bought off by special interests. They listen to hundreds of hours of testimony from experts in order to make the tough decisions. Few of us have the time or commitment in our lives to do the same.

We should give serious consideration to placing skilled and knowledgeable voters in a position to vote if we wish to elect the most qualified candidates and make the best decisions about ballot issues that are of paramount importance to our society. Special interest money should not control our elections. This is an absolute insult to our democratic form of government and sets a very bad example for the world.

Chapter 13

Military Draft and Public Service

There is nobody in America who understands and appreciates the sacrifices our military personnel have made for our freedom and democracy better than me. Every enlistee takes an oath offering his or her life for his or her country. That does not mean the geographic country, as some might interpret it. It is the citizenry of this nation and all the freedoms we enjoy, every single, solitary one of us.

So isn't it amazing that the majority of Americans make absolutely no sacrifice, not even community service, compared to the tremendous sacrifice that soldiers make? Would it be asking too much for every citizen to volunteer for some form of national or community service at some point in their lives before the age of thirty? Those who are not going to attend college could enroll in the military, the Peace Corps, or some similar organization. They might choose missionary work overseas. Those going on to college could offer valuable services either in their communities or overseas. Medical doctors, engineers, scientists, agriculture specialists, teachers, and so on could be of great value both in their community nonprofit organizations and overseas.

Imagine how much respect and gratitude this nation might gain if instead of spending our labor and money on military operations, we helped poor and deprived countries throughout the world. It would likely prove more effective than flexing our military might and fighting impossible-to-win wars.

There are so many areas in which people volunteering could make huge contributions to society: driving disabled citizens to doctor appointments and stores, delivering meals to the elderly and disabled, volunteering to work for Habitant for Humanity, delivering prescriptions and other necessities to elderly or disabled citizens, working at animal shelters, fighting forest fires—the list of ways to serve the community is almost endless.

Prisoners ... Perhaps a Valuable Resource

This nation is missing out on a valuable resource that is instead costing us billions of dollars a year. Most prisoners can be incorporated into the armed forces and work off their debts to society. They can be utilized in special forces that have special monitoring and specific missions of great value.

Most prisoners are punks who have just never grown up. This could be a very valuable experience in their lives that could open their eyes and give them the opportunity to learn the value of rules and regulations in society. If they complete their duty with valor and honor, they could be given a pardon or perhaps parole.

Society knows the value of military experience in getting teenagers to grow up and become men and women. There is no reason why this growing-up experience could not apply to prisoners and transform them into contributing members of society. This could be a huge gain for taxpayers and society in general. It certainly deserves a chance to prove its effectiveness. There certainly is nothing wrong with experimentation.

Just like any other experiment in social science, it will not be 100 percent effective. There will be trials and tribulations and lessons to be learned. Among those lessons will be the discovery of certain personality types that will not work out. A profile of a person's conduct in prison will give valuable input as to how well that person may qualify. If a prisoner volunteers, he or she could be given a series of psychological tests to evaluate their likely effectiveness. On the other hand, a bully in prison might make a great leader or soldier on the battlefield. Aggressive personalities often become the very best soldiers and leaders both in the military and in society as well. It all likely will require much study and experimentation.

These ideas certainly deserve strong consideration, because our prison populations are growing beyond our ability to house them. This problem is only going to become worse in the future due to the irresponsibility of our youth, the ever-increasing drop-out rate in our failing schools, and the ever-expanding discovery of mind-altering drugs. Society absolutely must do something different in the future, or we will be swallowed up by these problems.

Another issue concerning the military: many soldiers are charged with crimes while they are deployed in war zones. There is little consideration for how much stress our soldiers endure twenty-four hours a day, three hundred sixty-five days a year. There have never before been wars in which soldiers had to be on guard against the enemy so continuously, without breaks in safe zones.

The mental stress can drive people crazy and cause overreaction and poor judgment. Soldiers experiencing this kind of stress sure as hell should not be charged with crimes, and the nation where they are stationed should not be able to try these soldiers. The most severe punishment should be discharge from the service. Rape would be the exception to the rule. That crime is not caused by stress.

Chapter 14

Universal Language

Historians have universally claimed that the greatest problem in the history of mankind is the lack of communication. Since the English language is the universal business language and seems to be gaining a great foothold in most of the world, wouldn't it be a tremendous accomplishment for mankind to get the world to use a single language for communication?

We have a difficult time communicating in our own language. How can we have any hope of communication across many different languages? Some words or thoughts simply do not translate between many languages, and there is too much margin for error. Often, we are victims of nations with anti-American agendas that translate our actions and words to fit their agendas.

Wouldn't it be wonderful if the words and actions of our leaders and influential citizens could travel unfiltered to the world? Some of the greatest events occur in the English language. How can the world enjoy our great movies and cultural events if they do not understand the language?

With the advent of the internet, America can easily offer a software program that will help the entire world learn English easily. Our government should simply search for the best and easiest-to-learn software program. Then it should buy the program and offer it to the world on the internet for no fee.

I believe that millions of Americans wish we could receive the news and other cultural events from foreign nations daily. We could better understand their problems and views if our language was the same. I have to believe that the opposite is also true.

Let's face the facts. The reason there have been hundreds of languages throughout history is that mankind was divided by geography. Each tribe had to develop a method of communication among its people. There is no longer a reason for not having a single worldwide language. There are communication systems and inexpensive programs for learning the English language available for the entire world.

If we wish to solve common worldwide problems and gain a better understanding of international problems, we should invest immediately in programs to get the world on a level of understanding and communication. We give billions of dollars to foreign nations, and the masses do not even understand where those contributions came from nor why. As a result, most of that money falls into the wrong hands and defeats our purpose.

It's interesting that the United States can give millions, hundreds of millions, and even billions of dollars in foreign aid to nations. However, when that aid ceases, many nations continue to hate the United States. Sometimes, a change in leadership causes the tide to turn. Then all the good will is banished.

Many years ago, when I first conceived the idea of a universal language, I was open to other languages that might be adopted. Since then, I have noticed that it is actually the English language that is the universal business language. I have also been surprised to find that due to the availability of television worldwide, many citizens of foreign nations already speak the English language fluently. Many business signs in foreign nations are printed in English.

So I guess that the world has already spoken. English is the language of choice. I would also guess that it is the most descriptive and definitive of all languages. However, the language could sure use some work in order to make it easier to learn and understand. I mean a major overhaul. It's almost as if the people who invented many of the words were illiterate or arrogant or both.

Language seems to be almost sacred, just like religion. Nobody ever dares to question spelling or pronunciation. So the errors live on throughout history and make it very difficult for foreigners to learn and understand the English language.

One language issue I do not understand is why citizens who immigrate to America from Eastern European countries and former Soviet republics do not adjust their names to make them easier to pronounce. Those names seem to lack any vowels, and even a person skilled in the English language would have difficulty pronouncing their names.

Those immigrants have the right to change their names or adapt the spelling when they enter the United States. Millions of immigrants in the past have changed their names or at least their spelling in order for Americans to be able to pronounce them. Why would you wish to make it impossible? If you want people to know you, they have to know your name first and foremost. Many of those names leave you totally confused, exasperated, and without a clue.

Of course, there is also the issue of ridiculous and embarrassing names. Why people do not choose to change their names is beyond understanding. Let me tell you, people who are stuck with such crude names, that you do not owe it to your ancestors to continue the tradition ! Just because your parents did not have the intestinal fortitude to change their names does not mean that you should be stuck with a name that is uncomfortable to you. Your name and reputation should be of your own choice. Your name is one of the most personal possessions you own. You should be comfortable with it.

Chapter 15

Ten-Year World Peace Experiment

At no time in the history of mankind, to my knowledge, has there been an effort for world peace. There have always been wars, saber rattling, or nations building their arsenals for war.

Don't we owe it to mankind to at least prove or disprove what we can accomplish if we all lay down our arms and focus on how much better the world could be without war and the constant buildup of arms?

I am pleading with the world, for once in the history of mankind, to find out whether we can do better without the constant wars and threats of war. Instead, we might ask our enemies what their greatest needs are and how we can help with those needs, how we might intervene between other warring factions and help each one achieve prosperity through peace, assistance, and cooperation.

I am calling on all the superpowers and warring factions of the world to call a truce for a period of ten years. I am proposing a ten-year period during which all nations take a hiatus from manufacturing weapons, waging war, and training for warfare. Instead, we would all retrain our troops to engineer and build systems throughout the world that will enhance the lives of our enemies and other warring factions. We will ask our enemies what they most need. It may be a hospital, a school, an irrigation system, a reservoir, a dam, a water sanitation system, a power grid, teachers, agricultural technology, or a variety of other things.

Even if some nations would not choose to participate in assisting other nations, they would benefit immensely from investing in and building based on their own direst needs.

It would be similar to the effect on our nation of suddenly finding itself without crime. We would not need police, prosecuting attorneys, court staffing, prisons, prison staffs, probation officers, and so on. While that scenario is impossible, if there were no international threats, doing away with the huge expense of national defense could be a reality.

If all nations of the world put a moratorium on military actions and aggression, it might prove that mankind is capable of much better than we have ever imagined. It could turn the hearts of human beings and provide a beacon of hope for the destiny of mankind.

If we can prove that we can do much better than what has been the routine throughout history, then nobody will have lost an edge. I can't image that even the most wicked and evil of nations could turn their backs on the greater good that could be achieved in a world committed to goodness and compassion for all of mankind.

I know that the world has experienced less ambitious versions of the above proposals. It has been exhilarating and heartwarming to see how the world responds to nations struck by disaster. It is unbelievable how our inner compassion for each other comes out in times of disaster. The survival instinct of mankind suddenly kicks in, and all our differences become trivial. The greatest mystery of mankind is why we can't live our daily lives dedicated to the betterment and happiness of all mankind. Why is it that the majority of us revel in being better and superior to others? Would it not be better if we could all hope for happiness, financial security, and achievement for our neighbors? Wouldn't it be better if we could find more fulfillment in life by celebrating the victories and achievements of our neighbors, our neighborhoods, our nation, and all the nations of the world?

If we cannot live for a decade in peace, then there is little hope for the future of mankind on this earth. We will all just keep developing weapons that ultimately will lead to the destruction of all life in this world. It's unbelievable that after all these thousands of years, mankind is not yet civilized and that all nations still cannot work together for the betterment of all. What could the people of the world have to lose from this moratorium?

If all the powerful nations of the world pull together and pledge to stop all weapon manufacturing, military training, and military research and instead pledge to do all they can to help their enemies with their greatest social needs, we may discover a path to world peace and prosperity.

If nations are reluctant to participate, I would like to know what their reasoning might be. They would certainly be castigated by the world. I suppose the rest of the world could place an embargo upon those nations. If all nations stood together, they could force that nation into compliance. Nevertheless, it would be foolish not to participate and reap the benefits of cooperation.

If we all fulfill that pledge, what would any nation lose? If we fail to accomplish any success in this mission, what would any nation lose? We could just all go back to business as usual and build our weapons and armies to destroy mankind's existence. It would prove we are not capable or intelligent enough to live together on the same planet and that mankind is in fact worse than the animals and too ignorant to find peaceful resolution, hell-bent on our own extinction. The difference between animals and human beings is that humans use our intelligence to destroy, and mankind is not capable of living in a civilized world.

We all enjoy reports and statistics demonstrating achievement in our communities and nations. We should celebrate those achievements and pay strict attention to our failures. We should also appreciate other communities and nations that achieve prosperity and success. Those nations and communities provide a guide for the communities that are failing. We should all look upon those successes as a source of hope, inspiration, and guidance for all mankind.

Rogue nations and dictatorships should ask themselves what harm can come to them if we all lay down our weapons for a period of ten years and pick up tools to build a better infrastructure and assist our enemies who are suffering in poverty and despair.

Suppose we experimented with this idea and made such an offer to North Korea. If we could promise North Korea that we would help them become a strong, enterprising economic power like South Korea, how could they refuse our offer? Suppose we made an offer to Iran to build a nuclear power facility or oil refinery and maintain if for them. What would they have to lose?

If the entire world would participate, we could all spend one year retraining our troops for construction jobs, engineering tasks, water sterilization projects, medical work, agriculture, and a whole host of other humanitarian efforts. You might consider it turning the militaries of the world into a Peace Corps for a ten-year period, a ten-year period to determine whether mankind, for the first time in history, can prove that we can do better for the world than the destructive wars we have fought throughout history. Are we any more civilized and intelligent than we were in prehistoric times? Or will we remain on a path toward the eventual destruction of the world?

Chapter 16

Pharmaceuticals

I don't know what it is going to take to get our elected officials out of bed with the pharmaceutical lobbyists. This is the worst travesty I've ever witnessed in politics. Not only will our government not negotiate reasonable prices for our prescription drugs, but they allow the patent holders to blackmail other companies when the patent is due to expire. They pay them hundreds of millions of dollars not to manufacture generic versions of their obscenely priced drugs. There might as well not be patent expirations. You would expect, if anything, that the government would be shortening patent protection. Instead, government allows all kinds of loopholes to extend patents on expensive drugs. Laws are laws, so why are these extensions allowed? Kind of suspicious, isn't it?

When pharmaceutical giants come out with a new prescription drug that does wonders, they make a killing in the first year. If the patent expired in three years, they would still be rewarded very well and should be satisfied. The way the government protects them, you would think they had come out with the wonder drug of all time with absolutely no side effects. This might be worth long-term patent protection. However, all these drugs have serious side effects for some people.

What is really a travesty is that a good percentage of people cannot take these drugs, and some suffer severe side effects or even death. You can pay hundreds of dollars for a prescription. Yet if it doesn't work, you cannot take it back and get a refund. Our elected officials don't care as long as they please their lobbyist friends; they are the ones who count. They certainly don't care about the poor citizens who pay hundreds of dollars for experiments and have to throw them in the trash. You can't even legally sell them or give them to somebody who could benefit from them.

Strange, isn't it, that our immediate neighbors to the north and south can negotiate prices for these drugs that are half and sometimes even one-third the price that Americans pay. If that doesn't show you how corrupt and uncaring our legislators are, nothing will convince you.

I discovered something a few years ago that surprised me. Our federal government actually owns a number of patents or shares them with corporations. I have no idea how many there are, and I also don't know what our government gets in return. Somebody else can do that research. What I do know is that billions of our tax dollars are given out every year in research grants. Many of those billions lead to fantastic products and technology that provide billions of dollars in profit for shareholders. Does that not make taxpayers investors and shareholders in those products and that technology?

I would guess that the majority of products and technology come as a result of our tax dollars. Even if those innovations do not come as a direct result of our grants, likely the companies that discover them first started as a result of government grants. In other words, the billions of dollars these corporations reap are a result of the investment of our tax dollars. Should we not expect a return on our investment, or should we just stop investing?

The result is that the fat cats get fatter on our generosity and willingness to take risks for them. The taxpayers put up the investment, and if the research succeeds, then the private research and development companies step in and reap the rewards. We take the gamble, and they get the benefit.

Make no mistake—I am certainly not against capitalism and government investment of taxes. It has made America the most successful economic power in the world. It has given us the capital to invest in weaponry and technology to defend freedom and democracy in America and around the world.

What I am suggesting is that the taxpayers' investment and risk should pay dividends to some degree. The best way to invest those dividends would be in the social security and health care of all working Americans. This is what investors in the stock market do. They endeavor to secure their futures. The problem is that those who are financially well off keep getting richer beyond their needs, and the working class keeps getting poorer and obtains little financial security for old age or cannot afford medical care that will get them to retirement. The dividends from investment in research can become a partial solution to the deepening divide between the rich and the poor in this nation and around the world as well. America has an obligation to perfect democracy and be a beacon to the world by working toward solving the tragic and astonishing poverty and suffering in the world. It would help if our own health and welfare were sustainable. We have to do something to offset the hundreds of billions we spend on our military to keep the rest of the world stable.

Another issue that upsets me is that prescription drugs do not have adequate information on the bottles. They should all contain information as to what the drug is intended for—anti-inflammatory, muscle relaxant, antibiotic, blood pressure regulator, anticoagulant, antidepressant, etc.

They should also include information that informs patients of the best time to take the medicine: on an empty stomach, after a meal, a certain number of hours after eating, in the morning, etc. The label should also note if a particular drug is not to be taken with certain foods, prescriptions, or health supplements. All the manufacturers care about is selling their products, and they couldn't care less about whether those products work or whether they might be more effective if the patient avoids certain foods or supplements. All the drug companies give you is pages of possible side effects, even including situations that affect only one in a million people. In other words, they cover their asses. They cannot be bothered to study the mixing of different prescriptions, foods, or health supplements. I guess if the government cannot force these studies, it would be a good investment to create grants that would allow medical departments of colleges to study these situations. Prescription drugs should improve our health, not be detrimental to it. There is a whole lot of chemistry involved. Many chemicals simply do not mix.

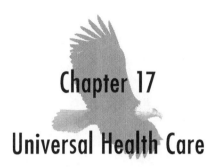

Chapter 17

Universal Health Care

Many citizens in this nation fear universal health care as if it were some socialist plot to force the wealthy to pay for everybody else's health care. To some extent, this is true. Taxing the wealthy and upper-middle class is how our nation became a superpower in the world. The wealthy or higher income earners have always paid the lion's share of taxes. This is the same method that has built churches, funded their social services for the poor of the congregation, and supported overseas missionaries aiding impoverished nations. Most churches request ten percent of a family's wages to be tithed to the church, which means that the most well-to-do members of the congregation pay much greater sums than the less well off.

The same formula has created a prosperous and powerful nation. I wish that I were rich or even well off. I would love to be able to pay a huge tax bill. That would mean I had done very well in my job or profession. I could live the good life, secure my future, and contribute to the betterment of the downtrodden. What better life could you live?

So yes, if we have universal health care, the wealthy and well-to-do will pay more. But aren't we already paying for health care for those who can't pay? Somewhere in our history, mankind decided we would help to preserve the lives of every human being. I believe some do not deserve that consideration, but my opinion is overruled by public opinion. I despise the worst of criminals and cover this in another chapter.

We can, however, do many things to place responsibility for health care in the hands of individuals. First of all, we have to consider how almost every form of insurance works. The main objective of health insurance is to protect against catastrophic expenses incurred in the event of a major health crisis.

There will never be any form of insurance that will be able to cover everything like Medicare does. And it is likely that we will soon find that Medicare cannot continue to cover all medical expenses. There have to be deductibles, and there have to be co-pays for every medical expense. Even low-income citizens have to pay certain up-front costs. Without their health, they may not be around to worry about rent, food, and other expenses.

Of all the expenses each of us prepares for in our budgets, health care has to be the number-one priority in our lives. You cannot provide for any budgeted items without your health. Any responsible form of family budget has to provide a certain amount each month to be set aside for medical expenses. I am referring to doctor visits and prescription expenses.

Many medical insurance plans and prescription insurance plans have a deductible or a co-pay (or both) for each office call or prescription purchase. This works in the insurance industry, and it would be wise for any universal insurance plan to follow that model.

Many people believe they should run to the doctor for every little sniffle, illness, or discomfort. What they fail to realize is that the body is by nature designed to fight off most illnesses and injuries. Most of these health problems will heal themselves given a reasonable amount of time. They often pressure their doctors to prescribe antibiotics that are not necessary and actually decrease the ability of antibiotics to fight diseases in the future.

This is the exact reason why many insurance companies or HMOs require a co-pay for doctors' office calls. All universal insurance plans should include a co-pay as well. There must be some incentive for individuals to use discretion when deciding whether to go to the doctor. Perhaps there would be a much better chance for the program to work if there were certain co-pays and deductibles for many other procedures.

Americans should accept the fact that universal health care will not work unless there are safeguards and disciplines built into it. Many will also have to accept the fact that it will not provide free healthcare.

Others opposed to universal healthcare should realize that we pay one way or another. We pay whether we realize it or not. We pay taxes to support Medicaid or other programs financed by the government. We pay exorbitant fees at hospitals or doctors' offices to counter or subsidize the expenses incurred by citizens who cannot pay. So, as you can see, there is absolutely no escaping the expenses of public health care. We can, however, provide preventive education. We can address serious health problems before they become catastrophic. We can charge a higher deductible or co-pay for those who abuse their health.

We can certainly take the profit out of health care insurance if we, the American citizens, choose to. It will likely require a national referendum or initiative, which is not possible under current laws. However, we can get rid of the slimeballs in government who represent insurance corporations and elect government officials who support nonprofits and national health care for all.

Probably one of the most important aspects of all might be tort reform. Lawsuits and liability insurance in the medical profession are the greatest contributors to expensive and unaffordable medical insurance. We all know damn well that to err is human. We strive continuously to perfect our trades and eliminate error. Yet there will always be human error or system failures.

So the question is whether the masses should suffer the consequences in order to reward a few victims and high-powered attorneys. Often, there exists a fine line between negligence and human error or unintended consequences. The problem is that there does not exist a reasonable compromise. Most often it comes down to a winner or a loser in court.

Then, of course, there are the unrealistic awards. They are often far beyond what a victim needs to live out his or her life in financial security and comfort. Just because a medical professional makes an error does not mean that the victim should win the lottery and penalize society. If half of the award was contributed to health care for society in some form, I might be able to accept some of the ridiculous awards.

Having stated my position on the above, I do realize there have to be penalties for incompetence and negligence. Some individuals are simply not fit for their occupations, and society has to weed them out. Oversight and mankind's pursuit of perfection will help to solve many of these errors and problems.

My advice to every citizen is that you are your best health care manager and your best resource for preventing errors from affecting your life. You simply cannot be careful enough, study enough, manage your health care enough, or question enough to make the correct decisions affecting your health and longevity. I could give examples of errors by medical professionals in my life; however, we all have stories in this regard.

Those who are willing to study their health, and health in general, are the winners in the health debate. They will discover preventive measures and cures, preventing much suffering and extending their lives. As I stated above, you are your best health care manager !

When I started writing this book over a year ago, I did not imagine what a dire situation this nation was in economically. Much of what I have written below was intended for normal or average times in America. I now have little hope that America will ever recover unless Americans are willing to make drastic changes and sacrifices in their lifestyles.

The bottom line is that now is likely the worst time in the history of America to finance any form of national health care. There have been recessions and there has been a depression in the past. There has always been hope that we would come out of these periods of economic decline. However, there will be no recovery this time unless there is a strong commitment from all Americans. The government will never be able to solve these economic problems; only the citizens of the United States will be able to turn the tables and create an economic recovery.

It is amazing to me that this nation struggles so much with the issue of health care. Generally, Republicans say it's all a matter of personal responsibility. I guess they've never put together a budget for a family based on the minimum wage or even a moderate wage. The math does not work out. Even if an individual purchases private health insurance, the door can close on him or her for almost any reason. Insurance is in business to make a profit. Insurance companies are not charities. If they can make a greater profit by denying coverage on expensive procedures, of course they will.

Now let's closely examine why we have Social Security and Medicare. Talk to people who are retired and enjoying those benefits, and they will tell you how pissed off they were when they were young and had all that money taken from every paycheck. Now they will admit that it was the best thing the government ever did.

Imagine what it would be like now if we had not enacted Social Security and Medicare. If we think that this nation is bad off with the health care situation these days, imagine if we had millions of retired citizens not just without healthcare but dying on the streets without roofs over their heads. As happened after the recent tragic events in Haiti, we could be sending dump trucks down the road daily to pick up bodies and dump them into mass graves.

Now imagine if the government had given citizens a choice whether to enroll in Social Security and Medicare and pay their monthly premiums. It would have failed miserably. Social Security and Medicare are forms of insurance geared for old age and retirement. Health care is insurance geared for those from birth to retirement. The only way to have coverage for all is for everyone to participate. And the only way for everyone to participate is to tax everyone's wages. You cannot legally force citizens to purchase health insurance. The Supreme Court will eventually find that the government has overstepped its authority on this issue.

Now let's examine the concept of insurance. We'll take auto insurance as an example. If only those who thought they were prone to auto accidents got insurance, how many would, especially among those who are young and feel invincible? So the law specifies that if you are going to drive on public highways, you are required to carry insurance. This is why auto insurance works—because we all pay into the fund. It's called single payer. It would work much better if government would utilize the technology that is available to prevent uninsured and negligent drivers from getting behind the wheel. That technology will be addressed in another chapter, however.

This theory is what makes Social Security and Medicare work. It keeps senior citizens from losing everything they have worked so hard for throughout their lives and winding up on the streets or, even worse, unable to afford life-saving medical procedures. It does not protect working employees, even those with insurance, from losing everything they have worked for. For many, a single health problem could financially ruin them for life.

So if Social Security, Medicare, auto insurance, private medical insurance, property insurance, labor and industry insurance, life insurance, liability insurance, and every other type of insurance in the industry works, why can it not work for all? There is profit in all insurance. Since health care is extremely expensive, there simply is not room for profit either financially or morally. Why does there have to be profit in health care?

Most of the types of insurance listed above not only work but also create a great profit. The reason they work is that millions invest in protection without knowing whether they will ever need the protection. The majority of home buyers would not carry insurance on their homes if it were not required by banks and mortgage companies.

You cannot force citizens to purchase health insurance. You can enact laws requiring citizens to carry health insurance, and the government can fine individuals for their failure to do so. If they don't pay the fines, are you going to put them in jail? We'd have to build a hell of a lot of jails. It's almost laughable !

The only method for creating a national healthcare program is the same process that created Social Security and Medicare. That process was successful by taxing wages, and the same procedure must be extended to health insurance.

Imagine if a child's health was insured from birth. From that point, either or both working parents would be required to pay taxes into a national health care fund similar to Medicare. The doctor would be required to report the pregnancy to the national health agency, and the premiums would be deducted from the parents' pay just like Social Security and Medicare deductions. Premiums would be deducted for all employees' health care in the same manner. All citizens who are physically capable of working would have to pay the premiums whether or not they were employed. When the citizens became employed, any back premiums not paid would be deducted on a small percentage basis over a period of time.

Now we reach the issue of profit in health care. It somehow seems immoral for a profit to be made from a person's tragic health problem. Are there not enough areas for insurance companies to make a profit? Can we not make health care off-limits for investors? If not, then why is it that hospitals and emergency rooms cannot deny medical attention to anyone? There is no profit for hospitals when patients come through their doors without a dime in their pockets. Hospitals cannot deny life-saving procedures to patients, so why can insurance companies? Isn't that discrimination?

It's too bad hospitals do not operate with billion-dollar profits, or they might be able to buy off our lawmakers.

Virtuous doctors are the ones who deserve to make a profit. The hospitals, clinics, medical research organizations, pharmaceutical laboratories, and others who create the wonders that save and extend lives—these are the people and organizations that deserve profits. I wouldn't mind putting my life and health in their hands.

We all complain about the obscene charges we receive on our hospital bills and the various specialists involved in medical procedures. Do we not have a clue as to why that is? Do you suppose the cost of care might be marked up to pay for all the thousands of patients entering hospitals every day with health problems from which these doctors and institutions will never see a penny? So for those who are defiantly opposed to socialized health care, I have news for you. You are paying for it ! It would be far cheaper for society to pay for these problems before they required serious and very expensive health procedures. A well-established preventative and educational health program for all would be far more effective than the progressive consequences of ignoring the cause and progression.

I recommend this tax be a progressive tax. That way, seasonal workers who earn a large amount of money for only part of the year would have their families' premiums or health care taxes paid in advance for when they are laid off. There should be no maximum annual tax ceiling, making it progressive to some degree.

All self-employed individuals should be required to pay monthly taxes toward premiums for themselves and family members. All citizens not working should be required either to pay premiums or to report why they are not working and earning income. This would be geared toward drug dealers, criminals, and those working jobs under the table. There are billions of dollars of tax revenue lost annually because of contractors and employees who work without reporting income and paying taxes. It is time for the government to catch up with these individuals who cheat honest citizens. This legal requirement will help in identifying these crooks.

I also propose a system of investigators who would show up at quitting time at places of employment and check the legal status of employees in order to determine whether those employers are employing illegal immigrants and whether they are reporting all employees for tax purposes. Perhaps there should also be a requirement for all employees to carry a special-issue Social Security ID card encoded with legal information that only government officials, police, or agents could decode with a special scanner. These agents could also visit construction sights and service sights to check on employee status. If OSHA can inspect safety regulations on job sights, it can also check the legal status of employees. This would be the greatest service government could provide for hardworking and honest employees and employers.

The bottom line is that national health care will provide a tremendous boost of jobs in America. The 30 million or more citizens who will suddenly be covered by health insurance will require millions more jobs in the health care industry. Our government and educational institutions had better be prepared for that demand.

We have a federal government in place in order to provide safety, national security, economic security, health, welfare, financial security, education, environmental protection, and so on. The federal government has been forced to provide all these services for its citizens because state governments have failed in most of these areas. Essentially, the federal government is the lifeline for citizens when states have failed to protect them. Many states throughout history have proven to have corrupt governments, and the federal government has found it essential for the strength of the entire union that all states remain strong and sound in all aspects of government.

Nobody can argue that the greatest endeavors our federal government has undertaken for its citizens is Social Security and Medicare. They are a kind of forced insurance, so to speak. When we are younger, we are all invulnerable and never expect that we will grow old and have health problems. Perhaps we should raise the age for voter eligibility to forty years of age when we are better prepared to realize the realities of life. Most cultures throughout history have relied on the wisdom of their elders. They certainly have not relied on glamorized political commercials that bullshit younger voters blind.

Now that a majority of states has failed to provide adequate healthcare for their citizens, the federal government has no choice but to step in and provide life-saving protection for all citizens. We cannot, as a nation with any kind of social conscience, allow our citizens to die in the streets. We cannot choose to make life-saving technology available only for the wealthy. Many will exclaim that it is a sin to abort a potential life, but apparently society has no responsibility to provide affordable medical care for the life of a child once it is born. It's confusing to me.

Probably the most effective method of controlling the extreme cost of health care would be for government to purchase patents on medical equipment as well as offering to purchase hospitals. Our government owns and operates veterans' hospitals, so there is no reason it couldn't operate publicly owned hospitals. Corporations that own the patent rights for equipment and technology would likely be willing to sell at some point in time, because at any time, a newer and better invention could make them obsolete.

With publicly owned hospitals and technology, we can bring down the costs of medical care dramatically. The same could apply to prescription drugs. Corporations that have made a killing selling patented drugs might be wise to sell their patents before they lose market share to newer and more advanced technologies. With the profits from these sales, the corporations can invest in new research and technologies. This endeavor will create much more affordable prescription drugs for the public.

There also need to be changes in the patent process. Our government officials should quit playing games at the expense of the public. There should be absolutely no extensions allowed. One of the most expensive drugs, Plavix, has been granted years of extensions, making the drug unaffordable to millions and causing premature deaths. This is an example of our government officials selling out to corporate powers. There needs to be an in-depth investigation into this process.

Additionally, our government should enact legislation that prohibits health insurance for elected officials paid for by our taxes. They need to pay their own way in order to learn to legislate from the perspective of average citizens. And pensions should be based on a prorated system according to the number of years an official is employed, the same as in the private sector. Forty years should be required for full pension benefits.

Lastly, I will address the most expensive burden on our national health care costs. Keeping citizens alive who are suffering unbearable pain and depression is the greatest plague on our health care system. Statistics prove that the greatest expense is keeping people alive who have no hope of recovery or a useful quality of life. Many of these people pray for and beg to die.

It would seem that if we have a right to life, we should have a right to cease our lives if we choose that the suffering and depression is more than we wish to handle. Essentially, the government is forcing citizens to suffer to the bitter end despite their desire to stop the torture. What a reward for a lifetime of labor and contributions to our society !

Many people choose their own methods of ending their suffering, which can be very painful and risks failure. Everybody should have the right to exit life peacefully.

Chapter 18

Social Security and Medicare

For decades, we have universally known that Social Security and Medicare would be in serious financial trouble in the future. The funds will completely dry up. Yet our government has not done a damn thing to adjust.

The greatest certainty in America is that Social Security and Medicare are going to go broke in the future. All that is in the trust fund are IOUs, and our federal government is essentially bankrupt. Given the trillions of dollars that America has spent on the stupidest war imaginable (Iraq) and little hope for an achievable end in sight, there is little hope that the federal government can bail out or even assist these agencies. There is only one logical solution.

Our elected officials know what has to be done. There are only a few things that can be done. Taxes or contributions must be increased. The sooner it's done, the less the rates will have to be raised in the future. Those rates should have been raised ten or twelve years ago. Instead, they cut the contributions. The age of eligibility for full benefits also has to be raised. It may become necessary in the near future to stop early retirement benefits. Most citizens are capable of working for many more years than our forefathers.

First, I must point out a few facts and realities. When Social Security was conceived, most Americans had either passed on or were in too poor health to work by the time they were sixty-five. Due to the miracles of modern medicine, Americans are living much longer and are in much better health beyond age sixty-five. Most Americans would not have had access to the health care that now keeps them healthy and alive beyond sixty-five if it were not for Medicare.

So the obvious solution is that Americans are going to have to work beyond sixty-five if they want Social Security benefits and Medicare to continue to provide the quality care that extends their lives. I know this will be a great disappointment for tens of millions of Americans; however, it is a reality we must all accept. However, it is a far better reality that we will live longer, have better health, and hopefully have sustainable incomes to live on.

The alternative is that we have incomes in retirement that would leave most in poverty and reduced health coverage that would not cover most life-saving procedures. The question is whether it is better to be alive, healthy, and working but unable to afford to live with financial security, or to be denied medical care to extend your years. Suffering and in pain is certainly not the way we wish to enjoy our retirement.

Actually, our elected government officials have known that there is only one logical solution for a long time; however, they do not have the courage and honesty to reveal the solution. If they had started making adjustments when the problem was outlined many years ago, the sacrifice of working Americans would not have been so difficult. They could have made one-year adjustments to the retirement age. Now, by the time they are forced to make the adjustments, they will be forced to put the minimum retirement age at seventy or beyond. If they had not been afraid to tell the truth, take appropriate measures, and risk their re-election chances, the sacrifices for Americans would have been much less severe.

There are solutions that can lessen these sacrifices and reduce the severity of the problem. There are many healthy and high-spirited Americans who would prefer to continue working if the government and employers gave them an incentive.

If employees have worked most of their lives, the government could resolve that those employees have already paid their dues. The government could make an agreement that those employees could continue to work without paying taxes (or with greatly reduced taxes for high-level earners) and continue to pay into Social Security and Medicare. These citizens would continue to build up the funds for Social Security and Medicare rather than depleting those funds. Essentially, they would be paying the premiums for their health care and taking that burden from society. This method could also take the burden off social services for those who cannot make it on Social Security alone.

There are many Americans who would embrace these incentives and continue to work. The incentives could continue to rise with age for those who love their work and are inspired to continue the occupations that inspire them. With improvements in health care and life expectancy, the age of sixty-five does not have to spell the end of being productive and contributing citizens in society.

With the retirement of the baby boomers, there will likely be a shortage in the workforce if the economy recovers. Having those baby boomers working and contributing to Medicare will take the burden off Medicare.

I believe a majority of Americans would choose to continue working and take home larger paychecks. They could essentially secure their financial futures and afford a better retirement lifestyle by working additional years.

The benefits for many employers would be that they would not have to pay into retirement funds or pension plans for these employees. The federal government might consider a reduced rate of Social Security taxes, since they would not be paying out benefit checks to those who are working beyond the retirement age for full benefits. Employees with a lifetime of experience and knowledge can be very valuable to a company as supervisors, dispatchers, or in numerous office or field positions.

There are numerous other solutions and incentives that could be applied to minimize the burden of this grave dilemma. We can offer senior citizens part-time employment, seasonal employment, less physical employment, management positions that take advantage of the expertise and experience of older employees, and government positions that may be valuable to society. We could start a new division of unemployment that specializes in placement of senior employees based on their experience in spite of their declining physical ability.

There are organizations that recognize the value of senior citizens, such as the Better Business Bureau and the Chamber of Commerce, from what I read in local newspapers. The government can also offer to subsidize retired workers for a six-month retraining period during which they begin work in new occupations. For citizens who have worked in physically demanding jobs all their lives and don't feel they would be able to retain their health if they continued in the same job, the government can offer retraining for jobs that are less physically demanding or a job-relocation program that requires little or no training. The government could also give preference to senior citizens when hiring in much the same way veterans receive preference in civil service hiring. This may force young employees to get further education or take their educations more seriously. Imagine a young applicant being rejected for a job because a senior citizen beat him or her out in skills and intellectual ability.

Senior citizens could be given tax exemptions for starting businesses and becoming independent of Social Security, especially if they created other jobs. Once again, the government and society should consider these citizens' dues paid as far as taxes are concerned. Other incentives could include building better Social Security benefits as they continue to contribute to the fund.

Another area seniors can be a great value to society is in teaching physical therapy to other seniors to prevent health failure that occurs rapidly due to stagnant lifestyles. We don't need young adults doing these jobs. Seniors would be much more credible and accepted and could be an inspiration to patients. It would allow seniors to set their own hours, days, and seasons of employment.

After all, this nation is facing a workforce shortage when the baby boomers start retiring. We will likely be recruiting senior citizens to start adult family care homes in their own homes; however, there will have to be incentives and rewards for doing so. Among those incentives should be preference for hiring other seniors and giving those business owners adequate breaks to get away so they do not have to be imprisoned in their homes and jobs. This is a very huge problem in the industry.

I recently had a severe problem with my right shoulder that was so painful I could not sleep at night. After two cortisone shots, the doctor informed me that unless I wished to face surgery with no guarantee, I would have to build up certain muscles to support the shoulder. He referred me to a physical therapist to learn those exercises. I informed him that I did not wish to visit the therapist over a long period of time. I suggested just a few sessions to learn the exercises.

When I arrived there, the therapist scheduled me for six weeks, with two sessions each week. After a few sessions and much improvement, the therapist informed me that I needed to continue the sessions. I objected but did not wish to make waves. At the end of the six weeks, the therapist informed me that they had contacted the doctor and the doctor had ordered another month of sessions. Now, I realize that they get you in the door and then try to maximize the opportunity. Nothing was different from the first few sessions, and I had already easily learned to perform those exercises at home or in the exercise gym I had access to.

I personally feel guilty when I see how many expenses my health problems have contributed. I do not wish to run up these expenses for Medicare if they can be avoided. I try to let the body perform its natural healing process before I go to a doctor. I really feel guilty when the above situations occur. The cost for therapy is obscene. Yet these people are out to squeeze every dollar out of the opportunity that they can. What a scam of the system.

Recently, I experienced extreme pain in my stomach and bowel problems. The doctor ordered a colonoscopy and diagnosed microscopic colitis. I inquired as to what might cause this. He stated that it is generally brought on by an infection. That is a red flag right there. Meanwhile, he put me on a thousand-dollar-a-month prescription drug that I started ten days later due to a conflict of medications. That apparently did not account for the pain I was originally experiencing throughout my stomach and lower abdomen. So he ordered a CAT scan. That exam came out negative.

A few days after the diagnosis of microscopic colitis, I discovered that I had a gum infection in an area that was difficult to detect. I started to treat that area with melaleuca oil. The stomach pains went away a few days later.

The point is that doctors might consider looking in patients' mouths before they order procedures that cost thousands of dollars. A person can have a gum infection for a long period of time without realizing it. I spend a lot of time every day brushing and flossing my teeth, yet I was not aware of this infection. These infections are also known to cause heart attacks. In the mean time, this oversight cost Medicare thousands of dollars. I am left wondering how much these unnecessary expenses drive up the costs of health care. We need a little more logic and oversight in our health care system.

These are not the only unnecessary extreme expenses in my life. I'm sure that we all have had similar circumstances in our lives. We just never question our doctors' integrity. That is dangerous territory. So the abuse goes on and on.

The federal government should consider investing 1 percent of Social Security revenues collected into the stock market or municipal bonds. Over a period of time, those funds would likely perform well enough to consider investing a greater percentage. After the lessons we have learned about the stock market over the past few years, it is unlikely that the market will ever plunge again.

Lately, many Republicans are proposing that Medicare be privatized. Medical insurance isn't expensive enough now, but they want to put the huge profits for insurance companies into the mix? Plus, insurance companies can decide which medical procedures they will pay for and which they won't. Who they will cover and who they won't. They can raise premiums to the point that many will not afford insurance.

Chapter 19

Research Grants and Patents

Years ago, I heard that the U.S. government owns certain patents. It occurred to me, shouldn't all the billions of dollars the government grants for research entitle the taxpayers to at least half ownership of the patents of the products and technology? Shouldn't the biggest investor be entitled to a slice of the pie instead of the fat-cat investors that move in after the technology is developed at taxpayers' expense?

Imagine how much more affordable medicine and medical technology might be if taxpayers owned a 50 percent share. What if half of the proceeds resulting from grants were invested into national health care? In some cases, it would be beneficial to the university or research organization if our government paid them generously for their inventions or discoveries. Then the government could develop the product or technology for market, especially in the medical field. The employees would simply work for the federal government, and the company could form a new division for further research and development.

I'm sure the government purchases military technology, so why not other technologies? Let me give you an example. There is a machine developed for sleep apnea called a C-PAP. All it consists of is a fan in a box with a hose attached to the nose. Yes, it has some electronic controls for increasing or decreasing air pressure, but nothing highly scientific. I don't know of any users who even like these instruments, for they are very cumbersome and annoying throughout the night. There is a long way to go before they are perfected to the point of comfort and effectiveness. These end up costing thousands of dollars when costs for management are considered. Medicare, Medicaid, and veterans' health care and insurance companies pay hundreds of millions of dollars a year to provide these machines for people with sleep apnea.

If they bought the patent, they could provide the breathing machines to patients for a fraction of the costs. In the mean time, the developer could continue research and development of a much better machine.

I know there are thousands more examples like this of medical devices that are priced ridiculously high. The government would be better off buying the technology, and the developer would be better off, because better technologies are always coming down the pipeline that could wipe them out.

These are just a few solutions that might lead to more affordability for healthcare. Isn't it time for citizens to get a return on their investments in research and development grants? Isn't it time to stop investing billions of dollars a year in grants to develop medicines the average person cannot afford?

I recently read of a new drug that will help those with muscular dystrophy walk or walk better. It costs one thousand dollars per month. Who in the hell can pay that kind of money every month for a prescription drug? I believe I would rather stay put in a wheelchair.

So the bottom line is that if the government can purchase and own military technologies, then why not medical technologies?

A better example would be a mechanism called Back2Life. You may have seen infomercials in regard to this device. I believe it is based on spinal decompression. It's absolutely amazing how well this machine improves your spinal problems. It costs about $150 at Costco.

When I bought it, I used it a few times; however, I was not in a period of severe backache or stiffness. It sat around for several months unused. Then one day I was installing a built-in microwave. I had problems in getting the duct work connected due to crowded space above, so I had to take the microwave in and out numerous times over a two-day period.

First let me explain that I have been diagnosed with severe arthritis and severe deterioration of the spinal column. I have had cortisone shots and physical therapy and have visited chiropractors hundreds of times in order to maintain my health. I have no business doing this kind of lifting; however, I cannot afford professionals.

By the time I finished the job on the second day, my back was so sore that I could barely walk. It seemed that every muscle in my back, legs, and arms had never been so painful. I considered taking medication, but I thought that this might be the supreme test for the Back2Life. Twelve minutes on the machine, and I immediately felt much better. By the time I went to bed, I had absolutely no pain. The next day I had no problems whatsoever. Now I use the machine about every other day.

So I could have been visiting a chiropractor, getting another cortisone shot, or eventually facing spinal surgery. It could have cost Medicare nearly a hundred thousand dollars. Instead, I manage my own arthritis problems and have not felt better in twenty-some years. Yet the cost of this device is not tax deductible, and neither are over four thousand dollars a year my wife and I spend on health supplements that truly improve our overall health and keep us out of the doctor's office or hospital.

There are numerous health supplements or herbal products that may or may not improve health or prevent health problems. However, certain popular products, such as glucosamine chondroitin, hyaluronic acid, MSM, CQ10, and metamucil are proven to work and sell like hotcakes. There is good reason that they sell so well. A product does not sell in mass volume unless it works well for people. The reason they are not tax deductible is that our elected officials are in bed with the pharmaceutical industry. These products are treated in the same manner as liquor and tobacco when it comes to taxation. So the bottom line is that people who take care of their health and use preventive measures at great cost are penalized by having to pay sales taxes on these products, and then they cannot even deduct the costs as medical expenses on their federal income taxes.

Another issue is that technologies that are developed as a result of government grants should have to be manufactured in America, providing jobs and industry here. It's our investment, so we should have a voice in creating jobs and promoting our economy. I would like to know how many elected officials would stand up for the majority of taxpayers' rights compared to how many would stand up for the fat cats in corporations. I guess we know.

Recently, the corporation that owns AT&T purchased T-Mobile. This is just another example of a few companies monopolizing the industry. This leaves just three major players in the American market. This will create much less competition, and consumers will likely pay more and have worse customer service as a result. There may even be collusion between the three remaining corporations.

This time, however, a German corporation, Deutsche Telekom, now owns AT&T and T-Mobile. Germany is a nation that refuses to aid the United States in military action against terrorism. We helped Germany to escape from Nazism, which resulted in their freedom and democracy.

Therefore, I am calling for a nationwide boycott on the purchase of services from AT&T and T-Mobile. We must take a stand against monopolization and foreign nations that are stamping out American corporations and pay no corporate taxes to the United States. This is especially true when such corporations are from countries that refuse to aid America in the battle against terrorism and vile dictatorships.

I would even be in favor of a blacklist of corporations that manufacture their products overseas and sell in the United States. However, there's a fat chance of that flying in America.

Chapter 20

Native Americans

In another chapter, I touch on how we did everything wrong in regard to the treatment and social security of Native Americans. We seized their lands and placed them on remote reservations. We gave them welfare checks, and they lost any incentive to survive. Most turned into alcoholics. They came into our cities and got drunk and violent. They murdered or were often murdered. Disease ran rampant throughout their race.

Our government built them homes and stocked them with furniture and appliances. They most often let those homes deteriorate, and when they ran out of money in the middle of the month, they would take appliances, windows, doors, etc. out of those homes and sell them. Education was almost a fruitless effort with the tribes.

As you can imagine, we not only stole their land and resources but also turned a thriving and proud society that was self sufficient into a welfare nation. If we had integrated those people into our society, this would not have happened.

Now the subsidies tribes used to get as residuals from mining and forest products are drying up due to environmental laws and regulations, and their reservations are becoming almost worthless in value.

One positive sign has developed in recent years. Due to tribal sovereignty, some Native Americans have been able to construct gambling casinos on their reservations. Most tribal reservations, however, are located in remote areas not able to draw consumers. That coupled with more and more states authorizing private casino operations within communities of their states and local governments becoming dependent on those tax revenues means that most tribes are left out of the competition.

The tribes that have good locations are building great success for their people. They are building good schools, health clinics, and social services. They are becoming very responsible, educated citizens and are taking on professional jobs to manage their successful ventures. It almost makes me feel good to visit a casino and leave with a deficit as all gambling is designed to do. It is so good to see a tribe become successful and self sufficient that I wish they were all afforded the same opportunity.

This brings me to my proposal, which can be a win/win solution for all of America. Since lucrative lumber and mineral rights are vanishing and hydropower dams have wiped out fishing resources for tribes, our government must come up with new resources to assure the sustainability of disadvantaged tribes. The only option available is to give Native American tribes exclusive rights to all gambling in our nation.

In order to assure fairness and equal distribution of gambling revenues, all tribes would have to form a confederation of Native American tribes. They might choose to sell reservation lands that are not suitable for casino operations and invest in locations more suitable or purchase private gambling operations in and around communities.

Las Vegas–type operations and all other local ventures would be required to deed 1 percent of their stock per year to the national confederation of tribes. Consider it a tax on all gambling operations. At some point, years down the road, the confederation would be wealthy enough to purchase and buy out the remaining stock. Even without that likelihood, in one hundred years, the Confederation could own all gambling properties and operations.

What difference does it make to 99 percent of Americans who owns these facilities? We don't know who owns them anyway, with the exception of a few billionaires. They have made their killing, and at some point it will be time for them to step aside in the best interests of America. If it were not for freedom, democracy, capitalism, free enterprise, and the laws enabling them to make their lucrative profits, they would not have their wealth. They now owe it to their nation to contribute compensation to Native Americans whose native land we stole.

A world court would likely approve of this method of fair compensation to the tribes. The tribes could all build their sustainability and secure their welfare well into the future. American taxpayers would no longer have to throw billions of dollars of their taxes into a failed bureaucracy.

America owes Native Americans big time, and this is the solution that would stop the billions of dollars of subsidies taxpayers waste on a failed welfare program. It's fairness and a win-win solution for the tribes and all Americans.

Chapter 21

Immigration

While America is a nation of immigrants, there has been a drawback to the absorption of immigrants from certain foreign nations. Throughout our history, we have given sanctuary to immigrants who could not live within nations ruled by vile dictatorships, autocracies, communists, Nazis, fascists, or any other tyrants. I guess it is referred to as diplomatic immunity. The problem with that is that we have robbed those nations of the individuals who likely would have fought hard for change and been the activists or freedom fighters who could have led their nations in the march for freedom. As Patrick Henry stated, "Give me freedom, or give me death"! Those nations desperately needed the leadership of these immigrants to oppose those vile factions.

So while our intentions were good, we may have paid a heavy price over the years by not encouraging those committed individuals to stay and fight for change within their nations. We cannot demand democracy. Freedom and democracy do not come easily, but they absolutely must be born within. It takes tremendous sacrifice. It takes activists committed to democracy to start a movement in any nation. A person recruits others who believe in the vision and commitment. Most of those types were given an easy out and a free pass to America. So we have essentially removed the very people who would have been most instrumental in reform.

Another issue related to immigration is that we keep absorbing people from overpopulated nations. We have our own population explosion under control. Yet we keep absorbing the overflow from nations that refuse to control their population explosions despite not having the resources to feed their people. There has to be some responsibility for all nations of the world to control population or we will wind up in a war of survival, fighting for natural resources. You could say that war is going on now with oil. It will be interesting to see how the fight for oil in the arctic plays out. Will there be a war over that oil ?

American universities have been very generous in sharing education and technology with foreign nations. It is a very noble gesture to teach technologies to foreign students who can then take knowledge back to their native lands and improve their productivity, agriculture, medical facilities, and so on.

The problem is that all too often these graduates apply for citizenship and stay in America. This hurts the nations we are trying help. If we are striving for peace and prosperity throughout the world, we have to have these scholars return to their native countries and contribute to their economies and education systems. Many nations are suffering from extreme poverty, disease, and starvation. These graduates are critical to their nations' survival. Often scholars can become leaders and catalysts for democratic reform and economic development.

Illegal Immigrants: Another Valuable Resource

America has a most serious problem to address with no apparent solution in sight. It would take hundreds of thousands more immigration police to round up the 12 millions illegal immigrants in this nation, and who knows how many years it might take. Unless the government is willing to invade the private residences of the wealthy, many will never be apprehended.

And how could our court systems handle the case loads of 12 million people? Who is going to pay for transporting 12 million people back to their countries of origin? If you remove 12 million people from their homes, you will create another huge gap in the real-estate market. In some states, such as Arizona, New Mexico, Texas, Nevada, and California, retail stores would close en masse. This would put hundreds of thousands of employees out of work. Our nation would clearly fall into a severe depression. There would be huge deficits in tax revenues both at the federal level and at the level of states and municipalities.

Let me lay out the truth. Government officials know damn well where the majority of illegal immigrants are employed. When this became a serious societal issue a few years back, I was expecting to pick up the newspaper every day and see several companies busted for employing illegal immigrants. Not going to happen ! Why, you ask? Simply because our economy cannot survive without illegal immigrants. If you removed all illegal immigrants from America, our economy would collapse overnight.

Citizens should demand that Congress quit using illegal immigration as a political football and demand reform that legalizes the majority of them. Let's get the hardworking, honest illegal immigrants paying taxes, Medicare, and Social Security and on the path to citizenship. What better way is there to prove their merit than by demonstrating their willingness to serve in our military?

Incidentally, I don't feel that impoverished human beings striving to survive in this world and feed their families are criminals. If they are involved in criminal activities, then they may be labeled as criminals. So let our government focus on the true criminals and get the rest legalized and paying taxes, Social Security, Medicare, and hopefully national health care. The difference is that we are now providing that health care, but they are not paying premiums or taxes.

There should also be a requirement for immigrants to learn the English language. That requirement would be a great advantage for all immigrants. They could better fit into our society, enjoy and understand our culture, and be better informed as voters and citizen activists for their people.

If I were moving to a foreign nation, the first thing I would do would be to study the language of that country before traveling there. I would not expect that nation to cater to my lack of consideration and irresponsibility.

Government is far too expensive without the burden of having to provide translators for every aspect of government and social services. There is also the extra expense of printing all paperwork in all these different languages. There are also cultural problems. How can we even hope to blend immigrants into our society without being able to communicate with each other? Language creates suspicion and a natural barrier between people. I personally always wish to meet and greet strangers and make them feel welcome and equal as citizens. If I cannot communicate with them, I cannot hope to accomplish that connection.

In many communities, we have citizens congregating into neighborhoods based on their ethnicity. Why do we suppose that is? Could it be that people by nature wish to assemble with people they can communicate with? If they cannot communicate, they likely will feel isolated and lonely.

It is absolutely outrageous that our society has to put up with these problems and expenses when there should be a legal requirement to learn the English language in order to obtain citizenship. It would be for the betterment of all concerned.

Have you ever tried to watch television with the volume off? Can you imagine being an immigrant and not being able to enjoy our culture or be informed of the news throughout our nation and world? We are doing no favor for these people by catering to their lack of language skills. If we would quit doing this and demand that they learn English as a requirement for citizenship, they would fit into our society and enjoy American life much more. And we would save millions of dollars that we currently spend to provide translators and duplicates of thousands of documents.

It is utterly amazing how many foreign nations have so many citizens that speak the English language these days. They are obviously aware of the advantage of speaking and understanding the universal language. So what is the excuse for the millions of people in this nation unable to communicate in English? If we quit catering to them, they will learn English damn fast.

Incidentally, there is a major issue that has come up in the past year in regard to the Fourteenth Amendment. It states that any child born within the United States is automatically considered an American citizen. We always like to brag about how wise our founding fathers were. Obviously, they had no idea of the problems that lay ahead. In those days, they welcomed all immigrants to our nation, as there were always jobs in an ever-expanding America.

I'm sure that there have been thousands of babies born to parents that were visiting America on business or vacation. I'm sure that they did not wish for their children to be American citizens when they returned to their native countries.

Therefore, the Fourteenth Amendment needs to be adjusted to state that a child must have parents who are legal citizens of the United States. So let's get busy legalizing the 12 million illegal residents who are not criminals. In a few more generations, those 12 million could multiply to 100 million or more.

Chapter 22

Mexico

We have continually witnessed our nation struggling with the impossible mission of securing its borders. I say it is impossible because it is neither physically or financially possible to build a fence that will stop smuggling and illegal immigrants. It is not difficult to build tunnels beneath the fence. Nor is it difficult to use rope ladders to scale the fence. Now the smugglers are utilizing ultralight aircraft that cannot be detected by radar. Where there are billions to be made in drug smuggling, there will always be a method. With these methods comes the possibility of terrorists utilizing the same routes to transport weapons of mass destruction, whether chemical or biological.

In light of the 90 billion dollars we have spent in the past ten years that will not even secure the border, why has there not been a proposal to study the feasibility of annexing Mexico into the United States. Would it be cheaper? Wouldn't U.S. citizens like to know? What could 90 billion dollars do to build a stable government and foster security in our neighboring nation? I'm not saying that we should adopt Mexico. I'm saying that we should at least study the pros and cons. Perhaps some sort of loose alliance could come out of the study that would give greater security to both nations and prevent the possibility of Mexico falling into the wrong hands.

The northern border of Mexico is impossible to secure. Now look at a map and compare the northern border to the southern one. A quick visual comparison will tell you that the southern border of Mexico is very manageable.

Mexico has long been considered an ally of the United States. Some of the presidents have been more cooperative than others. Imagine if they someday were to elect someone similar to Venezuela's Chavez. Suppose the cartels come to power and Mexico became an enemy of the United States and aligned itself with a rogue nation like Iran. Would we then have regrets about not bringing Mexico into the union?

So, as you can see, it could be very much to our advantage for Mexico to become the fifty-first state of the United States. It may be much easier to build Mexico into a democratic economic power than to leave the country in poverty and susceptible to becoming allied with an enemy. Believe me—because of the world's dependence on oil, there are numerous rogue nations that have more money and power than they know what to do with.

Mexico can become as prosperous a state as California, Nevada, Arizona, or Florida, a favorite vacation destination and place for retirement living. There are already millions of Americans who vacation there and millions more who retire there. Mexico has tremendous natural. Plus, with its warm weather, it could become a vacation and retirement paradise for millions of Americans.

The argument can also be made that America owes statehood to Mexico on the basis that we took most of the southwestern United States from Mexico. We took the entire United States from the Native Americans. We have been trying to make amends ever since. We gave them reservations in secluded areas to try to isolate them from our society. Then we gave them welfare checks, housing, schools, and every other thing we could to appease them. We gave them everything but incentive. We essentially turned them into an alcoholic, dependant welfare society. This was not much different than the policies that caused communism failed in the Soviet Union. When there is no incentive, there will be no progress economically.

If European powers invaded America in this day and age, a world court would order us out or demand huge compensation to the Native Americans. If we invaded the Mexican territories, which once included much of the southwestern United States, a world court would rule that we had to leave or make great contributions financially to Mexico, just as we did in securing the Louisiana Purchase from France and Alaska from Russia. Now, realize that some Mexicans are starting to demand that California be given back to Mexico. If they manage to make a legitimate argument to a world court, then the same could apply to Texas, New Mexico, Arizona, and Nevada.

Another argument can be made that America's appetite for illegal drugs is destroying the stability of Mexico's government. The cartels are becoming more and more powerful and dangerous in Mexico. Their security is so endangered that their government could fall overnight. We are responsible for their dilemma. We owe them statehood for our past land-grab and our illegal-drug dependence, which is threatening to cause their total collapse. Our appetite for illegal drugs has caused the drug cartels to rise to such power that the cartels could easily take over Mexico's government in the future.

These days, however, we are faced with a far more serious problem than the millions of illegal immigrants who are in the United States and the millions more trying to survive by making their way into the United States. The cartel presence has seriously threatened the tourist industry of Mexico. A nation already suffering extreme poverty is in danger of losing one of its chief industries. This will force millions more into acceptance of criminal activities and escalate the illegal drug trade. Mexico is a sovereign nation; therefore, we have no right to enter it and fight the drug cartels.

So should we ignore the solution until it is too late? Should we seize the opportunity before it passes? The drug lords are already penetrating our nation in Arizona. Drug wars and killings are occurring almost weekly. In Mexico, the cartels have kidnapped police and even made promises to kill one officer every day unless the police chief resigns. The next day, 70 percent of the police force resigned. Then the cartels put their own public officials in place. We do not need much imagination to determine where that will lead.

If the drug cartels succeed with their extortion in Mexico, the same could happen in Arizona. The media in Arizona is keeping these stories very quiet and off the front pages. Of course, they do not wish to scare millions of tourists away. However, when the national media picks up on these stories, it only occasionally publishes brief pieces on the inner pages of newspapers and broadcasts thirty-second soundbites on television. What happens in Vegas stays in Vegas—and apparently what happens in Arizona stays there too.

Is it then more ethical and beneficial for all concerned to incorporate Mexico into the United States? Especially when so many Mexican citizens wish to get to the United States and some die nearly every day while trying to get here? So do we seize the moment, or live with regrets for hundreds of years to come? This, of course, assumes that mankind can survive that long on its current path of self-destruction.

As a side note, who manufactures most of the deadly weapons the drug cartels use against their opposition? The United States, of course. Our police are not armed with weapons with anywhere near the potency of those weapons. We invented nuclear weapons that now threaten the free world and may ultimately end mankind's existence on this planet. Do we continue to invent weapons that will destroy mankind rather than focusing on how we might discover a method of diplomacy that enables mankind's survival and creating a prosperous world of peace and achievement for all?

For those who fear the loss of the great white Caucasian race of the United States, I have news for you. In case you haven't been paying attention, the Hispanics, Asians, Arabs, Africans and other dark-skinned immigrants are quickly starting to outnumber white Americans. In a few more generations, white Americans will be the minority. Essentially, it is not important to the future of the United States that the white race survive and remain supreme in America.

It is important that America remain the beacon of freedom and democracy. America must set an example to the world to show that mankind's survival depends on all the citizens of the world accepting that mankind can only survive if we accept freedom and democracy for all. Would we rather that the white race reign supreme or that all nationalities survive in peace, creating a world that proves that all races and ethnicities can exist together and accomplish greater achievement for all? It would be shameful if we did not extol the virtues of a greater world in the future for all nations, united in a covenant of peace and democracy.

Is Mexico's statehood at least worth study and consideration? Or do we continue failed policies until there is no option? If Mexico became a U.S. state, I would be the first in line shopping for a retirement home. With the current problems in Mexico, I would not even vacation there. Mexico deserves statehood. It beats the hell out of having Mexico fall into the hands of a Hugo Chavez or allying with a vile dictator like Ahmadinejad of Iran.

So here we are again, arming Mexico, and many of those weapons are falling into the hands of enemies. Recently, a report came out that the Drug Enforcement Agency has seen hundreds of military weapons bought at gun shops in Arizona and smuggled to Mexico. The DEA has chosen to do nothing to stop this, and the top management won't even grant interviews with investigative reporters about their actions. Even have a federal agency that was formed for the sole purpose of keeping weapons out of the hands of criminals is now totally corrupt. It was also reported that one of the weapons sold in Arizona to smugglers was traced back to the killing of an immigration official.

Consider that Iraq was once an ally of the United States. We built them into a military power. We provided intelligence, technology, and weapons in order to overpower Iran. Consider that Russia was well on the way to becoming a democracy until Putin came to power.

Now, with all of Russia's oil wealth concentrated in the hands of a small number of individuals who have a great deal of power over much of Europe and Asia, it is troubling what may lie ahead. I see little difference between Putin and Hitler. The only difference is that Putin has control of hundreds of billions of dollars in oil revenue and has much of Europe and Asia at his mercy. He is a young leader, and it looks as though he may have control of Russia for many more decades. His control does not allow any political opposition. Russia sells weapons and technology to rogue nations.

He is potentially more of a threat to the free world than Hitler was. I only hope that Mexico does not fall to the cartels or elect a vile dictator that Putin might cozy up to. The cartels can easily control elections by killing their opposition, and they have.

The same comparison can be made of the Taliban. The United States armed the Taliban to battle the Soviet Union. So, as you can see, the very nations we arm often become our enemies.

The bottom line is that if Mexico falls into the wrong hands, the United States will have a far greater problem on its hands than if we had invested in reforming Mexico and eventually bringing it into the union. There are various ways this could be done over a period of time.

Mexico could become a charter state for a period of years during which they would not have total statehood until certain reforms and goals were met. In the mean time, we might be able to assist in their efforts to put the drug cartels out of business. It would also serve to remove the threat of terrorists entering the nation at any point along a two-thousand-mile border that is seemingly impossible to guard by land, air, or sea.

One of Mexico's major industries was tourism. With tourism in the tank, Mexico's people are going to be more desperate than ever. That puts their nation in great danger of falling prey to factions that will cause unimaginable problems for the United States. Is statehood for Mexico at least worth study and consideration? Could the United States be at least a protectorate of Mexico, so that Mexico could give the United States authority to assist in its security and welfare?

Chapter 23

Cuba

I have been astonished for decades by the policies of the United States toward Cuba. I can understand implementing those policies during the Cold War, when Cuba was aligned with the Soviet Union. When the USSR disbanded, Cuba was no longer a threat to the United States. It was then time to drop all the embargoes and sanctions and develop friendly relations with Cuba. Now Cuba is developing relations with other rogue nations in South America. Soon it might become an ally of Iran if we continue to penalize Cuba. There are signals that Raùl Castro might be willing to open the door to change in that nation. We should be encouraging that transformation and offering help in every way we can. We need to stop dictating reform to our enemies and try friendly influential measures that could open doors for diplomacy, capitalism and democracy.

This is another lesson we should learn from the mistakes in the history of this nation. The United States should have offered statehood to Cuba long ago, before Castro came along. We would not have had the Cuban Missile Crisis if we had. That nearly resulted in World War III and nuclear war. Statehood should have been a provision of our establishment of a military base on their island.

Cuba can be an economic bonanza for the United States just as much as Hawaii has been. And the citizens of Cuba can end hundreds of years of poverty and suffering. It will also put an end to the problem of the thousands of Cubans who die trying to get to the freedom our nation offers our citizens.

We have an opportunity to open the door to Cuba now—or we can fiddle around until some dangerous foreign power becomes chummy with Cuba. We don't seem to be able to learn from the mistakes in our past and seize the opportunity when it arises. If the United States opens the door to commerce and tourism in Cuba, that nation will gradually embrace America's ideology and free enterprise. Within a few years, Cuba's economy could be thriving. With huge economic gains, new leadership will embrace free enterprise, and democracy will thrive. I guarantee it !

There is absolutely no reason for sanctions against Cuba. Why should we punish millions of its citizens and cause them to hate us? Their government will just continue to use that propaganda to teach their youth to hate us more. You don't make friends and influence people in this world by condemning them. You reach out a hand and offer assistance when they are suffering, perhaps even offering them statehood if they are willing to make reforms. Why do we need to create enemies of nations that are no threat to the security of our nation? We can only form strong diplomatic relations with nations to whom we give assistance, direction, and comfort. The basis of friendship between nations is just like the basis of any other friendship. Our government seems to think we can rattle the saber and condemn and isolate these nations. Of course they are not going to love us for it. This seems more like a perfect formula for permanent hatred, vengeance, and condemnation. These nations desperately need a hand up, not to be kicked down the road. If we would befriend these nations, we would be a positive influence. We must stop threatening and being feared and become a friend and consultant that will help meet their direst needs.

Chapter 24

Israel

Given that most of the Arab nations are at war with America in one manner or the other—either ideologically in a kind of cold war, economically, or through supporting terrorism—isn't it time to examine our actions in the history of Israel's statehood? This might be one of the most important lessons to be learned in the history of America.

The United States was certainly justified to support building a democracy and promoting capitalism in a part of the world that had never experienced democracy before. We expected that Israel would be such a great influence in the region that democracy would be adopted by other nations and spread throughout the Middle East. However, we underestimated the power and influence of their theocracies.

This has been the greatest failure in American foreign policy. We live in the present and react to the present situation without recognizing the ramifications down the road or the feathers that we ruffle by acting the way we do. Have we gone wrong in building the democracy of Israel in the middle of a billion people who have lived thousands of years devoted to a theocracy so strongly opposed to democracy?

We are directly responsible for building the nation of Israel. We have invested billions of dollars in it every year since 1947, when Israel was declared a state. Some used to refer to Israel as the fifty-first state of the United States. The Jewish people have built a magnificent nation with a military almost on par with America's. Of course, they have built all this through the generosity of American taxpayers. There would be no Jewish nation without the billions of dollars per year invested by America.

The cold war I mentioned above is caused by the condemnation the United States gets for supporting Israel in its battles with the Palestinians. Evidence for this war includes the involvement of certain factions of Saudi Arabian citizens in the 9/11 attacks and the involvement of numerous Arab nations in supporting the tragic bombing attacks in Iraq. It takes a lot of money to finance all these weapons and personnel. This financial support is coming from many different directions, and it all stems from the hatred of America for supporting Israel.

This was a very noble and well-intentioned gesture on the part of America. We hoped this experiment would succeed. The whole free world probably hoped we would succeed. We thought democracy would succeed, set a great example, and spread throughout the Middle East. The reality is that we created a hornets' nest, and it has had the reverse effect. The animosity has been building and building for over sixty years now. This is what created the anger and thirst for vengeance that resulted in 9/11 and so much other terrorism throughout the world.

Decades ago, Americans talked of Israel becoming the fifty-first state. It essentially is. We supported the concept of Israel becoming a nation from its inception. We helped extensively in building Israel, contributing billions of dollars a year. We donated or sold to Israel the high-tech weapons to fight their wars. If we hadn't built their military and infrastructure, Israel would never have existed. They would have been wiped out at the beginning.

Israel's military actions against Syria and Lebanon make them responsible for the fact that Hezbollah has become a political and military force that threatens Israel and the United States with the assistance and backing of Iran.

It is once again time for America to admit that our well-intentioned experiment failed and failed badly. On the other hand, we can boldly state that unless the entire Middle East unifies into some form of democracy, there will be unbelievable wars between the Arab nations in the future.

The economic war I mentioned above is demonstrated by the fact that many Arab nations are feeding the Palestinians weapons to attack Israel, and many Arab nations are feeding the conflicts in Iraq, Pakistan, and Afghanistan. The seemingly endless war in Iraq and Afghanistan is bankrupting America and is leaving us vulnerable to any other crisis that might develop. Those nations are giving America all the hell that is possible.

Unlike the situation we find ourselves in in Iraq, there is something America can do about the inflammatory situation we created in Israel. We can invite all the Jewish people to migrate to the United States and make this their homeland. Millions of Jewish people live in America very comfortably without the fear of daily bombs or nuclear attacks. Are those Jewish people going to hell because they do not live and worship in their proclaimed holy land? It's a simple matter of whether they value the lives of millions of their people or are willing to risk an inevitable nuclear disaster that could possibly destroy their entire nation. Which option would you choose?

It almost reminds me of the old strategy of drawing the enemy into a blocked canyon and then wiping them out. The enemy, unable to penetrate our nation, continues to draw our soldiers into their communities, where they set up explosives to kill our brave soldiers. It seems unfair to ask our soldiers to go into these territories to protect people whose response is to blow up our soldiers.

The terrorist war pretty much goes without saying. It is a way for numerous Muslim nations to wage a continuous war without being identified as a national enemy. There is no nation for America to retaliate against, because they all are in denial. They simply play the denial game, not accepting any responsibility for the terrorists originating in their countries. Don't they have intelligence agencies in their nations just as we do? Of course they do ! They also have millionaires and billionaires who keep supplying weapons to kill American soldiers.

We could not attack some of these nations even if we could prove their governments were behind the terrorist attacks. Why, you ask? Simply because it would interrupt the world's supply of oil. Our nation would be the one suffering the most. An attack on one OPEC nation could bring others into the conflict. This could be an unimaginable disaster not only for America but for the world as well. Imagine how the world would quickly turn against America at that point.

As much as Israeli government officials and Palestinian leaders talk about peace, the sad fact is that a huge majority of Muslims want no peace. They will only settle for Israel being wiped off the face of the earth, and they boldly state that fact. This is exactly why there can never be peace between Israel and the Muslim world. There are millions of Muslims who would rather die than have Israel exist.

So since America is directly responsible for creating Israel, which has led to terrorist attacks throughout the world, America is also responsible for cleaning up the mess. The only solution possible to diffuse this ugly mess is to bring all the Jewish people to America. Millions of Jewish people now live in America in peace and harmony with the rest of Americans.

There are many Arabs who are billionaires due to the wealth they have obtained in the oil industry. It should be no problem for them to buy out all the assets owned by the Jewish people. The Jewish migration to America could occur over a period of ten to twenty years. They could have the option of blending in with the rest of Americans or building their own cities in rural areas just as they did in Israel.

Hopefully other nations would be willing to absorb and welcome a percentage of Jewish people into their populations. It would certainly be a goodwill gesture alleviating the tensions and aggravation threatening the entire world. Those nations could prove they are willing to do their part to promote world peace and stability.

Over a period of ten to twenty years, the United States could easily absorb a large percentage of the 25 million Jewish people in Israel. We actually absorb many more immigrants in a ten-year period under normal immigration. For those people who are reluctant to leave their perceived holy land, I would say that if you believe in God and that he created this earth, then his entire world is holy land. Wherever you can live in peace and serve God in his vast world should be your priority in life.

Those who refuse our generous offer should be on their own. There should be no more military or financial support for Israel after a predetermined date of migration for all Jewish people. If people choose to continue living in Israel and agitate a billion people with their military powers and expansion of the Jewish empire, they should be on their own without the assistance of the United States, NATO, or the United Nations.

Of course, this deal would have to include a peace accord with the Palestinians and all the Arab nations according to which they would immediately stop all attacks and aggression against Israel, American embassies, and American allies or infrastructure.

I can't imagine the Jewish people could turn down such a generous offer from America. I can't imagine they would rather live in the hell they have had to endure for so many years, waking up every morning wondering which of their loved ones or neighbors would be blown up that day, wondering when some nuclear attack might wipe out all of Israel. Can they not see there is no future for a Jewish nation in this most hostile part of the world?

It is hard to imagine that any sane person would prefer to stand his or her ground in such an impossible situation. But then, religion has an almost insane effect on some people, so that they would rather die in martyrdom than live in peace and harmony. We will just have to allow those people to live with their poor judgment and decisions.

The Jewish people chose to invade a Palestinian nation, killing thousands and driving hundreds of thousands out of their country. Rather than trying to absorb and blend the Palestinian people into their nation, they chose to isolate them by building walls. They have also chosen to take over more and more territories from the Palestinian people. Since when does a nation at war with another take over the other's territory just because that nation won the war? If the United States had done that, it would have a huge empire. It is clear that Israel wishes to continue to expand its empire beyond its borders, and it will never cease to continue that expansion. Remember the Roman Empire !

If Israelis do choose to leave, there should be negotiations to reserve the rights of any and all Jewish people to visit Jerusalem and worship at holy sites. That right should also extend to Christian worshipers. Of course, those religions should also consider that if God created this world, then all of his creation is holy land and should be cherished as such.

The world has been living with this volatile situation for over sixty years and has been trying to prevent a potential nuclear war between the factions. We have not seen even an iota of progress. For all the talk of a peace accord and negotiations, the tensions continue to escalate. Many government officials in the United States and throughout the world continue to have a false hope that a settlement can be reached somehow. Currently, the violence between Israel and the Palestinians is calm. Of course, the Palestinians just suffered one of the most paralyzing defeats in their history. They will reload and strategize for the future; I guarantee it.

Author's note: I actually wrote this chapter over two years ago. Currently, the parties are starting their attacks all over again. They will never cease, no matter what peace accords are reached, not because the parties seeking peace are not sincere in their efforts but because there exist a billion people who resent having the nation of Israel in their land. There will always be terrorists bent on destroying Israel and feeding the attacks on Israel. It's simply an experiment that never worked and obviously never will. There is no reason that the United States should continue to support Israel when doing so causes a billion people hate us and carry out terrorist attacks aimed at us and our allies.

The United States somehow imagines that if Israel gives back the Golan Heights, the Gaza Strip, and the West Bank, the Palestinians will be completely satisfied and there will be peace. Well, Israel has made concessions by giving up some of those territories, and it has not accomplished a thing. Yet every year, the Jewish government approves the building of new subdivisions in Palestinian territory. Each side continues to aggravate the situation. So why should we continue to be the victim of these nations' refusal to negotiate or compromise?

We must stop exhibiting superpower military might, which much of the world interprets as bullying. We must form a strong world coalition of democracies and freedom-loving nations. All the nations of the world that benefit from democracy and freedom owe the United Stated big time.

There would be no democracy and freedom in the world without the extreme sacrifice of Americans. I hope all nations educate their citizens about this fact and try to model their countries according to the lessons we have learned the hard way and the resolutions we have arrived at. There is absolutely no reason why so many nations today and in the future should have to suffer the difficult sacrifices America and many other nations have endured to realize that we all have to respect one another and learn that we can live together despite our differences.

The most valuable lesson in the history of mankind is that there are strong differences between the various ideologies we live by. Realization of the fact we can live together with these differences as long as we don't force those ideals on the freedoms of others is the most difficult concession to make. Everybody wants to be a dictator to some extent. When we find a way to be respectful of each others' beliefs, that is when we become a civil society, a community, and a functioning world family. The future of mankind and the pursuit of world peace are dependent on this recognition. History has proven that forcing your ideology on others does not work and only leads to wars. America does not do enough to explain to the world that people with numerous beliefs and ideals live together in the United States in harmony.

Past generations have realized this and respected the United States for it. However, just as new generations of Americans have little or no knowledge of the extreme sacrifices of past generations, I am sure this information is even more lost with new generations of foreign citizens living under democratic forms of government.

The United States can no longer carry the burden of being the world's police, nor should it have to. We wonder why we cannot provide the quality of health care for our citizens that many other nations provide. It's simply because we spend hundreds of billions of dollars per year keeping peace throughout the world and for weaponry, military personnel, intelligence, and research.

This doesn't even include the billions we spend on boosting allies in these areas. We spend billions for infrastructure and social assistance for these nations, and they still hate us. They destroy the huge investments we make for them and kill as many of our people as they can.

We should be cautious regarding the build-up of nations that sometimes turn against us or other nations as Iraq turned against Kuwait in 1991. We are forced to defend the nation being attacked with our own weaponry. This should make us all nervous about providing technology and weapons that sometimes fall into the hands of the enemy and are used against our own soldiers.

Think of the billions of dollars we have provided to these people while so many of our own citizens suffer in poverty due to the lack of jobs. How long can we continue to invest in failed states before we ourselves become a bankrupt and failed nation? Israel has been thumbing its nose at the United States for nearly two decades now. Isn't it about time that we gave them an ultimatum? Start being cooperative, or you're on your own! And start appreciating the danger and damage your actions cause to the United States as a result of your arrogance.

These factions will absolutely never come to a peaceful existence. It will only continue to escalate to an eventual nuclear war. There are thousands of years of wars and hatred between these people that can never be forgiven. The Jewish people lost and dispersed throughout the world. Then, after World War II, they thought they could come back and take over Palestinian territory, killing or driving hundreds of thousands of them out of the territory the Jewish people craved. Then, in 1967, the Israeli army took over even more Palestinian territory and inflamed the already volatile situation.

Imagine if you were living in a Muslim nation and witnessed Israel moving in on another Muslim nation, attacking, killing, and driving your coreligionists out. Then imagine you witnessed them conquering even more territory. You would have to believe that eventually this evil empire would attack your nation and take over. You would fully understand that another nation across the world was supporting Israel and providing all the military might it used to kill and conquer your people. So who would you consider your real enemy?

You would surely decide you had better find weapons to defend your territory. You wouldn't be able to buy them from America, so where would you purchase them? From America's enemies, of course. So we have an escalation of arms throughout the world. Nations that could be allies suddenly find a way out of extreme poverty by manufacturing weapons they can sell at any price to oil-rich nations.

One lesson the entire world clearly understands by now is that money is the root of all evil in the world. If we are going to continue arming and assisting other nations, there will always be a market for weapons for those who oppose them. So how can we ever expect to get a handle on nuclear proliferation? How about if we stop arming other nations and put the burden of dealing with dangerous and threatening nations on the United Nations or NATO? It is in their best interests to take a stand if they cherish their freedom. The entire free world must unite and take a stand both diplomatically and by utilizing all available economic tools, such as boycotts and blockades.

If all the available alternatives fail, then we must strike the nuclear weapons facilities of threatening nations. It may start a war; however, it's far better to wage a conventional war now than a nuclear war down the line.

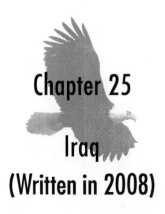

Chapter 25

Iraq
(Written in 2008)

Americans have become too comfortable with our military strength and power in the world. We fail to recognize that the mighty are destined to fail and have done so throughout the history of mankind. Why do you suppose this happens? Well, it's simply because it is the nature of mankind to knock off the big guy or the powerful. In sports, we love to see the underdog, knock off the champions. We love to see an underdog knock off the Yankees.

So while we are so admired and envied by hundreds of millions of people throughout the world, we are also the victim of billions of impoverished people who can never imagine living the life of luxury we mostly take for granted. There are millions of people preaching to hundreds of millions of people that we are the devil incarnate and an evil empire.

As Al Qaida and the Taliban continue to recruit suicide bombers in an attempt to wreak as much devastation and terror on society as possible, they will not hesitate to start a jihad or world war. We cannot continue fighting the war on terror on two fronts—Iraq and Afghanistan—without the help of our allies. We must humble ourselves by admitting that our experiment with democracy in Iraq did not work and that we are not capable of keeping peace in the Middle East indefinitely without the help of our allies. We must present a clear picture of what will certainly happen if we leave and how that will affect the rest of the world.

Patrolling neighborhoods in Iraq and making targets of our troops has got to stop. Imagine if we had foreign troops running through our neighborhoods day after day, year after year. That responsibility must be put on the government of Iraq, and the Iraqi people must be responsible for keeping their peace. I'm sick of hearing that their forces are not well enough trained. We train our police and soldiers in less than a year. We have been training theirs for nearly five years now.

What we need to do is retreat to remote military bases and be on call to assist the Iraqis when they have a major threat. Most of the assistance should focus on air support, intelligence, and training of their troops and police. We must give the Iraqis the equipment and intelligence to protect the Green Zone and their central government in Baghdad as well as other strategic government facilities.

The main thrust of our military should be directed at protecting the borders from insurgents entering from foreign nations. Iraqi military camps need to be built near all roads coming into Iraq, along with inspection stations. These inspection stations should be unmanned and contain the most sophisticated X-ray or imaging equipment available to examine cargo containers on ships and trucks to detect explosives, electronics, chemicals, and other hazardous materials.

This is where our allies can help. There are so many hundreds of miles of border to patrol that it would be virtually impossible for our military to cover those vast regions.

The bottom line is that the more we occupy Iraqi neighborhoods, the more they resent us and hate us. The more we attack insurgents in those neighborhoods, the more accidents we have that kill or maim innocent citizens and children. Then we become even more hated throughout the community. We should have learned by now that it is impossible to win a war in a civilian setting where there is no defined enemy. We have never fought this type of war or even ever imagined fighting this type of war. The enemy is often the people we are defending and helping to give freedom and democracy.

We need to imagine what it would be like if the situation were reversed. Let's say, for instance, that Iran had invaded our nation and was trying to force its strict form of theocracy on us. Most of us would fight back with every weapon we could get our hands on, even if we had to resort to suicide bombing to prevent the enemy from taking away our freedom and democracy.

—⁓—

I wrote the above nearly two years ago, and Iraq is now in danger of becoming aligned with Iran. Prior to our invasion of Iraq, I wrote to Congress that creating a democracy in Iraq would prove impossible. The country is 70 percent Shiite, the same as Iran. You cannot turn a theocracy into a democracy. In spite of the billions of dollars and thousands of American lives we have sacrificed, Iraq is now falling under the influence of the motherland of Shiite theocracy. It is the logical outcome for a nation that was born of the same theocracy as Iran. You cannot change a nation's religious creed. Israel has tried to force its religion and democracy on a region thoroughly entrenched in Islamic beliefs and indoctrination, and they have failed and created great torment and distress for the world in the past century.

The democracy we have tried to establish in Iraq is a corrupt sham. Trudy Rubin's editorial of July 14, 2011 offers a revealing report on the situation in Iraq:

—⁓—

Tehran appears to have Iraqi Prime Minister Nouri al Maliki in a head-lock. Once a politician who showed independence from Tehran, the unpopular Maliki has become dependent on the Iranian-backed Shiite group led by cleric Muqtada al-Sadr, who spends most of his time in the Iranian city of Qom.

Even more disturbing is the decision by Maliki and his Dawa Party to submit to the religious authority of Grand Ayatollah Mahmoud Hashemi Shahroudi, a hard-line Iranian cleric, rather than to Iraq's top Shiite cleric, Grand Ayatollah Ali Sistani. Shahroudi endorses the Iranian system of rule by a supreme cleric, while Sistani draws a line between mosque and state.

Maliki has facilitated the flow of huge numbers of Iranian pilgrims (no doubt including many Iranian intelligence agents) to the holy cities of Najaf and Karbalak, where Iran is building numerous hotels and restaurants.

This week, Iranian First Vice-President Mohammed Reza Rahimi is visiting Bagdad and has signed six agreements to boost economic, health, technological, and cultural ties with Iraqis. He is accompanied by scores of eager Iranian businessmen.

Iraq already depends on Iran for 10 percent of its desperately needed electric power (U.S. inability to help Iraq produce enough electricity, despite many aid projects, has bewildered Iraqis). More Iranian projects are on tap.

—w—

So, essentially I was right prior to the invasion. There is no way in hell to turn a Shiite theocracy into a legitimate democracy. If we can't stop Iran from funneling weapons and insurgents into Iraq, we may as well realize that Iraq and Iran are of the same ethnicity and same religion. Both will always be united in ideology. Trying to divide Shiite Muslims will do nothing more than lead to perpetual animosity, war, and tragic consequences. We tried doing that when we built Saddam Hussein into a military power to defeat Iran. We all know how that played out.

As long as there is a Shiite majority in Iraq, there will eventually be a theocracy and clerical rule as well as unity with Iran.

Chapter 26
Iran

The United States made its first mistake back in the '80s when Iran held our citizens hostage. Iran learned they could push us around, and they continue to do so to this day. We had the justification to bomb the hell out of their military installations and show them who they were messing with. Don't we realize that the billions of dollars they make from their oil can buy the best weapons in the world? They hate us, and they hate Israel. As soon as they can get the weapons to destroy us, they will not hesitate. They would be doing Allah's work, and we see every day how the new Muslim doctrine motivates its followers.

America is going bankrupt, and Iran has so much money it doesn't know what to do with it. Where is this going? They claim they are only investing in nuclear energy. If this were true, they would have no problem with America providing their nuclear power plants. Since they hate us so much, why not a compromise? How about if European nations build and operate the power plants? They certainly have the money to pay, and they obviously do not have the knowledge and ability to build the plants themselves. So why don't they prove to the world they are honest about their intentions?

NATO should make this offer. If Iran refuses the offer, it will prove that their intentions are to build a nuclear arsenal. Their nuclear facilities should be bombed out of existence immediately. Do we wish to go to war with them now or after they have developed a nuclear arsenal?

While we are on the subject of Iran, it should be pointed out that Iran is a Shiite nation. Shiites have formed the strictest theocracy in the world. Iraq is 70 percent Shiite. This is why getting the Iraqis to accept democracy is an impossible task. This is exactly the dilemma that Saddam Hussein faced. The Iraqis actually had more freedoms under Saddam than at any time in history. He constantly faced the threat of Shiites trying to overthrow him. The United States gave him the weaponry to fend them off. So the United States actually built Iraq into a military power in order to keep Iran in check.

You almost have to admire Saddam for his ability to keep order under such difficult circumstances. Apparently, you have to rule with an iron fist in that part of the world. Saddam managed to keep order in a country where we have tried and failed for nearly eight years now. The reason we fail is that Iraq is 70 percent Shiite Muslim, and a strict theocracy is in direct conflict with democracy.

There will never be permanent peace and order in Iraq. That's right ! I said never ! It will forever be the same situation as in Israel and Palestine. All that we will ever be able to accomplish in Iraq is to prevent it from starting a regional war or, even worse, a world war. We elected an idiot and a warmonger for president and we will be paying the price forever.

It is also questionable whether our presence in Afghanistan has done any good. Time will tell, of course. However, we must consider whether we are making progress or are only aggravating the Muslim world and creating a greater recruiting tool for terrorist organizations. We can be sure that Al Qaida and the Taliban forces are out there explaining to children and young men that we are an evil force that is invading their holy land, killing their people (women and children included) every day.

I thought that we were making progress in Afghanistan until this last year. Now it seems we are facing more opposition every day. It seems the longer we occupy their land, the more damage we do to our reputation and the more hated we become. This appears to be a great recruiting tool for the terrorists.

I am coming to the conclusion that it is impossible to wage a war on terrorism. The terrorists all seem to have roots in the Muslim world, and there are over a billion people who are diametrically opposed to Democracy, Christianity, and Judaism. This is an unbelievable number to recruit from. Added to that fact is the number of people dying every day, either directly or indirectly, as a result of our presence.

All of the billions we have spent to rebuild and improve their infrastructure are easily forgotten when their people are dying every day as a result of our presence. Money and material goods cannot fill the void of losing loved ones and family members. It's like I stated before regarding Iraq: all the good we may feel we are doing will never offset the carnage they witness day in and day out.

Saddam Hussein may have gassed over five thousand Kurds when he was in power; however, nearly a hundred thousand of Iraqis have died since our invasion. So how can the citizens of Iraq feel they are better off since our invasion?

If you apply logic to all of the above, you have to come to the conclusion that you cannot invade or occupy a nation containing terrorist roots without inflaming the situation. We should have learned strategic lessons by now. The only way to guard against terrorism is through better worldwide intelligence and strategic defenses for our borders. We might consider a temporary ban on Arab visitors to our nation except for those on official business.

We have opened our universities to millions of Arab citizens with the hope that they would learn the benefits of democracy and capitalism. We hoped they would go home and teach and influence their nations. Apparently, that has not happened. They likely were here to learn our technology, and some were here to determine a plan for striking targets that would wreak the most havoc upon us.

It is a far different world since 9/11. Yet we seem reluctant to give up the freedom of having our nation open to any and every visitor. I don't believe we are capable of tracking even a small fraction of visitors from the Middle East, let alone the millions of Muslims who have relocated to Europe and other nations.

I believe a majority of Americans would approve closing our doors to most Muslim visitors. Yet you will never find a politician brave enough stand up and promote this idea. I would have to say we are totally justified in closing our doors to these people until they get control of the terrorism breeding in their nations. Currently, they just ignore these movements and refuse to accept any responsibility. It takes vast amounts of money to finance terrorist activities, and these governments know damn well who is contributing. These nations have intelligence agencies, financial institutions, and tax agencies, just as we have. They know exactly what is going on, yet we are reluctant to make waves due to our dependence on their oil.

OPEC used to adjust the price of oil according to the ability of the nations of the world to sustain a healthy and growing economy. Lately, it seems they are attempting to bankrupt the democracies of the world. Of course, you have to realize that the easiest way to win a war is economically. This is how we won the Cold War against the USSR. They had a total economic collapse due to their lack of capitalism.

Chapter 27

Middle East Unity

The most essential thing America can do to bring stability to the Middle East is to encourage or insist on some form of unity in the Arab world. So much instability exists because there are numerous different sectarian beliefs, there is no democracy, and there are vile dictatorships and power struggles throughout the region. These nations have failed to understand they can peacefully coexist if they recognize their differences and work together. They need to understand that forcing their beliefs and doctrines on others only leads to needless death, bloodshed, and perpetual war between the factions.

It is nearly the same scenario that existed in the United States prior to the Civil War. We need to admit to the world that we encountered similar problems in building our nation, and we found a way to unify and overcome those differences. As a result, we have become the most prosperous and successful society in the world, a nation that has defended freedom for many nations seeking democracy in the world. Every nation we have given the opportunity for freedom and democracy stands firm in defending its freedom and democracy.

Another benefit of unity is that it enhances mankind's ability to respond to natural disasters and catastrophic weather events. When nations are unified, they are capable of stepping up to provide assistance to each other when in dire need.

The United States, the United Nations, and NATO need to sit down with the leaders of all the Arab and Muslim nations and convince them that there will never be stability in their part of the world until all of their nations unify into a united organization of democratic Arab nations. Most of their problems and animosity are the result of their own internal struggles. A major problem among those nations is that some have hundreds of billions of dollars in oil reserves and others have none. This would be the equivalent of certain states in the United States having billions of dollars in gold or oil reserves and not sharing the tax revenues with states that supply wheat and agricultural products. Each state contributes its natural resources, and as a result, we have built a strong and unified nation that spreads and shares its wealth. That wealth has created the ability to build a strong defense not only for our own nation but also for every nation seeking freedom and democracy throughout the world.

The world is becoming far too dangerous because of tremendous advances in weaponry and technology. These nations can no longer live with the possibility that a lunatic warmonger may come to power and gain access to nuclear power or biological weapons never before imagined. A unified Arab world can keep all nations in check and prevent disasters from occurring. It can also stop the arms buildup within each country by rendering it unnecessary. A unified military would protect them from any nation threatening another.

The United States will need the help of the European Union to convince the Arab Nations of the benefits of unity. It will need the support of NATO and the United Nations most importantly. It is in the best interests of all the nations of the world to maintain long-term stability starting in the Middle East and hopefully extending throughout the world. It will be much easier to solve conflicts if all the countries of the Middle East and Arab world are at the table and have a stake in the negotiations. Also, they must realize that all parties have to make concessions to form a strong union. This type of union will prevent the ascent to power of a vile dictator who would threaten the stability of the entire region. It should be clear to all North African and Middle Eastern nations that the citizens of those nations have reached the end of their tolerance for monarchies and dictatorships. It's time for those nations to sit down together and promote legitimate democracies and unity.

The most valuable lesson for the nations in the Middle East and perhaps throughout the world is that most of them are victims of the vile actions of their ancestors, who created the animosity that goes on to this day. A handful of miscreants turned nations against each other perpetually. Do your people wish to be forever victims of the depraved actions of a few in your history? Do you realize that if you had been born on the other side of the border, you would have developed an enemy's ideology and been at war with the nation you live in? Do you choose to perpetuate the animosity until you all destroy each other? History is full of examples of nations that once were at war with each other and are now allies and good neighbors. The United States, Germany, and Japan are examples of nations that finally sat down and worked out their differences following terrible wars. It is time for all the Arab nations to do the same in a spirit of unity. It's time for the monarchies, dynasties, and dictators of the Middle East and Africa to come to the table and determine whether their legacies will be to destroy each other or bring peace and prosperity to a billion citizens. To end the needless massacres, disease, poverty, and suffering and bring democracy, freedom, and comfort will require courageous leaders who are willing to give up their power and pass it on to their citizens—the greatest gift in those nations' history.

We all face mortality. Would you like history to reflect your brutality and the suffering of millions of your citizens or your courage and the sacrifice you made for millions by demonstrating kindness to your people?

Chapter 28
China

It seems that America has to constantly identify the next greatest threat to our freedom. During the Cold War against the Soviet Union, China was actually an ally to the United States. As soon as the Soviet Union collapsed, suddenly China became our main enemy and threat. There always has to be an enemy to justify greater arms buildup. First it was the issue of Hong Kong being unified back into China. There was rhetoric about that issue. Those poor people were going to lose all their freedoms and there would be total chaos. Actually, it seems that Hong Kong influenced China so positively that they are now becoming a capitalist nation.

We are also China's number-one consumer. Is China inclined to cut its own throat by going to war with the United States? China is waging a different war, an economic war, and they are kicking ass. This is how we won the Cold War against the Soviet Union. It wasn't because President Reagan told Mr. Gorbachev to tear down that wall. It was because the communist economy collapsed. They could not even feed their soldiers, let alone invest in weaponry to keep up with the United States. Their economy collapsed due to the lack of incentives. Capitalism won.

The United States has been at odds with China over Taiwan for decades now. The United States threatens to defend Taiwan if China tries to invade it. The United States supplies Taiwan with weapons, yet there is no way Taiwan could defend itself in a war with China. So essentially, we are adding fuel to the fire and creating an enemy for no good reason.

If Taiwan is taken over by China and the result will be the same as Hong Kong being absorbed into China, what would be the problem? It seems that the United States has to make a stand for no good reason and at the same time force China to build a million-man army and build weapons to defend itself against our threats. In the mean time, the Chinese sell weapons to rogue nations at odds with the United States or Israel. It's just another huge economic gain for China and more problems for the free world to fear.

There never has been a better time in history for China to invade the United States than now, while we are bogged down in Iraq and Afghanistan. The same could be said for invading Taiwan. They don't need Taiwan. China's economy is soaring.

My fellow Americans, can we not see that we are losing the economic world war? China is winning this war. However, I have no reason to believe that China has cause to go to war and destroy its economy by dropping its number-one business account. And what other countries would continue to do business with China if they were at war with the United States? China's economy would collapse overnight. China does not have a self-supporting economy. It is dependent on almost every nation of the world for its existence.

If we can make peace with China, it will likely open doors to peace and the reunification of North Korea and South Korea. North Korea's problem is poverty. If they could invest the billions of dollars they spend on their military in their infrastructure instead, they would likely become economically stable like South Korea. It happened in Germany, and it is slowly happening in Vietnam.

One thing I'm sure Americans have to realize is that the democracy and freedoms we live with may not work in such a hugely populated country. Let's take New York City as an example. Mayor Giuliani had to take a much firmer hand in order to clean up the crime that permeated that populous area; the more densely populated a region is, the greater the danger of government losing control of a population. You have to have stricter controls in such a massively populated area. Can you imagine what would happen if things got out of order in a nation with four times the population of the United States? You would have total chaos and a never-ending civil war.

On the other hand, democracy must be born within a nation. This will happen in the future in China as a result of capitalism.

North Korea is gradually learning the value of capitalism as it witnesses the rising economy of South Korea. It is time to open the door and offer assistance to North Korea. Continuing the policy the United States has exercised for the past half-century only serves to make those people hate us and fear us much more. This only leads to more arms buildup and selling weapons to other rogue nations.

America should stop exacerbating tensions with China. We need China both as an economic associate and as a military ally. If we had China's million-man army assisting our military in the Middle East, we could likely make great progress in achieving stability in the region. I fail to understand how Taiwan is any more integral to the security of the United States than Hong Kong was. It seems that this is the only issue standing between the United States and China. It creates military escalation and destroys the good will that could be enjoyed between two superpowers. China is not a terrorist nation as so many other nations are. We need China on our side in the battle against worldwide terrorism.

China is also on the verge of realizing how terrorism can eventually become a threat to it too. Eventually, China will realize its economic stability would be much stronger if they supported America's causes than it is when they impede our security. It is far better for the Chinese economy when America spends hundreds of billions of dollars on Chinese products than when we spend that money on fighting terrorism around the world. There is only so much money in the piggy bank. Busting the piggy bank in the Middle East will leave few dollars to purchase China's products, to say nothing of how it affects our ability to repay the hundreds of billions of dollars in debt China holds.

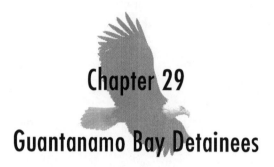

Chapter 29

Guantanamo Bay Detainees

I fail to understand why our federal security agents need to resort to torture in order to obtain valuable information. Often those suspects are going to lie just to satisfy their interrogators and stop the torture. They may at times not even have the valuable information we are seeking. Then we are only creating bad will for others we may wish to interrogate.

So why not utilize proven techniques? Just get them drunk! What happened to truth serums? You can take the suspects into a comfortable setting and give them their drink of choice. Vodka is almost tasteless in moderation. Soon the suspect will be asking for more and not even know why. Eventually, he or she will become your friend and spill the beans, just like any drunk. Some of the worst criminals in history have been caught due to the stupidity of getting drunk in a bar and spilling the beans.

There is nothing wrong with holding detainees offshore. It is only the methods employed at the facility that are the problem. I don't know any community that would wish to have terrorist suspects detained in its vicinity. Eventually, a plot by terrorists designed to attack the detention facility and free the suspects could endanger that community.

You cannot cite normal rules of engagement and detainment, because the war on terrorism will never end.

The government should, however, either try suspects within a reasonable time if there is enough evidence or release them if there is not. In doing this, we will gain worldwide respect for our justice system. Nothing in this world is worse than injustice. If we hope to steer the world toward freedom and democracy, we must set an example of justice for all.

Chapter 30

Unified Nations

M ost of the wars throughout the world could be prevented if nations of took a lesson from the history of the United States. All nations should take a close look at what made the United States the most powerful nation in the history of the world.

If we had not unified, chances are we might have had wars between states. We surely would not be the powerful nation we became, and we likely would have been overrun by foreign powers.

All the tragic wars and genocide that have occurred in Africa for hundreds of years could have been avoided had those nations unified in a democratic union. Those countries likely could have fought off the foreign and domestic powers that raped and pillaged their natural resources (something that continues to this day). If those countries had been unified under a strong central command and had been the beneficiaries of the wealth generated by their own natural resources, they could have staved off the invaders and blossomed into a strong democratic union, a union that would have provided well for all the citizens of a united Africa.

As sad as the situation is in Africa, it is far more dangerous and volatile in the Middle East. Rather than developing a strong democracy throughout the region and extinguishing the hatred and vengeance that has fueled wars for thousands of years, those nations continue to build greater animosity for each other. Their wealth goes into more powerful and destructive weapons rather than strong infrastructure, education, health, clean water, and a good environment for their people. The wealth their natural resources provide—hundreds of billions of dollars, in many cases—often is swallowed up by vile dictators or royalty, leaving the masses in extreme poverty.

Because of the extreme poverty throughout the region, the only hope is for young men to enlist in terrorist organizations. The volatility of the entire region in the Middle East forces most of the world's democracies to take on a role in preventing a disastrous war among those nations that would be the greatest threat to world stability in history.

It is time for all the Middle Eastern nations to come to the table and determine where their future lies. The United States has provided the lion's share of the stability in the Middle East for many decades. The extreme costs of the wars in Iraq and Afghanistan leave the United States incapable of continuing that stability. In much of the region, it is actually creating more instability.

It is past time for the United States and the free world to admit to those nations that they will not be capable of providing stability in the future. They will have to recognize that absolutely the only hope for their future lies in their ability to recognize they have all been victims of hateful and vile leaders in the past who started wars that continue throughout history.

Most of all, these people need to understand those born on one side of the border were brainwashed from youth to believe that those on the other side were the enemy. The reality most people fail to consider is that as human beings, we all live for the same thing. We all live for happiness today and a better future tomorrow. Continuation of the hatred and vengeance that has propelled war in the past will only destroy any chance for peace, happiness, and the betterment of our societies in the future.

People have to learn that past wars are not their responsibility. They were likely started by absolutely despicable tyrants who people alive today never knew and likely would not have approved of had they lived in that era. Many nations are the victims of past atrocities that have formed barriers and hatred for their neighbors. Each nation should study history and seek the truth that led to the wars. Perhaps your own leaders were in the wrong.

The United States must acknowledge that it is sometimes dangerous to arm one nation to balance the power in a region. It might be better to come to the defense of a nation rather than arm it. Arming Saddam Hussein is a case in point. He turned around and used the weapons to invade Kuwait. The United States defending against Iraq's invasion of Kuwait is an example of when we might be justified to launch military action.

Intervention and diplomacy would likely be a better solution for many of the disputes that create wars among nations. Arming one nation makes a permanent enemy of another. As a result of our actions, Iran is now one of the greatest threats to world stability, and its fear and uncertainty lead to the continued election of officials committed to overthrowing the military might of the United States.

It almost makes one wonder if countries would be better off staying out of these conflicts and letting the best nation win. If the winner arises as a threat to the free world, then there would be a target to aim for—whatever weaponry the winner is using to target other nations. This is how wars used to be fought—by knocking out weaponry and armies. That kind of war is very different from the wars currently being fought in residential neighborhoods with little or no benefit but an extreme amount of bad will. In this new kind of war, when the troops finally pull out, everything goes to hell.

All nations should examine how much European nations have strengthened since they formed the European Union. Asian countries should also form a strong union. South America may be on the way to becoming the most dangerous continent in the world. The drug cartels are growing stronger and more powerful every year, and they threaten any semblance of democracy and stability on that continent. With their power, they are able to place their own rogue leaders in place.

It seems no single nation has the military might and economic power to defend itself in this modern world. However, unified with their neighbors, nations would have greater diplomatic clout and military power. Continental alliances could provide political clout, enabling each nation to prevent rogue rulers from coming into power and becoming a threat to its neighbors. Out of union democracy and diplomacy would be born.

It would be very difficult to unify these nations. However, if enough countries unified for their self-protection, they would have greater strength to ward off the dangerous countries threatening them. Eventually, those other countries would see the benefits of unity. If a rogue country like Iran came into the region offering financial assistance and weaponry, it could become a serious threat to North America. It happened in Cuba, and it could happen anywhere in the western hemisphere.

In another chapter, I state that I would like to see Mexico and Canada become a part of the United States; eventually, even Central American countries could do so as well. You never know when a tyrant like Chavez in Venezuela might come into power in Mexico or when democracy might fall there due to the powerful drug cartels. Our enemies could then use Mexico's fall to be at our doorstep with nuclear weapons.

I believe that America has made a huge mistake by not continuing to expand. We can't seem to be able to push democracy onto foreign powers. However, we likely could invite others to join our nation. That direction could eventually lead to world peace. It may prove to be the only route toward that goal, but it seems to be becoming more impossible as time goes by.

Our goal of world peace and stability seems to fall farther away every year. Being a world power seems to be interpreted as arrogance even when our intentions are noble and justified. Perhaps we need to invite nations to join us in the pursuit of peace and freedom rather than waiting for them to fall prey to vile dictatorships and pose serious threats to our nation and the world. Is there any reason why the United States should have a limit of fifty states? There should be no limit to the methods used for the creation of world peace and prosperity. It worked for fifty different unified states, so why would it not work for many more?

America is a perfect example of how all nationalities and ethnicities can live together in peace and prosperity. We need to extol those virtues to the world every day and convince the rest of the world that unification is the only formula for peace and prosperity for all mankind. At the same time, we need to admit that we have made huge mistakes in our history and learned valuable lessons as a result. Other nations should avoid our mistakes if they hope to achieve peace and prosperity. Every nation in the world should ask itself which is its long-term goal: peace and prosperity, or war.

Chapter 31

Growth Curtailment

I don't know if the experts ever elaborate on the following issue. What happens when the world reaches its absolute saturation point for population growth? The problem likely is not that there is not enough land but that there is not enough natural resources: enough lumber, minerals, food, energy sources, and so on. And of course, there may not be enough of the most important resource of all: water.

How will a world economy sustain itself if it is only based on continuous growth and expansion? What happens to a world economy that will no longer support growth? Where will the jobs come from?

I believe this is an issue the next few generations will be forced to deal with. It is an issue that needs to be studied now, not after mankind finds itself in a crisis with no answers.

The world will be forced to answer the following question: Will the world be better off with fewer people or with billions more living in abject poverty, disease, starvation, war, suffering, and death?

We had better be prepared for answers and solutions, because any reasonably intelligent person can see the certainty of the coming crisis. We already witness hundreds of millions of human beings suffering in abject poverty and the suffering and death of millions of infants. How do we live with this? It's easy, of course. We just ignore it ! But it will be harder to do that when this situation comes to our doors or the doors of our grand-children. We may be forced to ask, Is this the best that we could do with the world we inherited? Abject poverty and suffering ! I guess that birth control is out of the question.

Chapter 32

Transportation Taxes

For many decades, the federal government provided the lion's share of funding for local roads, streets, and bridges. They also provided the lion's share of funding for state highways and interstate highways. The federal gas tax was instituted for the purpose of moving freight throughout the nation, which included moving freight to and through communities. Now, of course, we are spending all those billions of dollars in Iraq and Afghanistan.

It used to be that highway construction could nearly keep up with increases in population by expanding and building new highways. We were always behind, but we were always making progress in handling congestion throughout the nation. Now we are falling behind catastrophically. We can't build and improve roads to keep up with rising populations. Thousands of bridges are becoming more dangerous every year.

I have no idea how many states have an excise tax dedicated to highway construction and maintenance or how other states fund highway construction and maintenance. The State of Washington used to have an annual excise tax based on the average value of vehicles and also a state gas tax. When these taxes were initiated, they were for the sole purpose of highway construction and maintenance. Somehow, over the years, a large share wound up in the state's general fund.

During all the decades when the excise tax existed, there was a consistent revenue stream available for keeping up with the state's direst transportation needs. The state could repair and maintain roads and bridges and at the same time build and expand the most essential highways to handle increased population and congestion. There were always funds available for federal highway matching funds, and often the federal government supplied the lion's share of the funding.

Approximately ten years ago in the State of Washington, an antitax advocate named Tim Eymman convinced the voters that they should abolish the excise tax on vehicles. The wealthy who paid more tax for their luxury vehicles, multiple vehicles, and expensive recreation vehicles never had a problem paying this tax. It did not stop them from purchasing more and more expensive vehicles. They were paying thousands of dollars per year in excise tax. Yet the average citizens, seeing that they could save $100 to $300 per year, were delighted to approve the abolishment of the tax. Even those who drove very old vehicles and only paid $50 to $100 per year approved. How much more foolish could the voters be? Certainly, the wealthy loved the idea. However, the majority of voters are middle class to impoverished.

This tells me that voters should not be put in charge of or have a voice in determining the needs and financing of our transportation infrastructure. This is a necessary and essential part of the infrastructure of our communities throughout the nation. Just as with many other utilities and infrastructure operations, our government officials must make the critical decisions to keep commerce flowing, making the necessary improvements to avoid traffic congestion that would be costly for citizens and commerce. Government officials are the ones who study the facts, review the data and projections, and determine the most essential needs in our communities.

Until all citizens are forced to attend public meetings presenting all this information, our elected officials are the only individuals qualified to make decisions and appropriate funds to manage these urgent needs. Transportation is a vital utility just like sewers, water, garbage, and so on, and it is essential that government officials make the decisions required to keep commerce and citizens out of transportation bedlam and absolute dysfunction.

I'm sure most states depend on a state gas tax to build and maintain their roads and highways. So what happens in the future when the majority of vehicles are powered by batteries, hydrogen fuel cells, or other methods? The main source of funding for streets, bridges, highways, and even public transportation will dry up.

This formula for tax revenue has been flawed from the start. It should have been a natural assumption that vehicles were going to evolve to be more fuel efficient as the years rolled by. The tax should have been a percentage tax in order to maintain a consistent revenue flow. I recommend that all states and the federal government immediately make an adjustment to start addressing these huge losses of revenue. Clearly the gas tax should be a percentage tax.

I also suggest that states create an annual excise tax on all vehicles based on their value. This taxation would be the only method of funding the building and maintenance of roads, bridges, and ferries in the near future. This is a progressive tax that has never hurt the wealthy or prevented the wealthy from purchasing multiple expensive vehicles in the past. Progressive taxes are the only fair kind of taxation, and they have built the most powerful nation in the world. I might also add that progressive taxation has also created a nation with the wealthiest individuals in the world. In effect, progressive taxes have worked well enough to create the strongest nation in history. Additionally, most of those who pay little tax in their early years of employment generally wind up paying a greater share later in their careers.

It is a certainty that in ten years, the majority of vehicles will be powered by batteries, hydrogen fuel cells, or other technologies. How much revenue will be generated by fuel taxes to finance road maintenance and construction and public transit? An excise tax is the only method to sustain a constant revenue flow that will allow our department of transportation to perform its duties to keep commerce flowing and meet the escalating needs of the citizenry.

The millions of people who sit in traffic along freeways for hours each day do not enjoy the quality of life they deserve as hardworking Americans. Public transportation is fine for those who cannot afford to own and operate vehicles. However, there has probably never been another possession that can give individuals so much freedom—freedom to go where you wish, when you wish in privacy and security. Mankind will never give up that freedom. That is why there is such a proliferation of automobiles in rapidly developing nations like China and India. The only answer I can find for this problem is outlined in my chapter dealing with redeveloping rural communities and designing new communities.

One last issue on transportation: Why don't state legislators ban the use of studded tires on highways and streets that do not have snow or ice? We don't run with chains on dry or wet pavement. Our nation spends billions of dollars per year repairing the damage caused by studs.

Somehow, millions of us have survived without studs and without accidents on snow- or ice-covered roads. People should either learn how to drive in wintry conditions or park. The technology of tire design has advanced so much that it is absolutely unnecessary to use studs in this day and age. However, what is a billion dollars here and there for the legislators who spend our tax dollars?

Chapter 33

Local Government and Taxing Authority

There was a time in American history when it was necessary to have local governments, as townships were far apart and communities were very different in their cultures, identities, and ideals. Today, we are not so diverse in our culture due to television and other media. Economically, we all depend on each other.

Now many communities that used to be small cities and townships have grown together into huge metropolitan areas. Yet the majority of these areas still consist of numerous cities and townships. Most still choose to maintain their local governments. Worse yet, new cities continue to incorporate adjacent to existing cities. Can these citizens not see that this results in redundant equipment, resources, and management, creating much financial waste? This does not even take into consideration all the energy these communities waste in order to provide government services to their citizens.

It is an absolute fact that the larger a city is, the more political influence it has with the federal government. All these small cities crowded together could form one big city and have greater political clout. They choose to ignore this fact even if they would have to pay much more for government services. The desire for local control seems to outweigh the greater government grants they would qualify for, the duplication they pay for, and the greater buying power of larger corporations. Cities are corporations, and the larger the corporation, the more buying power and political clout it has.

It's not as if large cities or county governments don't have local representation. Most have district representatives just like our state and federal districts. Usually local control is the brainchild of a few angry political activists who did not get their way on an issue. So they become very active and convince local citizens they are being victimized. Sometimes, these actions even result in a different form of government, and often it's a worse form of government.

The best place to respond to elected officials if they have not served their constituents is at the ballot box. If those officials have made decisions contrary to the will of the majority of citizens, they are easy to dispose of. Yet some citizens choose to be dictators of public policy. The citizenry doesn't always identify its motives.

My solution to all these problems is to dissolve all city governments and place local control strictly in the hands of county governments. I will now outline my case for why this would be in the best interests of all citizens and fair to all.

First of all, there seems to be a migration of wealthy people from the inner city to elite communities, incorporated cities with local control, and areas under the jurisdiction of county governments. This allows those citizens to escape the tremendous expense of inner-city poverty and crime. Isn't that just wonderful! Citizens who work in the metro area and live in the suburban area can just wipe their hands clean of the financial burden of crime and all the social problems of the inner city. They depend on that city for medical services, legal services, social events, sports, entertainment, dining, and so on. Yet they expect the city's government to provide security and services with a tax base that is much smaller than the tax base in suburban areas.

Many of the spoiled brats of those elite citizens wind up in the inner city when their parents decide they can no longer afford to provide every little thing they desire. Youthful citizens and others failing in life do not migrate to suburban areas. They find temporary happiness with the drugs that are always available in the inner city. If they don't have the money, there are plenty of citizens who they can take it from. It should be illegal for the wealthy to escape the financial obligations of the metro area they live in by moving just outside the taxing district.

Many of the communities that are built in outlying areas have modern infrastructures and utilities. Those taxpayers are spared the tremendous expense of repair and maintenance that the inner city must pay for with limited tax revenues due to lower property values. Yet the residents of those outlying communities use the cities for employment and numerous services, which puts a great burden on the cities' infrastructure.

The worst injustice occurs in the creation of school districts. Tax-rich suburban areas can build better schools and facilities. They can provide better programs, better extracurricular activities, and hire better teachers and staff. Meanwhile, the inner cities rot away, property values decline, taxes decline, and many quality teachers fear working in crime-ridden neighborhoods.

Somehow, school districts always seem to be established in a way that separates low-income neighborhoods from wealthy neighborhoods. This apparently is a constitutional right that was granted in a time when communities were spread out over a wide area and autonomy was necessary.

There was a time when school districts were formed to serve rural communities as well as cities and unincorporated areas. The citizens who lived in rural areas lived there because that's where they made their livings. People who live in suburban areas adjacent to cities and form their own school districts do so mostly to form exclusive communities, escape the tax burden of the inner city, and spend their tax dollars on exclusive schools and facilities.

However, there are those who argue that you cannot deprive citizens of the right to form their own governments and school districts. Well, that would depend on how a state's constitution is written and whether it can or will be amended to spread the responsibility and expense for social problems and education equally among all tax districts within the state. To me, this is a form of discrimination against the lower-income residents of the inner city. They are forced to pay for and deal with most of the social ills of the state or county, while the elite suburbanites skate by and avoid responsibility. This is no way to construct a thriving and healthy society.

We may not be able to prohibit communities from forming their own governments without a constitutional amendment. State legislators can, however, take over authority of school districts, since they control a large share of funding for education. They can declare that there is only one school district in the state and that there will be equal distribution of educational funding. Not only should there be equal distribution of funding, but there should also be extra funding for failing schools. All the resources required to bring those schools and their students up to par with the most successful schools in the state should be put at their disposal.

This is where government officials can prove they are better equipped to make decisions than selfish voters. I'm afraid to tell voters that autonomy and selfish decisions in government are not going to work in society any longer. We all have to have an interest in saving every child and student in our nation.

The wealthy can choose to form their elite communities with elite schools; however, they cannot escape the severe social problems due to failing schools and impoverished inner cities. They cannot escape the problem of growing prison populations. Would you rather invest your tax dollars in quality education for all the children of your state, or invest in more prisons and the health and welfare of criminals?

I'm afraid to inform citizens that times are changing rapidly, and the autonomy and selfish independence that worked in the past is no longer going to work for America. America is rapidly failing, and I will describe the reasons why in another chapter. Apparently, most Americans have not studied history well enough to realize that all great empires are destined to fail. Stay tuned to find out why !

Chapter 34

Prison Explosion

How Society Functions

This section will focus on solutions and a perspective that I feel we, as a society, must adopt if we wish to put an end to the destruction of modern society. In order to put society into perspective and demonstrate how modern society works, which we take for granted, I will attempt to re-create our society as if I were explaining it to elementary students. I wish that our schools explained this to us when we were very young.

Imagine a cruise ship with thousands of people aboard that encounters a tidal wave, and for some unknown reason, all power and communications are wiped out. This ship is swept thousands of miles off course, and all efforts to locate the ship are eventually abandoned, and it is assumed that it has sunk. The ship's power systems fail, and the ship drifts at sea for weeks. Finally, the crew finds that an unknown island is in view and manages to steer the ship to the island, and the crew and passengers make it to shore. When all passengers and crew are safely on land, the captain addresses them. He tells them they have no idea where they are or if they will ever be found. All they can do is survive and hope they will eventually be found. Survival will require the best effort and dedication of every individual to making his or her best contribution.

There happen to be a variety of experts in the colony. There are a few doctors from different fields, agricultural engineers, farmers, carpenters, scientists, lumberjacks, and so on. Some are skilled hunters and fishermen. Some will be expected to step down from their areas of expertise, and others will be asked to step up and provide labor they might not be comfortable with.

The captain fully explains that all these skills are invaluable to the existence of the colony. If some choose not to do their part and take from their neighbors, it could create division or perhaps war. For instance, if the doctor were robbed and killed, they would not have the skills needed to treat a disease that could potentially wipe out the entire colony. If the surgeon were killed or disabled, there would not be a skilled surgeon to repair broken bones and treat other disabling injuries.

In other words, a society works because each person does an essential job that we all depend on at some point in our lives. If a citizen decides he won't do his part and chooses to rob or kill another citizen, the victim might be someone who provides essential services to society, such as a surgeon at a hospital emergency room. It might be a policeman, a fireman, or an emergency responder who saves lives.

Now, if enough of us choose to rob and kill to get what we desire in life, soon there will not be enough of the essential specialists left upon whom we all depend. Society would be destroyed. Nobody would be able to walk the streets, let alone obtain food and other essential goods to survive.

I am reminded of a time in high school when I got in trouble. When I returned to school, I was immediately sent to the counselor's office. He asked me if I understood why there are rules and regulations in society. He told me to imagine a society without rules and regulations. Cars would be tearing down the street at eighty miles an hour. Intersections would become wrecking yards and death traps. Pedestrians wouldn't have a chance.

He went on to point out how everybody would be robbing and killing one another. Then he asked if that was the kind of world I wanted to live in. That message has stuck with me throughout my life. I wonder why that lesson isn't taught routinely in school. Was it just because of my situation that I was fortunate enough to learn that lesson? It became my first lesson in logic, and I have based my life upon logic since then. Every fifth grader should be assigned to write a thesis on why we have rules and regulations in our society.

The Causes of Rising Crime

While America is quite concerned about how working Americans will be able to support Medicare and Social Security for baby boomers, here is another serious financial plague we are dealing with now that will become more and more insurmountable in the long term.

We can't seem to build prisons fast enough to house the dangerous criminals who prey on society more and more as time passes. There are several reasons for this trend. I will now point out what I feel are the major contributors.

First, both legal and illegal drugs are becoming more and more dangerous every decade and will only get more wonderful for the user and at the same time more dangerous to society in the future. The human brain is the most delicate and sensitive instrument in our bodies. Most drugs, whether prescription or illegal, are brain-altering chemicals. We've all heard the phrase, "You can't fool Mother Nature" ! That is exactly what many drugs do. I certainly am not implying that there are not a lot of good drugs performing miraculous healing, saving lives, and preventing much suffering. However, many drugs in the antidepressant category are very dangerous.

I personally had a terrible experience about twenty years ago. I had been on Lorazapam for about fifteen years, and it did a tremendous job controlling back pain and calming me down. At times, I forgot to put this pill in my lunch. I was thirty or forty miles away from home on the job. I seriously considered many times going to a pharmacy and begging for just one pill. Years later, I tried to get off the drug, and the doctor substituted another antidepressant. I experienced a strange feeling that I could not deal with. It was such a strange and uncomfortable feeling that

I wanted to kill myself just to get relief. I spent three days under my bed covers determined to fight it off. Consequently, I will never take antidepressants again.

Many drugs cause such irrational behavior that it is almost beyond belief what people will do either as a result of overuse or in order to feed their habits. They totally lose all rationality. We continue to witness these tragedies every day. These problems will continue to multiply in the future.

As this trend continues, eventually we will reach a point when each working person in America will be paying for a prisoner's room and board and health care. So where does it all end?

The sad reality of this situation is that many of these prisoners become secure and comfortable living in an environment where there is no stress about where they will get their next meal or where they will sleep that night. The social life and controlled security are likely more comforting than what they might face on the streets. So why not gamble when you get out and try to obtain the good life on the cheap? The worst that can happen is that you wind up back in a secure, comfortable place. It almost seems that many intentionally commit crime to get back where they are comfortable and secure.

It may seem absurd, but many criminals are good businesspeople. They work hard at their businesses, are committed, and have a special talent for overseeing all aspects of their criminal networks. It is very unfortunate their talents were not channeled in a better direction when they were young. I'll bet a majority of criminals who are in prison wish they had applied their labors in a very different direction.

The chief difference is patience. They wanted to achieve financial success overnight instead of realizing a long-term goal and exercising patience to achieve that success. Many of these people are not suited to work for somebody else. There are many successful businesspeople in society who were only able to achieve their success by working for themselves and building their own businesses.

The other contributing factor is the unbelievable way we spoil our brats. That's right! I said brats! There is no other way to describe children whose parents will go to great lengths to get them anything their hearts desire. They have to have the most expensive clothing that corporate America can provide. They have to have the most expensive toys that America can supply. They have to have the latest technology in communications and games. Parents certainly don't want to feel guilty or for their children to feel left out. They certainly don't want to lower themselves to expect their children to work for those things.

Then, of course, there are the sports activities and all the sports camps children participate in during the summer time. This gives up the chance for teens to work during their summer vacations and learn the work ethic and responsibility that will be so valuable when they enter the real world. Rather than teaching them to fish, we simply supply them with all the fish they need. When their parents are no longer around to provide the fish or can no longer afford the big fish their little hearts desire, these children will soon learn to go out and take fish from others.

For those of you who don't understand the above, let me put it in simpler terms. The more parents supply their children with everything they demand, the more they will demand. As they grow older, they will have greater expectations and demands. When you can't meet those demands, they will expect society to meet their perceived needs. That will eventually lead them to look for a cheap and easy way to obtain their desires. Some with find artificial happiness and fulfillment in drugs or alcohol. Of course, that will require more and more money, and we all know what that leads to.

At some point in the future, many couples will have to decide whether they can afford to have children because there will be so many prisoners to support, not to mention the children the prisoners leave behind. This is becoming a reality more and more every day.

Chapter 35

Prison Solutions

In the previous chapter, I identified the most serious factors contributing to the rise in prison populations. I didn't mention the thousands of criminals who get early release because of overcrowding. The greatest travesty is that many thousands are released due to a lack of funding for personnel in the prosecutor's office and the judicial system. This inhibits the prosecutor's ability to bring charges within a legal timeline. So these criminals walk and immediately go back to putting a burden on society. While there should be timelines for holding charged criminals or suspects, there should not be a timeline for trials. This is a travesty. Crime is crime, whether the justice system is overburdened or not. The same should apply to criminals or suspects released on technical errors. Retry them, but don't let them walk due to errors in trials or investigations. To err is human. To commit crime goes against the grain of a civilized society.

The only good news we ever get is when these criminals wipe each other out. This saves society millions each time it happens. Also, police should be authorized to use lethal force any time a criminal is in the process of committing crime and is displaying a weapon.

I would like to know why these criminals deserve the services and amenities other citizens work so hard to provide and sometimes pay for with their lives. These criminals are out there constantly interfering with the ability of honest, hardworking citizens to provide for their needs, security, and enjoyment of life. These criminals have established that they have no respect for those of us who work hard to provide the amenities they expect in life and take for granted. If the majority of citizens were criminals, would we have a society? Absolutely not ! It could not possibly exist.

The best justice society can hope for is that criminals get caught in the act of a felony and refuse to surrender their weapons so that the police are forced to kill them. Boy, does that save society huge amounts of money. Too often our brave law enforcement officers fall victim to these useless bastards; sometimes, even judges, attorneys, and other members of the judicial system fall victim to them.

Then these slimeballs get to live comfortable lives till old age without the stress or responsibility the rest of us live with throughout our lives. They also get medical care, room and board, and entertainment, while the rest of us worry about a major medical problem that will wipe out everything we have worked so hard for. Many of us will be denied life-saving surgeries or medical procedures. But we can afford these services for these worthless bastards.

If funding for the amenities of prisoners had to be raised by donations, I wonder how many donations would be made. If all citizens were mailed a monthly bill for the health and welfare of prisoners, I wonder how many would pay the bill. So why do we continue to finance their worthless existence ?

Therefore, I have come up with a logical solution that will save the judicial system and citizens billions of dollars per year. We should simply give these scumbags what they deserve: a lawless society.

I propose that criminals who either cannot understand the way society works or disregard those of us who do respect others should have the benefits of society taken away. They should have no access to medical care, entertainment, security, television, newspapers, radio, and so on.

The ideal situation would be to exile them to their own island, which should be surrounded by sharks. Let them fend for themselves. Since there are no islands available, I guess we would have to construct a concrete and steel island.

I suggest a concrete and steel fortress that will be impossible to escape from. There should be no prison personnel or employees. There should be one guard tower on the outside equipped with the most advanced monitoring technology available and an electric fence with a lethal voltage. Once a month, a truck should pull up to a chute to drop basic food supplies into the basement. These commodities might consist of flour, rice, beans, and canned fruit and vegetables—just the basics.

The prisoners should be responsible for cooking and preparing their own foods. They can create their own rules and regulations. If they choose to kill each other, that will be their problem, since they have turned their backs on a society that provided security, law, and order. If they have illness or disease, they should still be on their own, since they had no respect for the society that provided those benefits.

I will refer to this prison as the prison from hell (PFH). Of course, I am not so mean spirited that I would expect all prisoners convicted of felonies to be sent to the PFH. I do believe in second chances and, under certain circumstances, third chances. But I definitely would want anyone convicted of premeditated murder, mass murder, child molesting (when the victim is under twelve), some major forms of fraud, and some other criminal activities to be sent to the PFH. Other than those in the above categories, the PFH would be used for repeat offenders—those who have proved over and over that they have no respect for the rules and regulations of society.

I expect that over a period of time, the situation in the PFH would get so ugly and chaotic that it would become a great deterrent to crime. It might be so bad, in fact, that many criminals would prefer the death penalty. I have always felt that there should be a noose hanging in every jail cell or at least one in the outdoor exercise yard to provide entertainment. Prisoners should be entitled to this option if they prefer not to put a further burden on society.

My second proposal for the department of corrections is a true reform school. With the advent of the internet and the tremendous technology available in this age, a prisoner can obtain an education in almost any field or occupation. Many working and struggling citizens can only wish they had the time to study and improve their place in life.

If I were a warden, there would be nothing but educational programming and government affairs available on the prison television. If prisoners were exposed to enough of the problems government officials are forced to deal with, they might gain a different perspective and appreciation for society. It would be like being in a doctor's office waiting room and finding there were no magazines that met your particular interests. As a result, you might pick up a magazine at random and suddenly find yourself interested in a subject you could not have imagined being interested in.

If prisoners were subjected to the History Channel, Animal Planet, National Geographic, and so on, I predict that their interests and philosophies in life would evolve. Many citizens who were bored in school find that their interests evolve as they gain exposure to the real world. Many of us have regrets about not taking education more seriously, and many others choose to get that education later in life.

Essentially, I would like to see education offered via the internet to all prisoners. Those who do not have the aptitude for higher education could be offered trade skills, such as welding, carpentry, machining, landscaping, cooking, and so on.

Those who study and work hard would be rewarded with the right to view two movies and two sports events per week. At some point, the achievers would take a series of exams in their fields of study. If they acquired degrees, depending on the length of their sentences, they would qualify for early release. They would have to write a thesis on their goals in life and their thoughts about the rules and regulations of society. They would have to go before a parole board and take a lie detector test to prove their sincere desire to achieve in life and live within the laws. Some would have to enroll in a university to do actual lab work and gain hands-on experience in their fields. Some would be placed on the job as apprentices to gain field experience in fields like forestry or wildlife management.

The parole office would have a job-placement department and request periodical reports on the progress of parolees. If a parolee were convicted of a major felony, he would be sent to the PFH. That parolee would be declared a danger to society and not fit to live in society. I think we need to start assessing certain criminals as mentally unfit to live in our society. Just as we determine that some mentally ill individuals are a danger to society, some criminals are animalistic in nature and are a severe danger to society. They deserve to live in the animal kingdom.

Here is another solution I wish to offer. There are hundreds of dying or abandoned communities across the nation. If there are citizens living in those communities, the government should relocate them to other, more thriving communities of their choosing and provide a lucrative relocation package.

Prisoners could then be sentenced to live the rest of their lives in their own remote communities, just as settlers did in the pioneer days. With the electronic monitoring devices and technology available these days, prisoners could be securely kept in these designated communities. They will be instructed to live in a community, build it up, raise crops, and form their own rules and regulations. They would also have to consent to have vasectomies so that children would not be victims of their environment.

These criminals could either kill each other off or recognize the value of having people around to build a society from which everybody benefits. That is my proposal for dealing with ever-growing prison populations. As I stated earlier, the problem is only going to get worse in the future because of the irresponsibility of our youth and the even worse drugs that are sure to become available down the line. Prison and the death penalty apparently have not been a deterrent to crime. Perhaps allowing prisoners to develop their own little lawless societies will prove to be a deterrent. At least it will save billions of dollars per year in administrative costs, staffing, and medical care. There is a severe shortage of doctors and medical personnel in this nation. Why should good, law-abiding citizens go without medical care while these scumbags have all their medical needs provided for?

If the program succeeds, as I predict it will, it will make it easier for police to do their jobs. It will reduce the extreme financial burden on our justice system. I believe that the PFH will serve as an extreme deterrent for crime in the future. It's totally fair, based on the fact that most criminals have taken away the most valuable commodity from others—life itself.

—⁓—

I absolutely do not understand why the majority of citizens in many nations and states have agreed to ban the death penalty even for mass murderers. Can they not understand that these people are not human? That they have deprived human beings of life? That they have deprived loved ones of that life? The loved ones of the victims are the ones who are forced to live lives with huge holes in their hearts every day, suffering from unbelievable pain, loneliness, and depression. It's the survivors who are punished. I understand the issue of prisoners on death row who are later found to be innocent. However, there are many heinous crimes for which there are witnesses and solid evidence that proves guilt beyond a shadow of doubt. The Tucson tragedy is a perfect example. Yet there will be a trial costing millions of our tax dollars, appeals, and years of delay, all so attorneys can get rich at our expense.

People need to understand that the greatest gift of all is life itself. It is so very fascinating to see mankind's progress. That is the greatest regret I have about leaving this world—I will not witness the future of mankind. Even if a person is bedridden for decades, that person can enjoy the dynamic and evolving story of life.

Meanwhile, murderers are entitled to all of the above, plus room and board, medical care, security, entertainment, a social life, and the privilege of witnessing the events of the world unfold. No stress! They receive all these amenities and the wonder of life at our expense. It doesn't seem like justice to me. Being exiled in the PFH might be some semblance of justice.

The world has enough problems providing a comfortable livelihood for decent citizens. If we ever wish to have a civilized and peaceful society, we must leave the beasts behind and focus on providing for those who deserve a decent and peaceful life. Criminals have had their opportunities in life and have chosen to kill and cause suffering to the very people who provided those opportunities. It's time to quit penalizing honest, hardworking citizens for the sake of criminals.

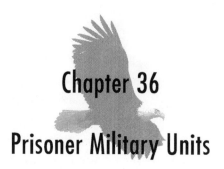

Chapter 36

Prisoner Military Units

America is finding it more and more difficult to recruit military personnel because of the Iraq war and perhaps also the war in Afghanistan. These are unconventional wars, unlike past wars in which the enemy could be clearly identified. It used to be that when you went to the front lines, it was army against army. The troops were on a mission, and when the mission was over, they went back to the safety of their barracks to rest up and recover from the stress they had endured.

We are now engaged with the enemy in civilian neighborhoods. We don't know whether the citizens in the neighborhoods our troops patrol are friends or enemies. Soldiers are often blown up by the very people they are trying to protect.

There is no safe place to retreat to for rest and stress relief. Twenty-four hours a day, three hundred sixty-five days a year, our troops are under stress. They try to be kind to the people they are supposed to protect, yet those same people will blow them away.

These situations are leaving a great number of our troops psychologically damaged for life—if they are lucky enough to make it home. It is almost as if we are giving our troops a prison sentence, and we are certainly increasing the chance that they will be so psychological damaged that their lives will be destroyed when they try to fit back into society.

Therefore, I propose that our military start utilizing a source that is currently a huge financial drain on society. Let's give prisoners a chance to grow up and contribute to society. It would have to be a volunteer program. If prisoners would like a second chance—or even a last chance—to turn their lives around and prove their worth to society, they ought to be given an opportunity.

We've all heard the phrase, "The army will make a man out of you". There is a great deal of truth to that. How often have we heard parents say that their sons and daughters went into the military as children and came back as adults? Most of the prisoners incarcerated are punks who have failed to grow up or have not had proper guidance in their lives.

Why not put certain young prisoners into a special military force where they will be given an opportunity to grow up and learn the value of the freedom so many have given their lives for? If the military is so adept at turning children into adults, why wouldn't it work for the many young people who have lacked guidance in their lives? What could it hurt to give it a try? If they are in a special force entirely made up of criminals, they cannot influence the regular troops.

The free nations of the world have adopted a policy against the death penalty even for the most egregious crimes. They condemn our policy of retaining the death sentence for the most extreme and violent crimes. Why not put those people on the front lines patrolling neighborhoods among the enemy? If they survive, they will have grown up and figured out how valuable their freedom is by having had to fight for it. They will likely understand why we have rules, regulations, and civility in society. Either way, they will have contributed to society rather than being a drain on it.

Many of our soldiers enter the military to build their lives. Many find a way to go to college who would not otherwise have had the financial means. We sacrifice the lives of so many good citizens, patriots, and potential scholars. Why not give the people who are a threat and drain on society an opportunity to discover how society progresses through hard work, sacrifice, commitment, and dedication to our fellow men in the trenches?

If we can sacrifice our good citizens, then why not sacrifice our bad ones?

If time proves that mixing the bad with the good does not work, then our military can form special forces that are composed of the prisoners only. Those units could man the front lines in many operations and be given an opportunity to prove their worth. It would be an opportunity for them to pay their debt to society rather than having taxpayers pay the cost of their incarceration.

Chapter 37

Crime and Youth

Our nation is really short on public service announcements. I don't know why our society shies away from such a useful and valuable resource. We used to use these services much more in decades past. It seems that the Church of Jesus-Christ of Latter Day Saints puts out more valuable messages for society than our government or the media in general. And there never seems to be a religious component to its messages—just great wisdom, guidance, and valuable advice for all.

I believe that the most valuable public service announcement would be to inform our youth that a career in crime is a dead end. Technology is advancing so rapidly that achieving any success in crime is virtually impossible. This fact should be preached and announced to society and especially directed to our youth.

It should be pointed out that there are millionaires in prison who thought they could beat the system. Our youth should be taught that there is no easy route to wealth and happiness in this world. You may build great wealth and temporary happiness or comfort by taking shortcuts; however, it will eventually all come crashing down.

If you wish to achieve success and security in your life, you have to work for it. Criminals are always looking for methods to avoid that work.

They wish to live the high life without putting in the honest work and patience necessary to achieve their goals. What good is it to achieve your wealth and enjoyment in life if it can all be taken away overnight along with your freedom? Freedom is the most valuable commodity in life. It does little good to have a million dollars if you are locked in a prison cell. At that point, you would likely exchange your million dollars for zero dollars and your freedom, if you could.

You children face crossroads throughout your childhoods. One road leads to school and the potential for a lifetime of success. Other roads lead to drug dealers waiting to offer you a wonderful high. Then they will recruit you into a career of criminal activity, and eventuallyly you will end up in prison. You will not enjoy losing your freedom and dreams and goals. Ask any prisoner !

It seems that this type of message could be used to create powerful advertisements. There are many goofy commercials these days that make absolutely no sense. A commercial that had a valuable lesson for our youth would grab the viewer's attention. Imagine a message about crime like the one above followed by this: "This message brought to you by Pepsi in association with your local police department".

Society throws enough money at crime after the fact. Why not throw a small percentage at preventive measures? How about a message like this: "Our nation is in desperate need of well-educated individuals to fill millions of high-tech jobs. Can you pitch in and help? Stay in school and realize all your dreams !

Chapter 38

Education Failure

This is the most important chapter in this book. This is why America is destined for failure, and America's failure will also mean the failure of democracy and the free world. If we don't open our eyes to the reasons for failure, I guarantee America will be just another great empire that failed. Unfortunately, if America and democracy fail, the existence of mankind will be short-lived.

There is absolutely no excuse for the failure of education in America in this day and age. The technology available for learning has developed by leaps and bounds in the past century. Computer technology, graphics, video illustrations, and numerous other methods now make it possible to absorb information much more quickly than in the past. It used to be that we had to use our imaginations to learn and use mere chicken-scratch illustrations in our books. I certainly wish we had had the clear graphics and video illustrations that are available today when I was in school.

I have heard for years from educational scholars and citizens that education is underfunded and classes are too large. Of course, there are a number of contributing factors. The reasons listed above are probably not even the most important such factors; rather, they are poor excuses.

Those excuses come from a society that fails to recognize how much harm comes when parents provide their children with everything they desire. These parents have grown up in an era when it is possible to provide so many magical devices at such affordable prices that it would have seemed like abuse not to provide your children with whatever new technology you could easily put on your credit card.

These same parents, who grew up in the best of times in America, fail to recognize that it was academic excellence that made America a leader in economic achievement and intellectual power. Now they want to make sure their children are the equals of rich and privileged children and are not deprived of any toy or technology. As a result, these children are never driven to play outside, which would provide physical health, exercise, and enjoyment of life. These parents are in fact depriving their children of the most essential component of brain stimulation—oxygen. There is no more essential element for the brain's operation than oxygen; lack of oxygen leads to depression and deprivation of pleasure, motivation, and intelligence.

Educational experts in past times recognized that physical exercise was an essential component of learning. This is specifically why educators in the past recognized the value of providing exercise in the daily routine. Of course, it would have been even better to have physical education classes every day instead of every other day, and the exercise should have been more strenuous but shorter in duration.

We all know that if we are falling asleep while reading or watching television, it is beneficial to go out and run or walk for five minutes to stimulate our brains. Even if we do the hundred-yard dash during a commercial break, it pumps enough oxygen into the brain to take it out of sleep mode. This phenomenon is most likely related to the way emotional problems can deprive an individual of the ability to sleep, consciously or subconsciously. The brain is most likely wired to address stress or unresolved conflict, so this is a survival instinct. Incidentally, worry about being able to sleep can become a source of stress in the same manner. Worry in the night was a necessary survival instinct in primitive times.

I will now get back to my original reasoning about why our children are failing. In past times, our children had exercise and play times, whether in the form of sports, hide and seek, or other games. We all enjoyed those physical exercises whether we realized it or not. It gave us a sense of euphoria we needed; however, we did not realize it. Riding a bicycle was not something our parents had to encourage us to do. Without realizing it, we were driven to get that oxygen high everyday.

Of course, the past few generations will not have any idea what I'm talking about. Those electronic games have been available for almost a generation now, along with computers, cell phones, iPods, Blackberries, and so on. By the time this book gets to print, there will likely be greater electronic marvels. My point is that we used to have personal contact with our friends during school and perhaps for a few hours after school. Now those contacts have no time constraints. If your child wishes to contact a friend at any time—even when he or she should be sleeping or studying—his or her social network is always available. The emotions that used to be expressed during the day in personal contact are now carried on practically twenty-four hours a day. Where is the time for study and learning?

I will now give you a perfect example of how this affected my personal life, even when I was a mature adult in my fifties. I realized, finally, that I had to learn how to use a computer or I would be left out of life and the ability to communicate. Unfortunately, my passion was sports, and I was drawn to blogging on a Seattle Mariners website. It instantly became an absolute obsession day and night. I had the longest list of things to do, yet all those things fell by the wayside for nearly eighteen months.

I had a great passion for telling it how it was in the sports world. Of course, if you wish to tell the truth about a sports fan's idols and heroes, you had better have a very thick hide. You are going to receive more abusive responses than you could possibly imagine. I could not wait to get up in the morning to read others' responses and often stayed up way too late corresponding with others. One day, I realized I was totally wasting my time and allowing strangers to destroy my integrity. Meanwhile, my list of things to do was growing longer every day.

I learned that there are many jerks out there who have personality problems, and the internet allows them to take out those problems on strangers without consequences. They can take out their hostilities on strangers without ever facing them, something they would never be able to do without anonymity. Essentially, they are the greatest cowards in society, and perhaps some are even social psychopaths. They certainly had an impact on me, and I can imagine how similar individuals might have an impact on children.

The bottom line is that today's children are so fascinated with their magical toys and technologies that learning to master toys, games, and technology has become far more important among their peers than any educational achievement. There is little time for study outside the classroom. When I was a child, I burned the midnight oil to work on my studies. I can't imagine students attaining a high degree of academic achievement without spending hours of the evening focused on their studies.

Therefore, I would advise parents to put their children's toys, games, and communication devices under lock and key on school days. If they achieve academically, they may be entitled to a certain amount of time during the week for those extracurricular activities. They should also be encouraged to participate in a sport activity or spend a set amount of time running, bicycling, or doing some other physical activity. We should not be raising couch potatoes!

The other issue that often irks me is the position of many that classrooms are too large for effective learning. When I attended school, there were usually thirty-two to thirty-five students per classroom. I never recall getting any individualized attention from a teacher unless I was in trouble. The only one-on-one attention I got came in the form of the comments teachers might occasionally put on my corrected homework. The bottom line is that you either understand why you are in school and that it is a once-in-a-lifetime opportunity, or you don't.

Out of my class in an impoverished neighborhood came several straight-A students and one who went on to be a nuclear engineer. They were Japanese students who realized that if they wished to get out of poverty, the opportunity to excel could be found at their elementary school.

So much for the oversized classrooms and lack of individual attention being the problem. I suppose if we all had private tutors, we might achieve better in school. Or maybe not! It would probably depend on our parents' ability to inspire and define the opportunity before us.

If I were a school superintendent, I would require that teachers spend the first day of school in every grade defining the importance of education for both the students and our nation. The teachers would walk the students around the school and point out all the construction and systems that make the building function. The teachers would point out every material, tool, and element in the building. Then they would ask the students a hypothetical question: If all the adults suddenly died, would you children be ready to step in and continue to build, manufacture, engineer, maintain and install all of the systems and materials involved in the operation of the building?

Then these students would be given an assignment to go out into their communities and write a report on all the jobs required to build and maintain the world they would inherit if all the adults were gone. It would be pointed out that education is the only way to acquire the skills and technological expertise that built all the fabulous buildings, homes, roads, bridges, electronics, machines, automobiles, and so on that are parts of their lives. It would then be pointed out that the more education the students receive, the more opportunities they will have to be successful in their personal lives.

It should also be pointed out that it is impossible to achieve goals without making personal sacrifices during one's education years. Choose to play too much and ignore your studies, and you will likely fail to achieve the success you are capable of. You will be kicking yourself for the rest of your life for making poor choices and neglecting the great opportunities that were there for the taking.

Furthermore, it should be illustrated that not all students have the capability to be doctors, lawyers, engineers, scientists, and so on. However, many people have built very successful and lucrative careers by doing something as simple as starting out in landscape maintenance. The more skills they learned in school, the better their chances of building successful and growing businesses. Many people have become quite wealthy by starting out in this field and growing very successful and lucrative businesses. Business skills require very basic education and do not require a great amount of science and math. Any amount of high school achievement or community college education in business will give you most of the necessary skills to achieve in many service areas.

Parents should make it clear to their children that their success depends on their effort in school. There is no guarantee their parents will even be alive from one day to the next. There is no guarantee their parents will be in a financial position to assist with their college educations. If their parents have a business or a career, there is no guarantee their business or career will not go under, leaving the family financially devastated. A major health crisis could leave the family financially ruined.

Children must be forced to face these realities of life. Parents and teachers must stop sheltering children from the truth and the sad realities of life. Each and every child needs to realize that his or her future depends on how seriously he or she takes education and how many sacrifices he or she is willing to make. I am reminded of the common phrase, "No pain, no gain"! This phrase usually applies to physical conditioning and training; however, it also applies to the personal sacrifices people make in their lives to commit more of their time to education.

Speaking of physical conditioning and mental sharpness, they go hand in hand. Society has been missing a great opportunity to give children a physical break from sitting at their desks for hours every day. Consider all the jobs and the money we pay out to employees to clean and maintain school buildings and property everyday. Now consider that the majority of children are never taught to do household chores or learn personal responsibility for cleanliness at home. They should have the opportunity to learn that habits of cleaning and maintenance can become as automatic as dressing and grooming in the morning.

I have personally hired many teenagers and young adults during my life, and I have found that their work ethic is absolutely appalling. I know many employers deal with this frustration every day. So here we have an excellent opportunity to teach our children great habits in school and save millions of dollars at the same time. There should be no janitors or other maintenance employees in any school. All students should take a five- or ten-minute break in the morning and the same in the afternoon. During that break they, should each be assigned a specific job doing maintenance of the school and its grounds.

This can also be a way for students to show their appreciation to taxpayers for their tremendous contribution to their education. Taxpayers donate all these fabulous facilities, and children can demonstrate their appreciation by providing excellence in the maintenance of the facilities.

Of course, the majority of parents will decide it is beneath the dignity of their brats to have to perform domestic chores. However, they are ignorant of the fact that this could be the best lesson their children could learn. Most of these brats leave home, whether for college or to begin independent living, and become such pigs that their lifestyles reflect negatively on their peers and turn off potential lifetime partners. This neglect takes a toll on society in the form of run-down and neglected homes and apartments, poor work performance, and a lifetime of bad habits, laziness, and obesity. It is so sad to witness neighborhoods where some residents keep up their homes and property immaculately while other properties are completely trashed. Schools can correct the failures of poor parenting by instituting these simple policies and solve a lot of social problems in the same manner.

Quite frankly, I am sick of the attitude of most children that schools are prisons or at least some form of punishment forced upon them. Some even decide to rebel against the institution by vandalizing the school, parks, or even private property.

I believe that if children learn to take ownership of their schools and parks by investing their labor in them, that may be one of the most valuable lessons they could learn, and they will begin to recognize the value of their parents' investment. Human nature dictates that you do not destroy that which you work hard to construct. You certainly will not win popularity with your peers by destroying the hard work and pride they have invested in their school or neighborhood park.

I also believe it would greatly improve children's attitudes toward school if, on the first day of school every year, they were directed to go door-to-door thanking taxpayers in their neighborhoods for building their school and providing for their education. They could also inquire if there might be some favor they could do for them in order to show their appreciation. Children might discover an elderly or disabled person needing some kind of help in the area. It might become a Saturday class project to clean up that person's property by picking up litter, mowing the lawn, pulling weeds, and so on. Teenagers might discover a person whose house needs to be painted.

The main emphasis would be on cleaning up the neighborhood, taking pride in the neighborhood, and at the same time giving a helpful hand to those in need. Of course, those who live in exclusive neighborhoods would likely have to venture out to more impoverished neighborhoods to assist those in need. I really believe this type of program would cause children to mature and develop good citizenship. At the same time, it would open their eyes to the reality of life and how their future will fit into the real world beyond their fun and games.

I have a theory that children at various ages have an innate desire to do something creative or profound. If not given challenges and direction, they will find destructive things to do just to satisfy their thirst to accomplish something dynamic. That desire can be directed toward a far greater reward and satisfaction if there are people in their lives to lead them in the right direction.

I have a great deal of confidence in children being able to take the lead in their neighborhoods and communities. As evidence of this ability, I would like to point out that many communities have adopted successful recycling programs because children have taught their parents the value of such programs. The same would apply if children were put in charge of maintaining their schools, parks, and other public areas. They would likely take a great deal of pride in their neighborhoods if they had a hand in sprucing up dilapidated properties. They certainly would not be likely to destroy neighborhoods they have worked so hard to improve and beautify.

Human nature dictates that if you work hard to build something beautiful, you will not allow it to be destroyed. This is the concept behind the success of Habitat for Humanity as compared to other government housing programs that have failed miserably in the past. The recipients of these homes have to be willing to work hard to build them. As a result, the homeowners take a great deal of pride in the maintenance and upkeep of their homes.

It is absolutely disgusting to see the amount of litter that has to be cleaned up in communities and throughout the nation every year. This creates an unbelievable expense for taxpayers and wastes tremendous amounts of fuel on collecting garbage. If all students took part in cleaning up litter along roads and public places each year, few if any would contribute to the problem.

You see, all these things are nothing new to society. There are church groups and organizations like the Boy Scouts and Girl Scouts of America that provide guidance to children. It should be obvious that this kind of guidance should be incorporated into the school system in order to provide direction for all children. Even summer camps at lakes and wilderness areas can be educational, fun, and rewarding for disadvantaged children. Even campouts at community parks can offer opportunities to build good citizenship, character, and social skills. All these programs can be instituted without religious context, which would make them more likely be accepted by all children and parents, and they may prove more successful than those with religious overtones.

Of course, most of these proposed programs are going to require teachers and parents both to step up and become community leaders dedicated to the better development and guidance of our youth. It will require teachers' unions to change their attitudes and commitments and realize that if we don't change direction, our nation will fail miserably. In parts of our nation, the dropout rate is near 50 percent and growing. When will teachers realize we have a crisis, and when will they be willing to make personal sacrifices to reverse this trend? Will it have to be when we become an absolutely illiterate nation and our economy totally collapses?

The future of America is totally in the hands of our public school teachers. Are they willing to step up and work for eleven months of the year?

We need all teachers to volunteer to teach at least six weeks of summer school. Too many children need extra help to learn their courses and avoid the failure that eventually leads to dropping out. Some could work summer camps and occasional Saturdays or weekends to shape the lives of our youth. I know of no other occupation that provides three months of vacation per year along with numerous holidays and various breaks. We might have to put the ball in their court and find out how dedicated they are to our youth and whether they will soften their union demands in light of the crisis facing our youth and the future of America.

I guess that if they are not willing to stop the destruction of our public school system, we may be forced to eliminate the public school system and vote to appropriate our taxes to a private system. The ball will be in the unions' court or it will be in the voters' court.

It would be best if the union teachers came around and made concessions; however, I believe there would be a multitude of parents who would volunteer to provide leadership and guidance for our youth at summer camps and to help with student volunteer community service. There are currently many citizens providing these services through the aforementioned organizations. Why would they not desire to reach the most vulnerable children in society?

I will also call on citizens who have achieved great success in their lives through achievement in education to step up and be examples to our youth to show how a strong commitment to education pays great dividends. I am asking these citizens to offer field trips to their homes or vacation retreats for students. Show off your assets, including your homes, vacation homes, cars, SUVs, boats, snowmobiles, ATVs, and so on. Then explain to those students that this is what they can accomplish if they take their educations seriously. Also, it should be explained that just one incident of an unprotected sexual encounter or a felony conviction can remove any hope of achieving your goals and aspirations for a comfortable and rewarding life.

Another issue that I would like to address is sports in public schools. Is it the mission of public education to be a farm system for collegiate athletes and professional sport teams? If this is their mission, they are up against very great odds, considering the miniscule chance that any given student athlete will have the talent needed to succeed in college or professional sports. I would guess that for every student athlete who achieves success in his or her sport at the division I level, ten thousand or more achieve success in academics.

I realize sports and physical fitness are an important and necessary part of education. However, if physical activity is important and necessary, why is it not essential for all students? This is why I propose that interschool sports and leagues be abandoned in favor of intramural sports in each school. Public schools should support sports in a format that encourages all students to participate.

The program should include a wide range of sports and activities. It might include the basic sports, such as football, basketball, and baseball along with track, cross country, golf, tennis, volleyball, badminton, and so on. Even chess or similar games could be incorporated during inclement weather. All students would rotate from sport to sport and chose their teams each month. This format would teach each student social skills and give each and every student an opportunity to find some form of sport and physical activity to adopt for the rest of his or her life.

Finding and pursuing some form of sport or physical activity is essential to one's balance in life. Sports are not just for jocks. All children need to experience this balance in life and discover which sport or physical activity best suits their personality and ability. It is also essential to each individual's social development. An individual can accumulate a great deal of knowledge and education; and yet if they do not develop a social fitness in their life, their professional life may become a failure.

I feel strongly that all students must be exposed to all forms of sports and physical activity in order for each to find the essential balance in their lives. The social and physical experiences of sports are essential to creating a well-rounded citizen who has the ability to achieve success in his or her profession. Social problems can be a great hindrance to a professional person's ability to perform a job with the highest degree of dedication, intelligence, and integrity. Success in society is all about teamwork!

Chapter 39

Gangs Are Enemies of Our Nation

There is a new and dangerous enemy growing in America and throughout the world: gangs. Our government seems to be almost defenseless to do anything about them. Yes, the government makes arrests when it can catch up with individual criminals. Our prisons are overpopulated with gang members. There always seem to be hundreds more ready to step in and take over their place in the market. They represent perhaps the greatest expense to our justice system.

Gangs or drug cartels are simply the greatest domestic threat to our public and the future of our children. We claim to be having a war on drugs in our nation. If we are in a war, isn't there a defined enemy? In war, don't we strive to wipe out the enemy?

In the 1920s and 1930s, we had problems with organized crime. We sent federal armed forces against those dangerous criminals. Today's gangs, drug cartels, and organized crime represent a far greater threat to our society than the mafia ever did.

I suggest that it is time we formed an armed forces unit to go after the enemy and mount a covert operation with the objective of wiping out the enemy and taking no prisoners. The enemy has to learn that we will not allow them to infiltrate our nation and destroy our society. We need a Dirty Harry attitude and willingness to use force.

Our youth need to learn that dropping out of school and earning easy money is not an option, that when you join up with a gang, you have joined up with an enemy of our nation. Enemies are subject to warfare and eventual destruction. Drug cartels need to get the message that they are the enemy of our nation and that they are subject to the same rules of war as any enemy and will be shot when they display their weapons. We also need to provide alternatives for our youth. Therefore, I am making this proposal in order to avert such warfare.

Due to the incredible growth in the number of single parents and the lack of parenting skills in this generation, we need to take a different approach. First, we need to understand the history of the public school system. When it was initially instituted, it was for the sole purpose of educating our youth. There were no school buses, and students carried their own lunches. There were no athletic facilities or other extra curricular activities.

Now consider what a huge bureaucracy the education system has grown into. Taxpayers provide breakfasts, lunches, school buses, gyms, sports fields, athletic equipment, music and theatre equipment, travel for all these activities, and all the personnel needed to provide these amenities. In addition, many communities provide breakfast and lunch on weekends and during the summer break. We provide just about everything except a roof over the students' heads, which many other government services provide.

Now I will provide a brief summary of my childhood. I was placed in a foster home at around two or three years of age. I have no memory of life prior to that placement, but I do recall a lot of violence. I was placed in a home with a woman in her seventies. She subsidized her late husband's railroad retirement and Social Security checks by taking in many foster children, some of whom got into trouble and were taken away. I was the last of those foster children.

This lady had four grandchildren on whom she doted and whom she provided with many gifts, including piano and dancing lessons. She had two pianos in her house; however, she would not provide lessons for me. She stated that she could not afford them. I used to pretend to play on it when she was not home.

As a child, I was taught to clean house every day. I was up at 5:00 a.m. every day polishing hardwood floors with paste wax, polishing all her furniture with furniture polish, cleaning windows, and scrubbing carpets with cleaning solvent. In addition, I had to wash clothes in a bathtub, ring them out, and hang them on clotheslines outside.

In exchange I got one pair of shoes, one pair of pants, one t-shirt, one flannel shirt, two pairs of underwear, and three pairs of socks at the start of each school year. If they got holes in them, I had to sew up the holes.

There was a park five blocks from home; however, I was never allowed to go there. Consequently, I never learned any athletic skills. I could not join the Boy Scouts or the YMCA or even have a paper route. Any of these activities would have interfered with my chores.

All my schoolmates had parents. I developed a huge complex about that and often told lies about an imaginary family at show-and-tell. I could get away with it, because none of my classmates lived near me. The other kids on my street attended a Catholic school. When I begged to go to basketball practice early in the morning, the woman whose home I lived in informed me that I had to do my chores in the morning.

Whenever a child welfare worker was scheduled to visit, I was told to lie about my activities and to say that I was very happy living there. I was told to tell them that I was active in the Luther League. She scared me by telling me that I would be taken away. Likely, that would have been the best thing that ever happened in my life.

When I was about eleven, I was allowed to mow and trim lawns for church members. However, I had to pump a heavy pre–World War II bicycle about four or five miles uphill to their homes. Often, she would borrow my earnings and lose them at the horseraces.

In fifth grade, it occurred to me that if I wanted out of that impoverished life, I was going to have to study hard, and I did. Learning did not come easily to me. With the exception of math, I had to do a lot of memorizing. My study site was a small pantry with a twenty-five-Watt bulb. Regardless of where I was in my studies, the old lady would get up and turn out that light after dark, stating that she could not afford the electricity. That was the worst of all her atrocities.

When I attended high school, the other children came from a wide range of economic backgrounds. I was very embarrassed by the ragged clothes I wore. Needless to say, by the time I was a senior, I rebelled and got into trouble. I did graduate and enroll in Washington State University. Soon, my life turned south based on the bad advice of the old lady's son, and I lost the greatest opportunity in my life. He informed me that it was my moral duty to marry and provide for the child even though my girlfriend's mother forbade me to marry her and threatened to put her in juvenile detention.

I tell this story in order to draw parallels to my proposal for all those lost and failing children in our society. Since we are providing all their services with the exception of housing, we need to strongly consider a special type of institution for children who are the products of poor parenting. I'm sure that there is a shortage of decent foster homes that truly have the children's best interests at stake. Many likely open their homes for financial survival in these difficult times.

I propose that we build compounds incorporating residence halls, a school, athletic facilities, a cafeteria, and other services into a campuslike setting.

Children that get into trouble, are neglected by poor parenting, or are constantly disruptive in school would be offered enrollment in this institution or, in some cases, directed to enroll.

Given an opportunity to live my childhood in this type of setting instead of experiencing the deprivation I suffered as a child, I would enthusiastically accept growing up in such an environment. While a traditional family setting with responsible parenting is preferable, many children would be much better off living their childhoods in the above setting. Far too many parents don't have a clue as to how to raise and inspire their children.

Children can develop close friendships and relationships with fellow students and faculty. They can learn responsibility by doing the necessary chores to maintain the facility, learning the concept of teamwork as a result. Most of all, they would get professional guidance in their lives.

There was a time in the past when wealthy families sent their children to professional military-type institutions for the school year. They obviously turned out well, or those institutions would not have existed for so long or developed such good reputations. It's time to re-create those institutions to serve our failing and troubled youth.

When you consider the immense and growing expense of the justice system, the police, incarceration facilities, parole and probation officers and the too-often tragic consequences of crime, this proposal should merit serious consideration and experimentation. It might be a last chance to save our misguided and neglected youth. Do we wish to have our nation turn into a criminal battleground like the ones cartels have created in Mexico? Artificial pleasure and greed are feeding this trend that gets worse and worse each year. We must stop our youth from being recruited into doing gangs' dirty work and offer an alternative in life that will offer a much better chance for development in their formative years and proper guidance toward a better future for their lives.

Chapter 40

Religious Rights, Tax Exemptions, and Public Entities

All religious organizations are given special tax exemptions regardless of what kind of country clubs or social activities they support within their organizations. Some religious groups also put pressure on public entities to make special accommodations for their religious beliefs and practices. These institutions are now required to set up special areas for religious practices and alter their schedules to accommodate religious schedules. Isn't there supposed to be separation of church and state?

Aren't these demands actually an effort to force religious beliefs on the rest of society? Aren't the efforts of religious groups to have religious displays in public places an effort to force their beliefs onto society? Why aren't they satisfied with their special tax exemptions and the right to display religious messages on church property that is visible to the public? They are also entitled to pay for messages and propaganda. Often those messages have direct political implications. Of course, there are few, if any, government officials, politicians, or candidates who will express any opposition to these violations of the separation of church and state. It would be the kiss of death for their careers.

I am also referring to Muslims who request special provisions for their religion. A public university should never be allowed to spend the taxpayers' money on anything connected with religion. If a person has a religion, he or she has a place of worship. If he or she wishes to sacrifice academics, sports, or other activities for the sake of religious practice, that is his or her choice. If a person chooses to participate in a team sport or other activity that depends on his or her presence, that person should be required to sign a statement stating he or she is available for that activity on any day when it is required. Otherwise, that organization is investing in an individual who cannot commit to the team.

What bothers me most about Muslim citizens in America is that I have never heard any condemnation of the actions of Muslim terrorists from their religious leaders. There are enough Muslim leaders in America to strongly influence the actions and attitudes of millions of Muslims worldwide. Why don't they do the decent thing and stand up and state that America is not an evil empire, that freedom and democracy are the best things that could ever happen to the entire world? Why do they wish to be American citizens if they are opposed to the ideology of America? Suspicious, isn't it?

Their lack of action in taking a political position promoting the goodness of Americans to the world makes me very suspicious as to their true agenda and presence in this nation.

America has likely allowed hundreds of thousands of Muslims to attend our universities over time. I'm sure we thought doing so was a good investment in democracy. We probably imagined these people would get an education here and at the same time learn the value of capitalism, freedom, and democracy. We likely expected they would return to their countries and educate their societies about the positive aspects of our society and the value of freedom of speech. Many of the leaders and people in high places in their societies have completed their educations in America. It appears that the influence we expected has had little impact on their nations.

So, I must ask, Would we be justified in closing the door to immigrants, students, and visitors from Muslim nations until they change their attitude and actions toward Americans? Is there not a pledge of allegiance to the United States of America for immigrants? I believe we might need an amendment to the Constitution.

The spread of Islam throughout the free world is a serious threat to freedom and democracy. Their populations increase at a rate five times that of other populations. It will not take more than a few generations before they outnumber the rest of the population. When that happens, the theocracy of Islam will wipe out democracy. Islam is the antithesis of democracy.

It's incredible that we spend trillions of dollars fighting terrorism overseas while the long-term threat is growing within our very nation. Wouldn't it be interesting to have a national referendum on banning the practice of Islam or any other theocracy opposed to the ideals of democracy and freedom within the United States? We could also declare that all practitioners of religious theocracy would be deported immediately with no opportunity for appeal. How many people would support such a referendum? It might not be politically correct, but I believe Americans believe that the sustainability of freedom and democracy in America and its influence on the world for eternity is far more beneficial than any political correctness. I'd like to see how many of our leaders would have the guts to stand behind the will of their citizens.

Can you imagine how the millions of Americans who have fought and died for freedom and democracy in this world would turn over in their graves if America fell into the hands of an Islamic theocracy? Would any of us be able to live with an America that had fallen to the extremist ideology of Sharia law a hundred years from now? Is that the world we would have our children and grandchildren inherit? Can we not see the forest for the trees? If you are Muslim and truly respect the ideals of America, it is time for you to stand up and defend the ideals of America and condemn the doctrines that America is an evil empire and that there must be a Jihad against America. Muslim Americans can have the greatest influence on the hatred of America in the Arab world. It's a patriotic duty for all Muslim Americans, just as it is a duty for all Americans, to stand up for America. If Muslims wish to extol the virtues of Sharia law, they should be deported immediately.

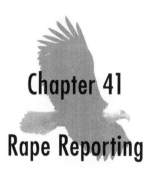

Chapter 41

Rape Reporting

One thing that has always bothered me is the way rape is reported and particularly the way it is not reported in a timely manner. First of all, we have to distinguish between rape by a stranger and date rape. One is much more serious than the other.

When you consider date rape, you have to realize that the woman finds the man appealing enough to go on a date with him. Along with that is the fact that the woman is eventually going to have sex with that man if they continue dating. Otherwise, she should not have been dating him in the first place. If the woman feels a religious or moral obligation not to have a sexual relationship until marriage or some other determined date, she should make that fact known prior to accepting a date.

Then there is the issue of engaging in kissing and arousal. A woman should never put herself in that situation if she does not intend to have intercourse. This is a poor way to prove your sex appeal toward men. You cannot turn a man on and expect him to stop on command. There are ways to get him off easily without intercourse. After a certain point, you owe it to him.

What I would like to propose is a program in which a woman could report a rape confidentially without filing criminal charges against the man. Those records would not be public information until or unless the woman chose at some point in the future to make official charges. This program could also allow for confidential medical verification and treatment in a timely manner.

There are numerous reasons why this program could be a valuable tool for the justice department. One issue I would like to address is the question of why wouldn't a woman immediately report the crime. According to public opinion, the crime of rape is more egregious than robbery, assault, manslaughter, attempted murder, and perhaps even murder itself. If you are robbed or assaulted, you call the police immediately. So why wouldn't a woman call the police immediately when raped? Shame is absolutely no excuse. Staying silent gives the rapist a green light to repeat the crime numerous times, and the next victim might be a child. Women who step forward to stop the continuation of this crime are both courageous and heroic and certainly are not in a position of shame.

That is why I am advocating a program that would allow optional reporting of the crime without having to file charges. This would give a woman the opportunity to change her mind at a later date if she decided the rapist had to be stopped. Most importantly of all, it would allow the justice department to track complaints filed that might lead to the conviction of a dangerous serial rapist. This should be considered a civic responsibility.

The situation sometimes also arises that a woman fails to win the love and affection of a man. She becomes embittered and vindictive. She arranges to have sex with the man and promptly reports having been raped. Judging by the actions and responses of some women on the television program *The Bachelor*, you can imagine how some would like to get revenge for being turned down.

I wonder how many innocent men have spent time in prison or had their reputations destroyed by false charges brought by vengeful women. This proposed system for reporting rape would give these types of women time to let the pain and heartbreak heal before actual and perhaps false charges are filed.

Another issue that needs serious examination is the incidents of female teachers having sexual relationships with boys. I have yet to meet a man who sees that any harm or crime has been committed under these circumstances. A male teacher who engages in sexual intercourse with a female student is creating a potential pregnancy for that girl. A boy cannot get pregnant! The girl's academic future could be destroyed. The boy would brag to his friends about what a great experience it was. The boy would go on with life the same as if he had masturbated. We all do that, regardless of the fact that some claim they don't. There is no such thing as stealing virginity from a boy.

I completely agree that the female teacher must be fired. But putting her in prison? Give me a break! Every guy I have ever discussed this issue with claims he would have loved to have sex with a female teacher, and some have even fantasized about having a sexual relationship with a hot teacher.

Reverse discrimination does not apply to these cases, despite lawyers' stupid arguments to the contrary. There is a big difference between a man and a woman and even between a boy and a girl. If the justice system cannot figure out the difference, it should give up its shingle. Lawyers are too stupid for words! How can we expect justice in our courts if we have these morons in charge?

There is no woman in the world who can rape a man. It is physically impossible. A man has to be turned on in order for the physical act to occur. Does the justice system not have enough real crime to deal with that they have to resort to dealing with these kinds of absurdities?

Now let's deal with real rape. This is often the committed by a stranger, and it should fall into the category of terrorism. Often, the woman does not know if the traumatizing experience is going to end with murder. So why does the justice system categorize such a crime using the same label as the one it uses for an overheated date? There should be a different way to charge those who commit nonconsensual sexual intercourse in that setting.

Can anybody in this world explain why the sexual terrorists should not have his penis removed before he is released back into society? It has been proven over and over that these deviants will repeat their crimes. Without their penises, they cannot repeat the crime. Is that too much logic for the justice system? It seems that the realization that getting caught would lose the only tool in their bag would be a tremendous deterrent.

On the other hand, I wonder if I'm running on all cylinders myself. I have always thought that the greatest turn-on for a man was how much he turned on his partner. I must have missed out on something somewhere along the line.

Another factor in determining how different kinds of rape should be tried and punished should be whether the victim was impregnated or contracted a venereal disease. Those factors always increase the severity of the crime and should also increase the severity of the ensuing punishment.

The bottom line is that there are many complexities, variations, and degrees when it comes to the crime of rape. Some logic and fairness need to be used in the prosecution of these crimes.

Chapter 42

Gay Rights and Marriage

The issue of gay marriage is quite damaging to modern society. Exercising a little logic and common sense could simplify this issue that tears society and families apart.

I don't know why so many people classify homosexuality as a sin when society accepts as natural so many birth defects and genetic mutations. Imagine if society told heterosexuals that their attraction to the opposite sex was wrong. That might be a poor correlation, but it might give you an understanding of what gay and lesbian people deal with throughout their lives. Enough of the condemnation. Either you get it or you don't wish to get it.

Now let's get down to the legal aspects of this issue. Marriage is a legal partnership between a woman and a man to protect their common property and the welfare of their children. In the business world, anybody can form a legal partnership to protect common investments, responsibilities, capital gains, and so on. Marriage is an identical legal partnership intended to share and protect common property and interests. Along with these common interests come legal rights to act in the best interests of the partner in cases of emergency or medical dilemma.

Now let's consider how the courts came up with common-law marriages. Two individuals shared a household for a number of years. Each contributed to that household in some manner, either financially or through labor and maintenance of the household. It becomes a legal partnership under the law due to shared expenses and investment.

This is the same scenario that gays and lesbians face. Let me give some other examples where domestic partnerships might cause courts to consider shared rights and responsibilities.

In this day and age, there are more and more people and family members who are forced to share households and assets for economic reasons. Let's say that two married sisters with children got divorced. Neither could afford to have a separate household, so they moved in together. The years rolled by, and each sister contributed to the mortgage, maintenance, improvements, and so on. If that partnership comes to an end, there should be legal protection for each party's financial investment in the property.

There are numerous relationships now in which people are forced to share households. They would be wise to file for domestic partnerships. In some of these relationships, one party may wish to have the other make life-or-death decisions on his or her behalf.

So in the eyes of the law, marriage is a legal contract to protect the interests of both parties in the partnership. Government has no legal authority to restrict any legal partnership. If they did, it would be prejudice and discrimination.

Marriage is only the license and registration of a legal partnership. The wedding is only the swearing in and confirmation of the legal partnership. The wedding is also a ceremony to share with family and friends. Government has nothing to say about a ceremony; it simply enforces the contract to form a legal partnership. Government is the issuer of the license, and the minister or justice is the notary public confirming the contract.

There was a time when the government and society refused to recognize or allow legal unions between African Americans and Caucasians due to religious beliefs. The ideology of that time is much like the ideology that now prevents unions between people of the same sex. People are trying to exercise control over the private lives of others, affairs that are absolutely none of their business. This is an equal-rights issue; same-sex unions should be guaranteed by the Constitution of the United State of America.

The justice department has no choice but to protect the equal-rights provision of the Constitution and the Equal Rights Amendment.

We don't like to see deformed babies and people with severe birth defects and abnormalities. Yet we accept those genetic defects and have compassion for those unfortunate people. Don't gays and lesbians deserve the same understanding and compassion?

When I observe gays and lesbians, I feel sorry for them—sorry that they cannot enjoy the beauty of romance and attraction to the opposite sex. Why can't the rest of society accept these genetic defects and feel compassion for them? Forget about the biblical story of Sodom and Gomorra. That story was written by religious people thousands of years ago who had the same prejudices as many religious people today. If it took thousands of years for us to accept people of different races as human beings, why can't we accept people with different sexual attractions as human beings who deserve the same respect?

We all have differing levels of sexual drive. This is what destroys many marriages, because one partner has less sexual drive than the other. It takes years for the true numbers to surface. Some people have no sexual drive at all. That same scale then runs below zero and into the bisexual zone and eventually into the homosexual zone. I am sure that some day genetics will spell out this scale and find the linkage. It is clearly a birth defect.

I wish society would stop labeling these people as sinners and outcasts. I rather wish they would understand this genetic mutation for what it is and invest in research that someday will cure this problem.

On the other hand, gays and lesbians should not flaunt their homosexuality in public places. It only serves to aggravate the problem of acceptance, and at times innocent gays and lesbians pay the price with their lives.

By the way, why are gay women referred to as lesbians? To me, that is a derogatory term that originated in ancient times. Why aren't they just referred to as gay ladies ?

The Constitution guarantees the right to life, liberty, and the pursuit of happiness. What part of that do people not understand? Yet people wish to exercise dictatorial powers over others when it should be none of their damn business. We have far more important matters in society to deal with than the private lives of law-abiding and productive citizens. Commit your dollars and labor to medical science that could solve this birth defect.

It would also help if gays did not flaunt their affection in public places. Men do not like seeing men kissing men; however, they do enjoy seeing women kissing women. Figure it out, and society will be much more accepting. Fight for your legal rights to form legal partnerships, and leave marriage to those who deem it sacred.

Chapter 43

Abortion

I've been puzzled for most of my life by the anti-abortion movement. I don't believe any of us are pleased that there are so many abortions—or any at all, for that matter. It is absolute irresponsibility that creates the situation.

On the other hand, are there not enough poor parents and neglected and abused children in this nation? Do we wish to have young women destroy their opportunity to attend college and make a secure life for themselves? Would we rather have taxpayers foot the bill for supporting millions more mothers and raising their children?

It seems abortion opponents would rather promote overpopulation of and all the tragic suffering that goes along with it instead of educating young people to the use preventive measures until they have secured their place in life and can afford a family. You would expect they would rather see young people reach a level of maturity that would allow them to build successful marriages, thus enabling them to give their children a success-ful upbringing.

Their only answer seems to be to teach abstinence, even though that method has been proven over and over to fail. Even those who take the sacred vow often fail. They fail to realize that all life is based on the natural desire to breed and continue the species. This natural desire is so strong that no amount of conviction or sacred vows can overcome it. It is a part of the beautiful connection between the sexes that cannot be denied.

Many religions forbid abortion and label it a mortal sin. I wonder how they would label miscarriages? Wouldn't that be a natural abortion? Or, if you believe life is a gift from God, I guess you might consider a miscarriage an abortion that is a gift from God.

Apparently, it is not only abortion but any form of protection that is sinful. Whether it is birth control, condoms, the morning-after pill, or any other method of preventing pregnancy, it is a sin and absolutely unacceptable to most religions. I wonder why.

Well, perhaps these beliefs go back to ancient times before people had sophisticated weapons. In those times, war almost always came down to numbers. Families were praised for their ability to produce large families. Why, do you suppose? It was simply because the larger your tribe, the better the chances of overcoming your enemy. This is exactly why religions have always glorified the virtues of large families. After all, most tribes and nations were affiliated with or guided by religion.

Here in America, the majority proclaim this to be a Christian nation. Those of Christian beliefs naturally wish to increase their numbers just as they have throughout history. If the masses are allowed to decrease the number of pregnancies, those numbers will diminish, so essentially, the anti- abortionists are imposing a religious belief upon society.

Religious beliefs cannot be a basis for law, regardless of majority opinions. Government must protect the rights of the religious and the rights of the nonreligious as long as neither group imposes its beliefs on society. One could write a book on the abuses of these constitutional rights that have occurred throughout the history of our nation and continue to this day. Somehow, the courts continue to ignore those abuses.

Furthermore, the sacred union of marriage is failing; over half of marriages fail these days. Teens and young adults who marry due to pregnancy are realizing they were not mature enough for marriage. They were not experienced enough in life to know what they wanted in a partner. People are so vastly different that it is difficult to find the right match. Most do not, and many others just wind up living an unhappy life together for the sake of financial security. Others will never find true happiness, because they expect too much or have their own demons.

Perhaps what is missing in society is proper education and counseling for our children before they approach that dangerous age—an education that would help them to imagine parenthood at their age and what would happen to their aspirations in life. How much money could they make with a limited education, and how much would be required to run a household and provide for a family? This type of education should be taught in schools, and perhaps it should be entitled "Family Planning and the Reality of Life". Flunk the course, and your goals in life fail before you get to first base.

We are in a dire situation with our nation's poor economy and the extreme failure of our education system. Can any of these problems be traced back to families that failed due to not getting proper education and not being prepared for life?

The burdens of all social problems fall on taxpayers because of parents without enough education to provide for their children, single mothers without education or careers. The question is whether we wish to have people birthing children who do not wish to be parents, resulting in so many children suffering, becoming drug addicts, or winding up in prison.

Our corporations, who are represented by the Republican Party, scream about high taxes, but they don't care about sending manufacturing jobs overseas. They rally against national healthcare. Did it ever occur to them that if they kept their manufacturing jobs in America, most citizens could afford their own health insurance? It seems un-American to allow America to go to hell while piling up obscene profits overseas.

Of course, there is blame on both sides. If unions did not get so greedy with their demands, the manufacturing jobs would not go overseas. So we as Americans have nobody to blame but ourselves. Can all parties get together and find compromise and make sacrifices that will get America back on its feet? After all, America can solve all its most serious financial and social problems if it can ensure employment for all able and willing workers. If America is thriving, we will all be able to afford health insurance, retirement, Social Security, Medicare, and superior education and solve many environmental and energy problems.

Otherwise, those who are working must continue to contribute to the health and welfare of those who are not. Instead of taxes going toward education, research, and infrastructure, they go toward providing food, shelter, and basic medical care for those in dire need. Americans do not allow their people to starve and die in the streets. Currently, a large share of our wealth and taxes go toward survival rather than investment in strengthening our nation.

When Americans are not working, they are not able to pay mortgages or purchase homes and other goods. The financial sector fails. When banks fail, there is no credit to obtain for purchasing homes, vehicles, and other merchandise. Nor are there finances available for business and industry investment.

So I ask corporate America and unions as well: Do you wish your taxes and profits to be dedicated to a stronger and better educated America or to social and welfare programs? It should not be a difficult decision. It's simple logic ! Logic is not based on emotion !

Our government and many charitable organizations send billions of dollars in aid to African nations and other nations throughout the world to fight the extreme poverty and suffering of millions of people. Religious organizations will not tolerate or preach any form of birth control, regardless of the fact that those nations' greatest problem is overpopulation and a lack of resources for survival. They force our government to withhold aid and education if there are any provisions for birth control. This is the greatest absurdity in the world. Keep encouraging overpopulated nations to breed like rabbits and wonder why millions are suffering and dying. In the name of God, I presume !

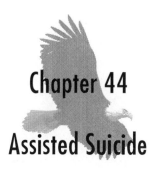

Chapter 44

Assisted Suicide

I hate the term *assisted suicide*. I'd rather it was termed *merciful termination*. I am very upset with our government for forcing its citizens to suffer in their declining years. Sure, we can attempt to take our own lives and perhaps wind up worse off for the effort. Some may be forced to choose to end their lives with tragic pain and suffering.

It should not be that way. You work hard all your life as a good citizen and contributing member of society, and then your wonderful government tells you that you must suffer until your dying breath. Worse for some of us is the fact that we have to suffer the indignity of having others clean our feces from our bodies for years. For many, this is worse than a death sentence. At least you don't suffer once you are dead.

I'll never forget my younger years when I made freight deliveries to convalescent homes. Sometimes I had to wheel freight down the hallways, and I observed the patients. Most of them were in a vegetative state. I'd say hello to them, and they could not respond. What the hell kind of a life is that?

First of all, I don't wish to be a burden on society. I don't want people to remember me in such a deteriorated state. If my mind is not sharp and coherent, then I will not be the same person. Most of all, I don't wish to have to bear the indignities listed above.

Life gets less fun for most of us as we age. Society evolves so much over time that it becomes difficult to understand and enjoy. You long for the good old days when people had fun. For decades, people went out to bars or nightclubs and danced. Now everybody goes out to sports bars, whatever those are, to sit on their butts and drink. I guess that's a result of the growing obesity rate.

The bottom line is that there is little joy in life for many once they reach a certain age. All they do is sit around suffering while they wait to die. They don't much enjoy modern culture. Some of us do not wish to be a financial burden on the medical system, because we feel we are robbing our grand-children and future generations of medical care and creating tremendous debt for society. The last year of your life can be more expensive than all the medical care you have received up to that point. Why would we wish to cost Medicare hundreds of thousands of dollars to keep us alive and in so much pain? This expense is born by society and future generations. Is there any wonder our nation cannot afford health care and Medicare is going broke?

This is one of the greatest injustices that the government can inflict on its citizens. The right to die peacefully and with dignity when you know that the time is right should be the reward for living a respectable life.

Too many throughout history have misinterpreted the commandment "Thou shalt not kill". We know what killing is, and it has nothing to do with merciful termination. There were no painless methods of terminating life in biblical times. I bet many millions wished there were. I guarantee you that there are millions today who wish their lives could be terminated without the guilt religion puts upon them. All they can do is pray many times a day that God will put their lives to an end and end their suffering. I wonder if God says, "You have not suffered enough yet".

Well, I am here to tell you that I'm not sheepish enough to allow religion or the government to dictate how much I suffer before I die. If you have a right to life, you also have a right to end that life when you choose. You will not go to hell if you have lived a decent life and lived by the golden rule.

Isn't it strange that killing in war has nothing to do with the com-mandment not to kill? How can that be? Perhaps the commandment should have read, "Thou shalt not kill except in wars, but then killing is just magnificent".

I had a friend who had severe diabetes. This man was an avid fisherman and hunter. He was told his legs would have to be amputated. He realized that his life would never be the same. He would not be independent and able to take care of himself. He would not be able to do the one thing in his life that he lived for.

With no notice to anybody, he quietly got into his vehicle in his garage and turned it on and ended his life. We should all have the right to end our lives when they are no longer enjoyable or of value to us, especially when continuing to live would be a burden to our loved ones. This is a personal decision we should all be entitled to consider. Many of us wish to be remembered for who we are, not as a deranged substitute nobody knows or wishes to know.

Is there no dignity in dying?

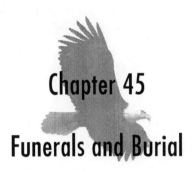

Chapter 45

Funerals and Burial

Why do people choose to burden their survivors with elaborate and expensive funerals, caskets, vaults, headstones, plots, and so on? If they could see their corpses inside their caskets a year after death, their rotting carcasses would likely repulse them. Because most caskets are air tight, that rotting will still be there hundreds of years later.

Personally, I choose to have my remains disposed of as sanitarily as possible. I would like to have my ashes dusted over a lush mountaintop so they can go back into the stream of life. If my survivors would like to plant a tree and place my ashes in the hole, that would be the best memorial I could imagine. I would not wish to burden my survivors with a great expense, and I would not wish to contribute to wasting space that society may need in future years for a better purpose than storing my rotting carcass.

Why do people feel that their remains should be preserved? Do they believe that their DNA is going to be reconstructed by some miracle? That they won't get to paradise if their remains are not available? What do they suppose happens to those whose remains are lost at sea or are incinerated in a fire or a natural disaster like a volcanic eruption? Is God going to lose track of you? If people truly believe that their spirits go to paradise, why are they so concern with their remains?

Incidentally, regarding those people who protest at the funerals of soldiers who have made the ultimate sacrifice for our freedoms: Why don't the citizens in those communities come out en masse to screen and obliterate their message? They should let them know that they are the ugliest Americans in history and that they do not deserve to breathe our air. I'm afraid that I might get thrown in jail if they ever came to my community.

Chapter 46

Right to Bear Arms

I believe at some point in the future this nation is going to have to revisit the Second Amendment—the right to bear arms. First of all, when the Constitution and that amendment were written, there was no police force or organized military to protect citizens from foreign militias or even organized enemies from within. So citizens had to have some method of protection. Our nation depended on all citizens to come to the defense of the nation if we were attacked by foreign powers. Armed citizens were essential in those times.

I have no problem with citizens carrying guns, providing they are used with discretion and for honest protection. The problem is that way too often, they are used for crime. Too often, they are used with catastrophic consequences. Too often, they are used in emotional situations, resulting in colossal regret in the aftermath. Too often, we read of children obtaining these weapons and killing their siblings or friends. Too often, we read of accidental deaths from the mishandling of weapons.

Not often enough do we read of citizens using their weapons to kill or disable criminals.

The tired old argument is that when guns are banned, only criminals will have guns. Well, they will for a while—until there are no more guns on the market. As each criminal is arrested, guns will be taken out of circulation. If guns are banned and citizens hand them in, there will be far fewer guns obtained in burglaries. When gun shops go out of business, there will be no burglaries of gun shops to supply the criminals.

Am I the only one who is deeply bothered to read or hear of domestic disputes ending tragically because a gun was handy when things got heated or of people dying in an assault by a mentally disturbed individual?

Sometimes, I wish only women and the elderly had the right to bear arms. But then there are women and elderly people who can be mentally and emotionally unstable. However, the most serious problem with weapons now is that they are used by people who are under the influence of alcohol and drugs. People lose all rationality when they mix weapons with those mind-altering chemicals. As a result, our communities are becoming more and more dangerous as time passes. Everybody feels they need weapons for protection, but then they wind up using those weapons in the heat of the moment, often when they are under the influence.

It is so sad to me to read of all the deaths caused by these situations. I'll bet there are hundreds of people who regret every day that a weapon was available during a time of emotional disturbance.

I'll bet that there are thousands of people in prison who regret one brief moment that ruined their life. I'll bet there are some who even wish there were no such things as guns.

Here is a consideration government will have to deal with in future years: Would the citizenry be better off with new weapons that will become available that will disable someone who is a threat to their safety? If you can stop a criminal in his or her tracks by causing the criminal to lose consciousness until the police arrive, then for what reason would you need to have a gun? You would have the ideal method of self-defense. If we can use anesthetics to put patients out prior to surgery, then why not a weapon that can fire a blob of anesthetic in the face of a perpetrator?

Weapons have evolved to be unbelievably powerful. These are war weapons, certainly not anything a citizen needs for self-defense. Many citizens seem to be hell-bent on owning these types of weapons in order to defend against the perceived tyranny of their own government. Do they not understand the concept of majority rule and the principles of democracy? I guess that those citizens ought to identify themselves as anarchists.

If the citizenry is to continue being armed with these weapons, I wish they were required to get an education on how to use and store them. I wish they were required to have some kind of psychological examination to determine if they are fit to own a gun. Education would lead to knowledge that there are times when emotional problems can lead to regrettable situations that destroy lives. The same applies to alcohol or drugs. Ideally, everyone who owns a gun would have to own a gun safe that could not be accessed while drunk or under the influence of drugs, similar to vehicles that cannot be started when the driver is under the influence.

What bothers me most of all about gun rights and the National Rifle Association is that they do not advocate responsibility along with rights. They encourage training, but they never advocate that licensing be tied to education, training, or psychological examination. You would expect they would want to have guns out of the hands of nuts and mentally unstable people. Why is there not a National Responsible Rifle Association (NRRA)? The saddest fact of all is that they accept no responsibility when a child gets hold of a gun and kills another child or parent. At least you would expect them to advocate legal requirements to keep guns out of the reach of children.

The NRA is always saying that when guns are banned, only criminals will have guns. That will be true for a while, until the criminals are arrested and the guns are confiscated. Yes, weapons will be in the hands of criminals, but they will become less and less prevalent as time goes by. In the mean time, thousands of needless deaths will be avoided because of the difficulty of obtaining deadly weapons.

Another huge problem our government is dealing with is that Americans citizens sell arms to drug cartels in Mexico. Anything for a buck, no matter how many lives it costs. These war weapons should not be sold to anybody other than the police and the military, and the government should oversee and regulate those sales.

I have a proposal that might solve many problems. There was a time before the 1960s when you had to have a liquor license to purchase liquor or be served in a bar. So wouldn't it be wise for our government to require a federal weapon license in order to own, buy, or sell weapons?

The licensing process could involve a criminal background check, a weapons education course, a psychological examination, and possibly some other requirements. All weapons sales would be recorded and linked to a license. Wouldn't this be a great tool for law enforcement officials to use to track illegal sales across borders?

Chapter 47

Celebrities and Superstars

I t is time for America's superstar athletes and celebrities to recognize the power and influence they can have on the social problems and crime so prevalent in neighborhoods across America. Without the people supporting them, they are nothing. If people quit going to professional sports games or movies or quit buying their music, these celebrities would be looking for jobs just like millions of other people. Most of these individuals won the lottery the day they were conceived. Sure, most all of them have worked hard to achieve success; however, for every one of them, there are millions of others who worked just as hard and never achieved superstar status. The bottom line is that these stars have been gifted with the right combination of genetics.

You could say they owe a debt to society for the good fortune they inherited at birth. They have tremendous power to change the world. Some do ! And I congratulate them, and the world appreciates their convictions and moral contributions.

I would like to see much more of this type of contribution from the stars. Imagine African American superstars going into impoverished and drug-ridden neighborhoods to recruit young men to put an end to drugs and gangs in their neighborhoods.

They could start their march by going from home to home and asking who will join their army and become committed to cleaning up the neighborhood. They could create a critical mass of people who are committed to putting these bastards out of business. The recruits could teach their children that these negative forces are only out to destroy their lives and get rich by preying on them.

Superstars could reach out to young boys in these neighborhoods and teach them the responsibility of having only protected sexual intercourse until they are ready to accept all the responsibilities of fatherhood. They might be asked if they would like to leave their children fatherless and neglected.

They might be taught by their heroes how important it is to get all the education they can. The stars might ask for leaders in their neighborhoods to step forward and commit themselves and their neighborhoods to better achievement. They could ask young males to stand together to end the trend of fathers who abandon their children, leading to hopelessness and lack of guidance for the youth in their neighborhoods.

Then the stars could request monthly reports on the progress of those they have recruited and promise to return one year later, at which time they could hope to find that the army of committed young men they left behind has made great strides.

I am not referring to African Americans only. The heroes of all races and ethnicities can inspire and spread the kind of influence that is so very badly needed in thousands of neighborhoods. There are no individuals in society who can influence our youths as effectively as sports stars, musicians, and Hollywood celebrities. Collectively, they have the ability to change the world. I wish they would form a powerful army in order to influence our youth.

Chapter 48

Stalking the Stars

I am very disturbed by how our government allows the media and the general populace to interact with our famed stars, be they Hollywood stars, athletes, government officials, musicians, or celebrities from other fields. The reward for great accomplishment in life should not be a loss of privacy and harassment everywhere you live, visit, or travel. Many will say that this is the price of fame. Well, I say bullshit. Every citizen should have a right to privacy along with the constitutional rights to life, liberty, and the pursuit of happiness.

The actions of the paparazzi amount to absolute harassment and stalking. Why does the government not arrest these individuals and charge them with stalking and harassment? If I followed another citizen around taking his or her picture, asking questions, interrupting his or her privacy, and so on, I would be arrested.

The paparazzi should not have the right to hang out near a person's residence. They should not be allowed to follow famous individuals while they travel or stalk them during their daily commutes. They should have to apply in advance for any photographs, recordings, or interviews with the exception of public appearances. Even then, they should be required not to interfere with anyone's privacy, passage, or travel.

I'm sure there are many people who choose not to acquire fame because they don't want to lose their privacy or peaceful lifestyles. We lose a lot of talent in government because of the constant scrutinizing of candidates' private lives. The media should not be allowed to delve into the personal lives of candidates and elected officials unless they are breaking the law in some manner. The exception would be if the individual gives permission to the media to delve into some personal aspect of his or her life.

Stalkers who seem obsessed with a certain celebrity should be arrested and required to have psychological counseling. If that does not stop their stalking, they should be required to wear a GPS monitoring anklet.

We do not need to know if a government official has a companion outside his or her marriage. It has little to do with how well that person performs his or her job, just as an extramarital affair does not affect a doctor or mechanic's ability to perform his or her job. Writing about a citizen's private social life without his or her permission should be illegal.

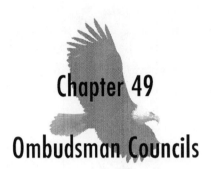

Chapter 49

Ombudsman Councils

For many years, our city has been struggling to determine the perfect person to oversee citizens' complaints about police inequities and abuse. I imagine many other communities face the same problem. The police want someone who will represent their position, and the American Civil Liberties Union wants to be represented as well.

It's difficult to find a neutral individual who does not have ties to the community and might therefore employ prejudice or favoritism. This is practically impossible, because any local resident would most likely not want to see a local government body sued. This would be very costly to the local taxpayers and the government's budget. That citizen might not wish to see the justice department become corrupt either. It is nearly impossible to find a qualified local citizen who is neutral enough to satisfy all parties.

Past ombudsman councils have had little power and have been easily overruled by the police chief. The ombudsman the community was seeking would have more power and would report his or her findings and recommendations to the mayor.

I wrote a guest editorial that was printed in the local newspaper. I felt that when the most qualified individual was found, he or she would oversee the police actions of the city only. The population of the unincorporated county is greater than that in the city, and county residents are without the representation of an ombudsman.

My recommendation was for a state council of ombudsmen. That would give every county in the state the benefit of police oversight—even the small counties that cannot afford the luxury of an ombudsman. There is even more opportunity for police abuse and inequity in smaller communities.

On the other hand, in many communities, there may not be a need for an ombudsman for many years. With a state authority, there would always be a service available for any community in need. There would be no local ties, prejudice, or favoritism. In other words, there would be complete neutrality. Best of all, each county would pay for this office on a per capita basis. No local government would have to pay a full-time official whose service might not be needed for years or occasionally.

A state council would send an investigator or two into a local community to investigate any alleged improprieties. They would take their findings to the state board for a ruling. This would provide complete oversight, justice, neutrality, and minimal expense for all counties in the state. It would be a practical solution to a problem that exists throughout our nation.

Chapter 50

Professional Juries

There is nothing in life that disturbs me more than corruption and unfairness in the government and our justice system. It brings out my almost uncontrollable passion and compels me to demonstrate these inequities. I have little respect for many judges, let alone attorneys.

Years ago, an attorney asked me to serve in a mock jury trial. Having never served on a jury before, it was an eye-opening experience. Our jury had many questions about the facts and testimony presented to us. When we were finished, we had a meeting with the attorney and presented these facts. He informed us that this is the way it is in our court system. Juries cannot request additional information, facts, or answers to questions. It's the most outrageous absurdity in the justice system. The citizenry is supposed to respect the justice system, yet they are forced to make their decisions without knowing what the hell is going on? I'm afraid if I were a juror in many of these trials, I might erupt.

What kind of justice system is this? Are trials just a game where the best team wins and justice takes a backseat? Is this why so many guilty parties walk—high-profile attorneys who can manipulate juries? Questions that need to be answered are ignored.

Citizens are actually short-changing themselves with a jury system that was born in a time when the justice system had no choice but to depend on local citizens in small communities. Now a majority of working Americans do not wish to have their lives or jobs interrupted by serving on juries. This leaves the justice system with leftovers, not necessarily the most intellectual or educated minds in our society. It interrupts families' lives and jobs. They most often do not get reimbursed anything even close to what they would have made at work during the same time. So we essentially get the leftovers of society. The justice system does not get the professional and intelligent people needed to make the best decisions, because they have critical business to tend to. There are numerous excuses to get out of jury duty.

Now I understand how murderers like Casey Anthony get off scott free. Juries are simply not intelligent enough. Another factor might be that the whole jury could be opposed to the death penalty, even if they stated during jury selection that they were not. What better way to stop an execution than to serve on the jury in a murder trial?

It's almost pathetic how trial lawyers manipulate the minds of unintelligent citizens. A general public that loves to see a common citizen win the lottery is another factor. Little do they realize that they are putting most of the financial burden on themselves and society as a whole. Many businesses and corporations also bear responsibility because of their negligence, arrogance, and corruption. I just wish to see justice served both ways. A professional jury could better determine actual damages and set fair awards that don't penalize taxpayers or cause insurance rates to escalate.

The jury system causes huge problems in civil cases. They bring in fresh faces for every trial, and too many of the jurists are like television fans who enjoy seeing contestants become millionaires. High-powered attorneys feed these juries bullshit to cloud the issues.

Once-in-a-lifetime jurors are likely not aware of the tactics attorneys employ to manipulate their passions and emotions. A skilled juror would see through these tactics. Rookie jurors can easily assume a game-show mentality, wishing to see big winners and large payouts from the deep pockets of corporations or the government. If they could see the huge awards that are given out daily over the course of a year, they would likely begin to realize that ridiculous awards come at a tremendous cost to society.

Therefore, justice would be much better served if we had professional jurors. Prelaw students or people with some experience in law enforcement or the legal profession would be ideal professional jurors. It would be the equivalent of medical students serving a residency in a hospital. Professional jurors could be aspiring attorneys or social workers or members of many other professions. The bottom line is that they would become experienced in their jobs. They could more easily determine guilt or innocence. They could arrive at fair and reasonable awards in civil liability trials. They would not prey on the deep pockets of the government at the taxpayers' expense.

Most of all, attorneys would not spend endless hours making frivolous arguments to green or inexperienced juries. This would likely cut down significantly on the length of trials. It would drastically cut the immense expense of the justice system.

Paying professional jurors a fair wage for their service would provide society with greater justice, save the tremendous costs of unwarranted financial awards, and reduce the filing of frivolous lawsuits. I feel it would be the best investment taxpayers could ever make; it would result in greater justice and save money as well. This system of jury selection would save endless hours or days of jury selection before each trial.

Additionally, it would not interrupt the lives and jobs of citizens who can scarcely afford to take the time off, and it would save employers the loss of key employees.

The justice system is an extreme expense to society, and there is no escaping that expense. Taxpayers have a reasonable expectation that their taxes buy the most efficient and most absolute justice possible. Bringing in inexperienced jurors every day cannot result in justice. Many trials these days involve government institutions or services, because the government has the deepest pockets financially. Trial lawyers simply have to prove the negligence or irresponsibility of any party related in some fashion to the actual guilty party. It becomes simple for a trial lawyer to make a connection that will win the lottery for his or her client. This is why so many parties are listed in a typical lawsuit. And this is why I am advocating for profession juries. They would be experienced and less easily influenced by manipulative lawyers. They could much better distinguish between honest claims and prevarication. This would be a huge gain for society, because society does not mind paying for legal justifiable claims against the government and insurance companies if the claims are honest and justifiable.

On the other hand, lawyers will jack up the damages beyond belief. Damages in civil suits should be based on the reduction of a person's earning power, not on that person's ability to live life to the fullest extent. Yet many awards are so extreme that you are left asking, "How could the damaged party ever need that much money to live his or her life in comfort and financial security"? Well, the obvious answer is the greed of attorneys. This is where professional juries can better serve society and better distinguish between actual damage and ridiculous awards.

Judges and Justice

You would expect judges to be prepared to serve justice when they reach the pinnacle of the justice system. It seems obvious that they should have a thorough knowledge of the law, yet many seem to lack common sense and logic. Some judges allow their political views to affect their decisions, and others are just plain corrupt.

What complicates the justice system is the history of the law, which offers many loopholes. I don't understand why decisions fifty to eighty years ago pertain to this day and age. First of all, those decisions could very well have been errant and prejudiced. Society is constantly evolving and becoming much more complicated. Yesterday's decisions do not necessarily reflect today's justice and the complications of law. Justice is a constantly evolving process. It demands a justice system of logic, common sense, and evolution. Certainly, justice is not served by finding loopholes in ancient laws and decisions of the past.

There are many lousy attorneys who just don't know how to present the facts and ask the right questions. This is where juries could be of great assistance in trials. Most professionals in a given field, such as medicine or the law, receive similar educations, yet it is difficult to find a competent doctor or lawyer. The difference is that some have more logic and common sense to bring to bear on their educations. If attorneys were not so expensive, it would be better if each party in a trial were represented by a team of attorneys instead of just one. Many attorneys simply do not have the ability or talent to put things into perspective, and these incompetent attorneys omit many pertinent facts.

Another issue that seems to be ridiculous and is tremendously expensive for taxpayers is the way the justice system sometimes moves trials out of a community because of publicity. Does the Constitution not state a citizen accused of a crime should be tried by a jury of his or her peers? Peers are the people living in your community, not people living across the state or in another state.

Responsible citizens read newspapers and keep abreast of news throughout the world. If you could move the trial completely out of the nation, you *might* find jurors who have not read news reports of the crime. News reporting is a twenty-four-hour-a-day phenomenon throughout the world. You might find a few remote areas of the country where citizens are completely without knowledge of criminal arrests and the facts surrounding the crime.

Facts are facts, and evidence is evidence. This is what trials are about, not rumors, speculation, or the prejudices presented in the media. I'm sure jurors are instructed to base their decisions on the evidence presented in the trial. After all, don't most defense attorneys make public statements to the media so that when the evidence and facts are presented in the trial, the defendant will be exonerated?

Chapter 51

Courts and Justices

N ow I wish to address the apparent holiness or prestige of judges. Why do we assume that judges are honorable? Most come from a pool of attorneys. We all know how honorable attorneys are. Their job is to present the best arguments in order to win for their clients. It matters little whether they lie or distort the facts.

Judges come from this same environment. Many are no more honorable than the attorneys I described above. So why is everybody in a courtroom required to rise when a judge enters? There are just as many corrupt and unfair judges just as there are corrupt and unfair members of any other occupation. Judges get approved, appointed, or elected based on approval by the bar association, which is made up of attorneys. Often, their approval is based on how favorable they have been toward other attorneys' interests. Human nature prevails here just as much as in politics.

Nobody should be allowed to rise as a judge enters a courtroom, and nobody should be allowed to address a judge as "your honor". Honor is an unfair assumption. It is only an opinion or a kiss-ass tactic employed by attorneys or defendants. "Sir" or "Ma'am" would be a more appropriate form of address.

Now let's address our sacred Supreme Court. We like to pretend Supreme Court justices are apolitical. This is the greatest absurdity in our nation. Of course they are political. Every individual has a political leaning. It is human nature.

In order for our nation not to be victimized by these political leanings for as many as five or six decades, no Supreme Court Justice should serve for more than ten years. The world is constantly changing, and too many justices are old-fashioned and out of touch with modern realities. Others are forced into decisions based on their personal interpretations of an antiquated Constitution. Everybody seems to have his or her own interpretation of the Constitution, just as there are various interpretations of the Bible. Our entire nation should not be tied to the prejudices and political leanings of a Supreme Court Justice for his or her entire career. This is absolute injustice! Let's get over this honor bullshit. Most Supreme Court decisions are political, and the justices demonstrate this fact nearly every day. If we could bet on their decisions in Las Vegas, we would all be winners.

If we could take these Supreme Court decisions out of our country to be decided by a foreign court with no political connections, we would likely get fair decisions handed down.

Our Constitution and certain amendments are too old-fashioned and out of date for this evolving world. It is time for a constitutional convention, a long and thorough study of how the Constitution needs to be tweaked to adapt to the modern world. It makes no sense to try to apply a caveman's constitution to an astronaut's world.

The world and society are constantly changing. We should not be tied to old rules. The founders were wise and noble in their time. However, if they lived in this age, they likely would have very different opinions on matters. The founders should not have a vote now or in the future. Democracy is based on the opinions and votes of the majority in the present. The vote of citizens today should always prevail over the rules and regulations of yesteryear. It is now our democracy, and tomorrow it will be another generation's democracy. The Constitution is not written in stone. The amendments to the Constitution are proof of that fact.

The best evidence that the Constitution needs to change is the right to bear arms. When the Second Amendment was introduced, there was no organized military. We have since determined that it is essential for our nation and each state to have professional armed forces. The right to bear arms was essential at the time, because we did not have local police forces to ensure our protection.

When judges ban cameras in court trials, what is the justification? Could it be that they don't wish to have the public realize how incompetent or unfair they are in their rulings? The public is entitled to attend trials. So what is the difference between attending in person and viewing a trial on television? The lessons that can be learned from watching trials are valuable tools for all of society. A better understanding of the law for the viewing public would be a great asset to the justice system. Watching trials would provide valuable lessons for potential victims and might act as a deterrent who those who feel they can beat the system.

Why is it that so many high-profile trials in which the evidence is solid go on for weeks, costing taxpayers millions of dollars? If a bank robber is caught in the act, why does there need to be a trial at all except for the sentencing? Isn't it just a case of running up the bill for attorneys at the taxpayers' expense? While we are hard at work, attorneys are running up our tax bills by thousands of dollars with their bullshit.

The worst threat to our justice system is the ability of attorneys to file lawsuits on behalf of corporations with billions of dollars, essentially destroying an individual or a small business. Individuals or small businesses simply cannot afford the extreme costs of court and attorney fees that would be required to defend themselves. Just another win for the fat cats and the government officials that are in their pocket !

I also propose that everyone who testifies in court or before an investigative committee should have to be hooked up to a lie-detector test. This would be true and absolute justice. That is why I like the *Nancy Grace* show. There are so many lies and exaggerations in court that it is sickening. Too often, the lies lead to injustices. There is nothing that interests me as much as true justice. Conversely, there is nothing that angers me more than injustice, and you witness it everyday in this society.

As long as we are discussing honor here, I might as well address our Congresspeople. They like to refer to themselves as "the honorable Senator" or "the honorable Congressperson" when addressing on another and on their letterheads. There is nothing honorable about them ! They make their decisions based on keeping their power. They sure as hell do not care about their constituents. Their souls are for sale to the highest bidder.

If they were honorable, they would not be running up a catastrophic debt that will destroy our nation. They would be taxing according to the nation's need and raising taxes to cover the cost of wars, not putting billions of dollars on a credit card. They would not be charging taxpayers more money for interest than for the services they provide.

An honorable congressperson would make his or her decisions based on what is best for the citizens, not for corporate powers. A better description of these rats would be "dishonorable slimeballs".

Chapter 52

Liquor Laws, Taxes, and Marijuana

'll start this chapter with a few stories about things that happened many years ago. Early in my life, I was a heavy drinker. Many years later, I was out at a particular restaurant for dinner and dancing on New Year's Eve. The bartender was a lady I knew from many years of frequenting a bar she worked at.

At times, if I feel that waitresses are overwhelmed by customers, I go to the bar and order a drink. Having been there since dinner and expecting to stay through midnight, I ordered water with the drinks. The bartender seemed put out by that request and mumbled something about amateur night.

On another occasion, I was sitting at a bar discussing politics with another political activist who later was elected to the city council. He also owned the bar. After a few drinks, I ordered coffee. Later, I ordered a drink again and was refused. I asked the owner why I was refused. He said this was the policy he has instructed his bartenders to abide by. Since he was himself drinking and a customer, he could not overrule his employee.

I think you see where I am going here. People who drink responsibly are either shut out or insulted. Well, that is not the end of these stories.

I spent most of my working days working a blue-collar job. We worked in extreme heat on a very physical job. Often, we left the job totally dehydrated and headed for the local bars. We were thirsty and put the drinks away. What we needed was a gallon of water. What we got were many alcoholic drinks. The more friends and co-workers who gathered, the longer the buying of the rounds went on. The longer the good times went on, the more difficult it became for individuals to bail out. It was easy to get stuck in a situation that dictated that it was your turn to buy a round. Sometimes, these hardworking individuals became the victims of dehydration and tragedy. If I were king, bars would be required to serve a glass of water with each alcoholic drink. It's strange how a person will drink water if it is sitting in front of him or her. Water serves two purposes. First, it satisfies your thirst and keeps you hydrated. Second, it stops you from drinking too much alcohol in an attempt to satisfy your thirst. It gives you a much better chance to get home without incident.

At one point, I became friends with a local talk-show host who was very astute politically. I and others encouraged him to run for the state house of representatives. After he was elected and established, I approached him about a few ideas I felt would benefit society. He felt that the legislature would never go for my suggestion of serving water with alcoholic drinks. It's no wonder there are citizen initiatives. I guess the government is on the side of liquor establishments and their ability to sell more drinks without consideration for the consequences.

I have frequented bars where people gather to do shots several times a night. It's as if the drinks sitting in front of them don't provide enough liquor. They revel in getting insanely drunk. These are adults, not college students. There appears to be no education about drinking except the fatal lessons people learn when it is too late. It is sad to read of the tragic deaths that occur every day as a result of lax laws and a government that ignores the problem.

So these are some of the revisions that I believe would save thousands of innocent lives and still allow citizens to party.

First, I suggest that bars designed only for drinking be banned. Don't worry; the jobs, taxes, and contribution to the economy will be made up in other ways and actually create more economic gain. Restaurants will be allowed to serve alcoholic drinks to dining customers.

All entertainment events involving alcohol, such as musical performances, dancing, comedy shows, and so on, would have to be located and performed at a hotel or motel. Attendees would have to book a room for the night in order to attend. Attending one of these events would require a hotel reservation and checking your vehicle into a locked parking facility for the night. Any individuals leaving the facility early would have to take a breathalyzer test to prove sobriety and would not be allowed to re-enter.

This would create greater commerce for hotels, give the public a better opportunity to party hearty, and remove any worry about DUIs or death driving home. It would give the hotel industry a great boost in the off season, which in some areas of the country makes up eight months of the year. It would be a boon for the hotel industry, would allow people to party hearty without fatal repercussions, and would eliminate thousands of needless fatal accidents.

I will not go into detail here; however, this would also be a great tool for law enforcement agencies. This type of regulation would allow people wishing to party to do so in a safe environment without the possibility of drunk driving. The current laws are a joke and almost border on entrapment. The police can sit down the street from a bar and arrest anybody leaving late at night. If anybody has a better idea of how we can put an end to these needless tragedies, I'd like to hear it.

Marijuana Laws

The laws regarding the possession and use of marijuana are another joke. Which is the more dangerous drug, liquor or marijuana? I don't even like marijuana; however, when I was younger, I spent time around enough people who used marijuana to realize that people are not dangerous when under its influence. They usually are laid back, funny, and nonviolent. You'll almost never find people getting into arguments or fights when they are under the influence of marijuana. You sure as hell cannot say that about liquor. There might be problems with liquor and marijuana in combination; however, I am in no position to evaluate those scenarios. Most of the tragic deaths and violence in our nation are the result of alcohol.

While I am writing this chapter, Michael Phelps is being crucified by the public and the media and will likely to be arrested. Many celebrities, athletes, congresspeople, judges, politicians, and other public figures have experimented with marijuana. I believe that I have read statistics indicating that over 60 percent of adults have used it. The government should get the message that when a majority of citizens ignores a law, there is no point in having that law. If the majority of people consider a product to be harmless to their health and well being, then it is time to re-examine the usefulness of the law prohibiting that product.

Wouldn't it be interesting to give a lie-detector test to every citizen and find out how many professionals and high-profile people have used marijuana? It would be humorous to expose so many hypocrites. Candidates and politicians running for office realize that if they took a pro-marijuana position, it would spell the death of their campaigns. It would be almost as bad as stating that they don't believe in God. If enough well-respected people in high places would step up and take a pro-marijuana position, it could easily make it onto the ballot.

Legalizing marijuana would allow the government to tax its sale and sell it in state-licensed liquor stores. The revenues would be huge and could fund the war on dangerous drugs. It would keep people out of prison who don't need to be there. This would save the citizens hundreds of millions in justice department and incarceration expenses. The police could then focus on dangerous criminals.

I smoked marijuana approximately ten times in my younger days due to peer pressure. I finally learned not to inhale (like Bill Clinton). All kinds of chemicals affect people differently. It never agreed with my system. I'll never forget my last experience. It was many years after the early days of marijuana popularity. Marijuana apparently had become more refined and potent through genetic engineering. I took a few hits off a tiny joint, and it disoriented me terribly. That's when I realized that marijuana was getting dangerously potent. I do not expect that the majority of people would want to indulge in marijuana that potent. How would they have a choice, though? It is not regulated.

So if the government legalized it and regulated marijuana, it could prevent it from becoming so potent and a danger to the public. It would put a stop to ruining decent citizens' lives and careers. Personally, even though I enjoy drinking, I would rather see liquor banned than marijuana. Liquor is far more dangerous to society than marijuana. I guess I would just have to buy bootlegged liquor—as would millions of others.

That's what happens when you ban something that is hugely popular. The citizens ignore the law, and then a new industry pops up to serve the need of those who see no harm in the product. The cost to society becomes colossal—the costs of investigating petty crimes, of maintaining the courts, of prisons, parole, and probation. All the while, the justice system could be focusing on the real crimes that seem to be so overwhelming to keep up with.

The federal government has a chance to allow states that have approved marijuana use to test its effect on society if they will just stand back and allow state governments to take the lead. Instead, big brother is going after local and state officials, threatening to charge them for doing their jobs in regulating the industry. By their actions, they are going against the will of voters and exercising fascist procedures.

As I stated before, I have never liked the smell or influence of Marijuana. However, when you suffer from the pain of arthritis, it can wear you down to the point of wishing for any relief. I read recently of statistics that show older citizens are resorting to marijuana for pain relief. Since it does not agree with my lungs, I wish it could be available in pill form. Since tobacco smoke is damaging to the lungs, it seems likely that smoke in any form is harmful to one's health.

Many States have legalized Marijuana for medicinal use through citizen initiatives. They are allowing entrepreneurs to grow and sell this product with a doctor's approval. Allowing this method of sale is exactly the wrong thing for the government to sanction. There is no control over the strength of marijuana. There is the chance of people damaging their lungs with the smoke. After smoking marijuana, I personally went to the emergency room with severe chest pain when I was a young man.

If Marijuana is legalized for medicinal purposes, it should be in the form of pills or capsules. The strength should be controlled by the pharmaceutical industry. There should be a tax to pay for the regulation of this new industry.

The use of marijuana absolutely should not be allowed in the workplace. If you are on high-strength controlled pain medication, you are advised not to work, as it can be very dangerous and your work can be poor.

I would like to see public service announcements that warn of the extreme danger of mixing alcohol and drugs. These announcements should state that some of the most heinous crimes and tragedies occur when people are deranged by the effects of these combinations. Perhaps our major brewers could sponsor these messages in the same way that they warn people to know their limits and never drink and drive.

Prohibition of Drugs

What bothers me most about the prohibition of drugs is the size and viciousness of the drug cartels. They are becoming so powerful that they are essentially taking over the governments of many nations, especially in South America. That same power is threatening the government of Mexico and likely will spread to the United States. Of course the United States is the world's biggest market for illegal drugs. My, aren't we proud Americans?

Is it not time to realize we have lost the war on illegal drugs? What has to happen before we surrender and try a different approach? Do we wait until the cartels start taking over one community at a time? Until our police officers and public officials start resigning as they have in some Mexican cities?

The federal government would be wise to create public service announcements on television detailing the tragedies that occur in Mexico as a result of America's consumption of illegal drugs. They need to show the public the carnage, terrorism, and damage to Mexico's tourist industry and economy. They need to ask drug users if they wish to be responsible for destroying a nation and allowing terrorists to take over a nation on our border, which will put them in position to launch attacks of mass destruction on America. Some corporations would likely be proud to finance these messages, especially those that have a financial stake in Mexico. These lessons should also be taught in schools at every level.

I would be very much in favor of legalizing all drugs. The taxes generated would be tremendous. With those taxes, we could educate children and adults extensively about the extreme danger of drugs to our lives and health and the ways they can destroy lives and careers. A similar strategy seems to be working in the campaign against cigarettes, which are far less dangerous to society than drugs.

I recall a time when citizens were required to have liquor licenses in order to purchase liquor. We could require citizens to have drug licenses in the same way. In order to purchase a license, you would be required to complete an extensive educational course on the hazards of drug use and the danger of addiction. You would be exposed to the testimony of people who have seen drugs destroy their health, careers, families, and lives. Teachers should teach these same lessons at every level of school with a passion for getting through to every child.

I have to believe that if drugs were legalized and controlled, the revenues generated would pay for all the negative effects, including the institutionalization of those who abuse drugs. The greatest benefit, however, would be that legalization would put an end to the drug cartels threatening our society. Even the crimes committed for money to purchase drugs are a huge drain on society and the justice system. Wouldn't we be better off if we supplied drugs in a controlled environment to those who are so desperate that they would kill for their next fix? It would be an opportunity to reach these individuals and provide rehabilitation and guidance. Would the addicted not be better off if they were provided with medical and professional assistance instead of the assistance provided by drug dealers? Yeah, they will give you help if you sell for them and provide leads to expand their business.

The bottom line is that we must better educate children about the dangers of drugs. They should be taught that when they decide to take their first dose of these drugs, they have chosen to destroy their lives. Their peers will tell them that these drugs will make them feel wonderful. They will not tell them that their lives will be destroyed as a result.

We are obligated to provide rehabilitation to those who have chosen to take drugs. However, if they fail to take advantage of the help that society provides, then we must stop aiding and abetting these individuals. They cost society millions of dollars, because they are totally worthless and unable to support themselves. The government should place them in an institution and give them all the drugs they want. If they choose to overdose, then they have chosen drugs over life. They should sign a legal contract that relieves the institution providing the drugs of all liability and states that they, by their own will, choose to participate in the program. This program would put the drug cartels out of business. It's time to quit catering to drug addicts' failures. There are millions of Americans who desperately need medical attention and cannot afford it, and they suffer the consequences when drug addicts and criminals are given priority over them.

We damn well better find a better approach to dealing with illegal and dangerous drugs, because American society is in danger of becoming a failure in a world that depends on America to provide hope and guidance for all humanity.

Of course, we can stay in denial and keep failing. History proves every day that money will corrupt individuals and nations. There is so much profit in illegal drugs that when you take one dealer or supplier off the streets, many more are ready to move in and benefit.

It always bothers me that the government and society are reluctant to try different methods. Laws are written, laws are changed, and laws are disposed of. Laws are not written in stone for all eternity. Yet we are always reluctant to experiment and try different approaches, even when other nations have success with a different approach. Life is about trial and error. Society should not be so averse to experimenting, especially when failed experiments can be disposed of.

Of course, if we legalized drugs, society would have to adopt many more regulations to protect employers. There would need to be strict rules to prevent people from showing up for work under the influence of drugs, just as now one cannot show up for work drunk. Employees would have to be willing to be subject to blood tests any time their employer suspected they might be impaired.

Mood Enhancing Discoveries

There is one thing society and science never seem to discuss or realize. We are all different in our natural or sober states. Some people spend most of their lives on a natural high. Others spend most of their lives in a state of depression or at least without feeling that natural high.

You can easily tell an individual's natural mood by his or her personality. If someone speaks boisterously, smiles a lot, and has a spring in his or her step, it is clear that person is just full of energy and life. On the other hand, there are people who are very quiet, seldom smile, and generally live a life of depression. If you have a natural high, you cannot control your enthusiasm for life.

It has always amazed me how many people can live their lives, socialize, and have a ball without liquor or drugs. They participate in sports and outdoor activities like hiking, skiing, kayaking, swimming, and biking. They also gravitate toward success in their careers. They essentially enjoy life and all the challenges they encounter.

The same differences can be seen in children. Why do some of our children approach education with so much enthusiasm and desire? It isn't always parental guidance that instills desire in children. Some children simply have that natural enthusiasm for learning and achieving. If we could give all children that natural high and mood, we could achieve a huge gain for society. We would not have to deal with children who lack motivation and drop out in order to seek artificial happiness in their lives.

Would it not be a tremendous gain for all of mankind if every child enthusiastically achieved all they could in this world? Perhaps we could put an end to terror and crime instead of spending billions of dollars fighting crime and terrorism.

The point I want to make is that we have to develop the chemistry to give those people living a lifetime of depression a lift. We have to invest in research that will develop better drugs or treatments that are safe and lift those people up.

I can never forget some of my fellow students in high school whom I considered to be geniuses. They were practically straight-A students. Years later, they were working very modest jobs for modest pay. What happened here? If I had their ability, I would be a research doctor or a scientist ! Is it lack of desire on the part of these people, or is it just a natural high that drives the achievers in the world? It's time to investigate this problem and discover the genetic code that separates the winners and losers in society.

A percentage of the revenues from taxes on liquor, drugs, and cigarettes should be solely dedicated to research to solve these problems. If you can tax the hell out of cigarettes, you certainly could institute a modest tax on all of the above that would raise billions for research.

Most people do not feel the natural high that many of society's highest achievers do. As long as there are drugs that make people feel better, they will pursue them. Society would be better served if we came up with safe and inexpensive drugs. If we do not, our problems will continue to escalate.

St. Johns wort has been proven to be a great mood-enhancement tool. However, at first, people did not realize that you have to be active in order to feel the benefit. It stimulates a natural high when accompanied by exercise.

The government would be wise to invest extensively in research into ways to enhance mood. That can pay huge dividends for society and solve many societal problems.

It's time for the pompous people in society to step up and admit that they have natural gifts and realize that the majority of people lack this benefit. Let's get all our children and citizens on the road to achievement and spread our solutions throughout the world.

Depression and depressed people cause the greatest societal problems in the world. We need to commit to safe and sane cures. One more item I would like to throw in here. I don't know much about cocaine; however, I have rarely read about anybody going crazy on cocaine and killing people. I have never used it, because I have a healthy fear of cocaine addiction. But

I know many successful and high-profile citizens who indulge in cocaine as a recreational drug.

This might be a good place to start research into drugs that can elevate the moods of the many depressed people who never experience the natural high I described above. Perhaps there are chemical properties that can be altered to make drugs less addictive and safe for individuals who need that extra help to elevate their mood, spirits, or desire to excel in life. If scientists can discover an ingredient, herb, or supplement that can be applied to foods just as certain vitamins are required in bread and other foods, we may give a great boost to people and solve many societal problems.

Depression destroys far too many people in our society, and the pursuit of an elevated mood drives great numbers of people to alcohol and other dangerous drugs. The costs to society are immeasurable. It's time to invest in research and find safe and healthy alternatives. Heavy taxes on drugs can fund the research and development of these alternatives.

Bartering Is Cheating Honest Taxpayers

While we are on the issue of taxes, I would like to bring up another issue that robs the treasury of the people. We who pay taxes for goods and services both to the federal government and local governments are cheated by the well-to-do professionals who are in a position to barter for many of their goods and services. Why is skirting taxation legal? Well, actually it is not. However, when have you ever heard of anybody getting arrested for failure to report financial gain obtained through bartering? The very same could be applied to people who work under the table for cash. How many billions of dollars could our IRS collect if we could put a stop to this cheating? If we all bartered or paid cash for services, we sure as hell would not have funding to provide government services. Perhaps we should put an end to currency and all payments over one hundred dollars would have to go through a bank.

Chapter 53

Entrapment

I am really disgusted with our justice system and one particular television network. The methods the law uses to entrap citizens should absolutely be prohibited in the Constitution. I'll cite an experience I had in which I was nearly the victim of these methods.

When I was a young man, I remember driving down a street in our city that was known as "Hooker Row". I had driven down this street many times and seen many of these ladies. I viewed them as nymphomaniacs until years later I came to understand that it was in fact drug addiction that drove them to this desperate lifestyle.

One day I was driving down this street and saw a magnificently beautiful lady patrolling the avenue. I was instantly in love. I had to drive around the block and view this magnificent creature one more time. I felt that if she was this beautiful and also a nymphomaniac, she was the perfect match for me. Maybe I would just ask her out for dinner or a night of dancing.

Ah, but it finally dawned on me. This lady was far too beautiful to be patrolling for prostitution. She was obviously a plant for a sting operation that the police often used in this area. So what if I had pursued this lady and she had made me feel like I needed to put up some money to get next to her? I probably would have bitten. I might have done anything to get acquainted with her.

The bottom line is that I likely would have been arrested for innocently trying to get acquainted with the young lady. I would not have been in this situation if the police had not put such a beautiful lady out there. Does the law go too far in enticing innocent people into a crime?

Speaking of crime, isn't the justice system burdened with enough real crime without focusing on prostitution? Wasting time on antiprostitution laws is part of why we are losing the drug war. We are wasting millions of dollars that need desperately to be spent on the serious crimes that plague society. Why do police have all this time to crack down on the harmless rights of citizens to engage in natural sex acts? As if ordinary citizens do not have to pay for sex. I guarantee you bureaucrats that if you don't buy your significant others gifts on Valentine's Day, you will not get any sex. If you don't pay for it throughout the year in some manner, you are not going to obtain sexual favors. Marriage is a form of prostitution. If you don't provide material things or services, you are not going to get sex. In effect, you are bartering for this service.

At one point, I owned a very nice four-plex in the wrong part of town. At the time, I knew little about real estate; however, I was conned into buying this property by a real estate salesman. I worked hard on this property for over fifteen years in an effort to provide decent housing for people. Many of the tenants destroyed the apartments and left owing months of rent. There was no retrieving the lost rent, as these people usually had no jobs and many were on public assistance. You would expect public assistance to pay for a roof over their heads; however, that's not the way the law sees it.

During one period, things became ugly at the four-plex. I had three vacancies for months. Two families came along with children. I rented an apartment to each family. They paid the first month's rent, and I never saw a dime after that. I gave them eviction notices. They ignored them. Weeks later, I confronted them and let them know they had to evacuate.

Meanwhile, I was working in an adjacent apartment. They came in there, obviously drugged up, and I had the impression they were going to kill me. They did not know that a friend of mine was in another room.

He stepped into the closet and called 911. The police arrived just as the tenants were kicking in the bedroom door to get me. After I finally got rid of them, the police informed me they were two of the most notorious criminals in town.

One day, a pretty little blonde arrived with an infant in her arms and asked to rent one of the apartments. I rented to her and never saw her again. When the rent was overdue, I knocked on the door, and it opened. Inside were about a dozen African American guys drinking and smoking pot. They stated that the lady was not there but that they would inform her that the rent was overdue. As the months went by, I couldn't even locate this lady to serve an eviction notice. I finally notified these guys they had to leave. They came after me and asked if I wished to die. I notified the police, and they informed me that this was a civil matter and I would have to take care of the problem in court.

In the mean time, these guys were running a drug operation out of my building. All day and all night, one or two of them stood by the curb waiting for customers. I watched this going on. They stood there motioning their customers to the back parking area, where they completed their deals. I came home from a visit across the state at 4:00 a.m., and there they were at the curb.

I notified detectives on the drug task force, and they informed me that they were aware of the situation; however, they were keeping tabs on it in an attempt to determine who the supplier and others at the top of the drug ring were. In the mean time, I was left with three vacancies, because nobody wanted to live in that environment.

One evening, I went the four-plex to work on something, and I noticed about twenty police cars and a paddy wagon in a Bingo parking lot about a block away. I walked over to find out what is going on. An officer informed me that they had just had a major prostitution sting. I could not believe my ears. All the serious crime involving drug dealers and gangs in our community, and they were more concerned with who was having sex with whom?

However, I'm well aware of the forces behind it all. The churches in every community lean heavily on public officials regarding what they consider sin. Religious groups are well known throughout history for trying to influence public policy based on religious belief. They are probably the most powerful influence in elections. If we didn't have our Constitution and freedom of speech, we would be no better off than the Taliban.

Another alarming issue is the way the justice system uses entrapment procedures that totally destroy lives and families. NBC's *Dateline* seems to be very proud of its sting operations that entrap numerous citizens by lining them up with supposed teenagers to engage in sex.

First of all, I doubt there are very many children out there who are vulnerable to these potential child molesters. If there are, then there must be a lot of irresponsible parents and teachers. I would guess that is the reason *Dateline* is able to catch so many fish with their entrapment schemes.

I do believe that this is a very good method for finding and locating potential suspects. A database of suspects could be very valuable for investigations of actual child molestation. However, to arrest people and destroy lives based on a crime that may never have happened without the bait makes a travesty of justice. It makes for good television. I don't even have a problem with that issue. However, to throw an innocent person in prison based on baiting should not pass muster with the Constitution.

I don't know much about child molesters and what drives them to the crime. I do have an intuition that these individuals are unattractive or socially clumsy to such a degree that they can't get to first base with the opposite sex. Therefore, they prey on the young and vulnerable. It is similar to how people are driven to seek company or sexual contacts on the internet. If they had the attractiveness and personality to make contacts in person, they would not have to resort to finding dates on the internet or in wanted ads. A certain percentage of those who flunk the internet test likely resort to preying on children for sex. If prostitution were available for those who are physically and socially disadvantaged, perhaps there would be fewer rapes and less child molestation.

What about the wealthy married man who has a girlfriend set up in a plush apartment and lavishes her with expensive gifts and luxury living? Is that not prostitution? Is he not paying for sex? When have you ever heard of somebody getting busted for that? So I guess whether you are a criminal or not depends on which end of the pay scale you live on.

In a nation or state not controlled by religion, government would simply declare that sex is a personal freedom and therefore it is none of the government's business who has sex with whom. (That is, unless a man ignores the responsibility of supporting the children that result from sexual activity.)

Now, don't give me that song and dance about health concerns and the spreading of venereal disease. If the general population used the precautions that responsible and regulated prostitution operations use, there would be little venereal disease. I'll bet the police and the justice department would rather spend their time and resources pursuing real crime that damages people's lives and property.

At some time in the future, when the world is overpopulated, society will be glad that gays and lesbians are not contributing to the overpopulation of the world and that people can enjoy sex of their own free will without bringing unwanted children into the world.

Another issue I will address in this chapter is polygamy. Have you ever been in love with two different people at the same time? Perhaps you wished that you could marry both. Tradition should not be any excuse for a law. Personal freedom and responsibility should be the government's prevailing priorities. What somebody does in his or her private life should not be the government's business unless there is abuse, child neglect, property liability, or damage to others in society.

The only problem I might have with multiple marriages involves financial considerations. Can this individual provide a home, health, and welfare for more than one partner? Are all partners in full agreement to the union, and are all parties in agreement about how to divide the assets in the event of dissolution of all or part of the union? Those should be the only concerns that the government should have. Anything else amounts to religious rule by one religion over another and government intrusion into the private lives of citizens. I guess the government would have no authority over these scenarios if the parties did not marry. I don't believe that it is illegal for a person to have two or more sexual partners living under his or her roof. So why prosecute the legal partnerships, especially at a time when marriage is becoming a thing of the past ?

Chapter 54

Financial Institutions

I don't get it! There was a time in the history of this nation when we had laws against monopolies and laws prohibiting interstate banks. There were very good reasons for those laws. History had proven that they were absolutely essential for the economy to function. Yet all that legislation and wisdom seems to have been swept under the rug in the past few decades. I can't believe the apparent corruption of society and the government.

We have a Securities and Exchange Commission that is supposed to protect the financial investments of Americans. Yet it appears to exist for the purpose of protecting all the illegal and corrupt dealings of the millionaires and billionaires.

Our elected officials appear to be beholden to the power and money of the rich. Who can get elected without a ton of money? The corporate powers dictate to our government officials what they can and cannot regulate, and any official who ignores their commands soon finds him- or herself out of office. It seems that these slimeballs can get away with anything unless or until somebody goes to the media to blow the whistle on them.

The government is supposed to provide oversight and regulation, but this corruption has gone on for a decades. Somebody must be getting paid to look the other way. It's hard to believe that after hundreds of years of careful legislation and oversight, this corruption was able to go on for so long.

Now many of the largest banks and financial institutions in our nation are failing. Yet small community banks are doing well. Has our government taken notice? Absolutely not ! This is one of the major factors contributing to the collapse of our financial institutions. These giants have little financial interest in the stability of their assets, as they can simply pass them along to another institution to get somebody a bonus for writing a great number of loans. These transactions do not happen in small community banks. Their daily business is tied to every transaction they make. They know their customers and do not make blind decisions to pad their books.

So perhaps it is time to go back to prohibiting interstate banks and the rules that prohibit monopolization of markets and industries. It's well worth a study. Many mergers and acquisitions are designed to stamp out competition. There is never any consideration of the careers, livelihoods, and communities that are affected by these mergers and acquisitions. It seems that every transaction is approved if it will contribute to the rich getting richer. Is that better for society and the financial health of the nation? Time will tell ! Or is it telling now?

Another issue that disturbs me—and I cannot figure out the justification for it—is the fact that any individual can have as many credit cards as he or she wishes. Why does anybody need more than one credit card? It only encourages higher debt and higher interest rates. There is a reason why credit cards have limits. When the bank issues the card, it supposedly has checked your credit history and debt–to–income ratio.

If other cards are issued, it defeats the purpose of those calculations and limitations. The banks are actually trying to do a favor to their customers by keeping their debt under control and keeping people living within their means. So when another financial institution issues a card to that customer, it undermines the bank that issued the original card.

Therefore, I propose that legislators protect financial institutions and customers by allowing only one credit card per individual.

Credit rating institutions actually penalize people for closing credit accounts. What the hell is that all about? You pay your bills responsibly, get out of debt, and don't need a particular credit service any more, and you get penalized for your responsible management of your debts.

It's almost as if these credit reporting agencies are in business to promote debt. If you don't charge up a storm on a regular basis, you are not a good candidate for their club. I can't express my disdain enough for those people and their methodology.

The bottom line is that credit cards should be issued on the basis of affordability. If you have too much debt for your income, you should not qualify for a credit card. If you freeze those accounts and have a record of making regular required payments, then you might be eligible for a new card.

What the hell is wrong with teaching people to be responsible for their debts and keeping their debt loads manageable? That used to be the way banks operated. They needed to be assured that you could handle your existing debts before they extended additional credit to you.

Is it any wonder that the national financial system has collapsed and spun the world and our nation into financial ruin? Is it any wonder that millions of people are losing their homes because of mortgage obligations that any responsible individual should have realized could not be met?

Now, what about those adjustable rate mortgages? Shouldn't they be illegal? Wouldn't that have prevented the collapse of our mortgage market? It seems that the new generation ignores all of the values, principles, responsibilities, regulations, and ethics that have been developed throughout our history.

Laws and regulations were created to prevent the destruction and collapse of financial markets and industries. The collapse of the mortgage market has proven that adjustable rate mortgages are a poison to the market.

The Stock Market
There is a solution that can prevent the stock market from going into a free fall. It seems that every time the president sneezes or a foreign leader makes a threat, it sends the stock market spiraling downward. Stocks

should be treated the same as certificates of deposit. If you withdraw early, you pay a penalty.

This would encourage long-term commitments and minimize the hasty and foolish dumping of stocks. It would be a stopgap measure to stabilize the markets. At least some stocks that are dependent on growth, research, and development should be protected in this manner. If our nation wishes to have stability in the stock market, then stocks should be treated like certificates of deposit and should be subject to the same regulations and penalties.

Stocks are meant to be long-term investments in commerce, not week- or month-long investments.

Chapter 55

Condominium and Real Estate Failures

O ur nation has faced the greatest real estate failure in our history in the past few years. New condominium towers and new housing developments have failed all over our nation.

Imagine being a buyer in one of these promising new developments. Maybe you bought in early, and then the developer was unable to sell more of the homes or condos. You were promised a recreation center and many other amenities. Suddenly, you find that the developer is bankrupt and unable to finish the project or that most of the homes or condos are being foreclosed on. The neighborhood consists mostly of vacant homes with weeds growing high in the front yards. The condominium building is mostly vacant, and none of the promised amenities are finished or open.

I have a solution that may alleviate many of these tragic situations. The federal government should step in and start a relocation program. Let's say that there were three or four condominium towers in a community that were failing or unable to sell many of their units. Officials should study the situation and choose the project that has the most units sold and then buy out another failed project and offer the people who live there an opportunity to relocate or transfer their ownership to another project. In other words, the government should help to fill up the project that has the best chance of succeeding. The government could repossess other projects and hang onto them until the market rebounds and investors are interested in paying close to fair market value for the properties.

The same could be done for failed subdivisions. The government could choose the one that has the best amenities and chance of success and give homeowners an opportunity to relocate from other failed neighborhoods. This would build strong neighborhoods and allow the government to sit on the others until the market recovers.

Filling a subdivision with homeowners will also fill schools and parks with children instead of creating half-vacant schools and dangerous neighborhoods.

Without strong neighborhoods, tax revenues will fall short of being able to provide essential services. Mostly vacant neighborhoods fall prey to vandals, drug houses, and vagrants, all of which creates a very dangerous situation for remaining homeowners. You cannot expect to grow tax revenues from failed neighborhoods or bankrupt developers.

If this situation exists in a proposed home owners association, then the home buyers are often cheated out of their investments, because the developer fails to provide the amenities promised and the area becomes dangerous to live in.

Many times, when these homes are foreclosed on, the bidders purchase them for rental investment. We all know what can happen to a respectable neighborhood when renters move in. Even some buyers, if the price is low enough, can drag down a neighborhood.

I might have a suggestion for the security of the vacated neighborhoods.

We might consider offering free temporary housing to police officers, military personnel, or other armed government employees. How much would criminals wish to mess with these people? It's just a suggestion !

Chapter 56

Property Ownership

People purchase property based on the perceived value of the land for housing or agricultural development. If, by blind luck, that land happens to contain tremendous value beneath the surface in the form of petroleum or valuable minerals, who should profit from that value? In my opinion, every citizen of that nation should. Actually, in my opinion, every citizen of the nation should own the nation's land, and it should not be for sale. You should be entitled to rent or lease that land for as long as you live. When you and your legal partner pass on, the land should go back to the nation. It could then be designated for the public good or sold or leased to the highest bidder.

It is entirely conceivable that a handfull of billionaires could eventually own all the property in our nation. Is that the destiny of America? In my opinion, this could be very dangerous to democracy and free enterprise in future generations.

So should any individual actually own the land of a nation or its mineral rights? Or should the nation own it? A better future exists for a nation's citizens if individuals only own the lease on the land for the duration of their lives. I will explain the reasoning for this below.

There are too many brats who are born with silver spoons in their mouths these days. If their parents wish to secure their futures, there are numerous ways to do it. It should not be legal to pass on property owner-ship to an individual who has not worked to earn that land. Far too much property is falling into the hands of individuals who did nothing to earn it. Most often, they blow the proceeds.

America is in danger of being totally owned by foreign powers. I don't even consider American billionaires to be much different. Too much wealth equates to too much power, and this is very dangerous to a democracy. Do we want foreign powers to own America and all the mineral and oil rights to the land? How much power will American citizens have if most or all of the land and its mineral rights are owned by foreign nations? Is it not better in the long term that the land and its mineral rights belong to the nation? Can we foresee serious problems in the future if foreign nations control our na-tion? Don't we already have enough problems now that huge corporations in America own too much property and have too much control of Congress?

I have come to this conclusion after many years of observing people stealing from, raping, and killing citizens in Africa and South America. Nations on those continents contain billions if not trillions of dollars of wealth, and that wealth often is seized by force. Foreign corporations and wealthy individuals take all the wealth of the land, and millions of those nations' citizens suffer in poverty. How wonderful it would be if the citi-zens of those nations benefited from the great wealth that their nations produce. This is likely the greatest injustice in the history of mankind. Hundreds of millions of dollars go into the pockets of the powerful, while the ordinary citizens of those nations live out their short lives in poverty, starvation, disease, and hopelessness. If there has ever been a noble cause for the United Nations to embrace, this is it. They could solve some of the biggest problems in the world and improve the future of mankind.

You might say that this is those nations' problem, but the reality is that we are on course to have it happen in America. More money, property, and assets are concentrated into the hands of fewer people every year. Much of this wealth was not even earned but was handed down. Often, inherited assets are mismanaged and lost, which often affects the future of numerous families. If major businesses and corporations are mismanaged, they go under. Then foreign nations move in to take advantage of the crisis.

Chapter 57

Illegal and Uninsured Drivers

Since the invention of automobiles, they have had a costly impact on society both financially and through the lost lives of loved ones. Criminals, drivers under the influence of drugs and alcohol, and accident-prone drivers continue to skirt the law, causing much unnecessary suffering, death, and expense to law-abiding citizens. Why does society put up with it?

If we could eliminate this type of driver from our highways, even low-income citizens could afford insurance. I believe technology has advanced to the point where it would be simple to prevent these lawless individuals from plaguing society.

This endeavor is going to require many changes in laws and manufacturing processes, and the ignitions of old vehicles may need to be refitted. Currently, we use technology to prevent drunk drivers from starting their vehicles when drunk, and used car dealers and financiers use technology to prevent vehicles from starting if payments are not current.

I propose a new type of driver's license with a computer chip that acts as the ignition key. It would be somewhat similar to the key card employees use to access doors at work or travelers use to access hotel rooms. Automobiles would have computer chips matching the VIN number in the ignition system to the driver's license chip.

Automobile manufacturers would be required to install key cards and encoded chips in ignitions systems. These systems should be installed in a heavy steel box in a location impossible to tamper with. It would be similar to the black box on airplanes. It might also be encoded to send out an alert to the department of licenses when tampered with.

Your driver's license would be encoded with your identification, and that license would be your ignition key for your personal vehicles, company vehicles, rental vehicles, and so on. Your license key would be sent to your insurance company or agent, and they would issue the license when you purchased insurance.

All vehicles, foreign and domestic, would be required to have smart ignitions encoded with information exclusive to each vehicle. Each vehicle also would be required to have a global positioning chip and an alarm to notify authorities if the ignition were tampered with or removed. If battery power were cut to this system, it would also transmit a signal to authorities. Imagine how society could put an end to auto thefts with this technology.

If your license were suspended, you would not have the ability to start any vehicle. If you did not have current insurance, you would not be driving. If you were convicted of possessing illegal drugs, you would not be issued a driver's license during a probationary period. If you were convicted of driving under the influence of drugs or alcohol, the same would apply.

Imagine what a great security tool this would be for people who own rare and expensive vehicles and classic cars. Imagine how this could reduce insurance premiums for all drivers by making it essentially impossible to steal vehicles. And the most valuable benefit would be that this system would end the killing and maiming of thousands of innocent citizens. It could eliminate a great deal of suffering.

How many times have we heard of a vehicle going off the road and over a cliff with no witnesses? Some of these people are discovered after several days of searching, just in time to save their lives. Most are found too late. You can imagine the suffering they endure before they die. Many more are never discovered and become missing persons who are never found. How valuable a tool would this system be if you had a loved one disappear under these circumstances?

Later on, as the technology becomes less expensive, iris identification could also be incorporated as well as intoxication detection. This could prevent first-time offenders who are not aware of how inebriated they are from making fatal mistakes. Unfortunately, this happens all too often. We often ask, "How could this happen? He or she was a responsible, law-abiding citizen" !

The ignition system could also contain a computer chip that could track stolen vehicles, criminals, parolees, illegal immigrants, terrorist suspects, and so on. Even rental cars could be encoded to track foreigners, potential terrorists, or even members of drug cartels.

Earlier, I mentioned that new vehicle manufacturers would be required to install these smart ignitions. This would leave millions of older vehicles without the technology. Owners of these vehicles, if they had clean records without any DUIs or drug possession convictions, would not be required to install the smart ignitions. If they wished to let their teenagers or other family members or friends drive their vehicles, they then would be required to have them installed.

Visitors to the United States could simply present a driver's license and proof of insurance from their native countries to the rental car company. The rental company would issue a temporary driver's license for the rented vehicle. In the same manner, a visitor who purchased a vehicle could be tracked if he or she overstayed a visa—an invaluable tool for the Department of Homeland Security.

The department of licensing would have the sole purpose of testing new drivers and those applying for reinstatement. Renewing drivers' licenses would be the responsibility of local insurance agents. Drivers would take the renewal forms they received from the department of licensing to their insurance agents. Upon payment of insurance premiums, the agents would issue drivers' licenses for specified vehicles.

Insurance companies without local offices could simply make contracts with local, independent insurance agencies to issue licenses.

I might be getting into dangerous territory with this idea, however, so these issues will likely require much study. Driving is a huge expense, and I doubt the cost of smart ignition systems would render driving unaffordable. The societal gains from removing irresponsible drivers from our highways would be huge. But that benefit would pale in comparison to the ability to put criminals out of business. How could burglars operate without vehicles to haul their goods? Not very well! How well could drug dealers operate without transportation? As you can see, this could be the greatest crime-fighting prevention tool ever. Grounding criminals would be very valuable to the law-abiding citizenry.

This is the solution that we have always hoped for but never imagined would be possible. We can get chronic drunks and drug users off the roads. These individuals have little or no regard for the lives of others. Law enforcement agencies can track criminals and potential terrorists. What a tremendous tool for the justice department this would be! At the same time, we could do away with one of society's greatest expenses, get the worst violators off our highways, and make life very difficult for criminals.

This technology could be a great tool for teaching our youth about responsibility and freedom. The realization that they could lose the right to drive with one foolish act would teach responsibility. Is one night of partying worth the loss of a freedom someone has waited years to obtain? Our youth would have to seriously consider this question. One drug or alcohol conviction could lose that privilege for years. They would also have to face the realization that revoking this privilege might very well save their lives or the lives of others. Our youth might be able to understand that the rules and regulations of society are actually there to protect and their ability to reach their goals in life.

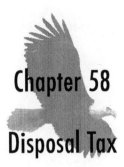

Chapter 58

Disposal Tax

M any years ago, I witnessed industrial businesses dumping hazardous materials in disused parts of their property. This used to be standard procedure for many businesses before laws and procedures were enacted. These laws do not, however, mean that all businesses take the time, trouble, and expense to dispose of hazardous materials legally. Nor does it guarantee that contractors and homeowners obey the law or do the proper thing for the environment.

How many people are willing to drive ten to fifty miles to dispose of a gallon of oil-based paint or used solvent? How many small contractors will take time from their busy schedules to take their used or leftover materials out to a disposal site and then pay a disposal fee? I have a feeling most of those materials go down the drain or into garbage cans, dumpsters, or vacant fields.

It has always bothered me that many of us take the time to separate recycled materials and participate in recycling programs (as any good citizen should), and yet there is a large number of irresponsible people who don't give a damn about the world, the environment, or the rest of us. Many will even stoop to disposing of garbage in recycling containers, their own or a neighbor's.

So why does government make recycling voluntary? Why not make it mandatory? Why not charge those who don't recycle double disposal fees?

Waste disposal is a huge expense for society. Most waste has to be hauled hundreds of miles to landfills. Some communities use incinerators to dispose of garbage, releasing all kinds of harmful gases into the environment, including mercury. These incinerators cost hundreds of millions of dollars to build, and then they charge citizens a hundred dollars a ton in disposal fees. That encourages some people to dump their garbage wherever they feel they can get away with it. Some even put the burden on charities by dumping waste at their doorways at night, which puts a huge burden on those charities. Garbage disposal is one of the largest expenses for many charities.

Improper or illegal disposal can be a health risk for society. Therefore, I propose a 0.1 percent sales tax on every product sold to pay for the eventual disposal of that product. I'm aware that the proposed amount would require much study. Certainly, some materials are more expensive to dispose of than others. The tax on those materials would have to be higher to reflect the additional expense of disposal.

These taxes would totally fund the waste management departments of each community. The disposal tax paid upon purchase would fund the pickup and disposal of every product from couches to hydrochloric acid. We charge fees for battery disposal and oil and tire disposal, so why not do the same for all products?

Why would anybody dump hazard materials down a drain or into a river? Why would anybody dump their garbage in the countryside? Why would anybody dump a useless couch or appliance at the gate of a charity at night? All these individuals would have to do is place their items by the curb or, for larger items, call for a pickup.

This tax could also fund composting, and how beneficial is that for the environment, the food we eat, and our health?

For many years, I have shaken my head in wonder when I read of the expense of hauling garbage hundreds of miles to landfills. The trucks are very expensive, labor is expensive, and fuel is expensive.

Every community has rural property on the outskirts of town. With good engineering, these communities could build mountains with all this garbage. In most communities, these mountains could then become sledding hills in the winter and great waterslide parks in the summer.

In the mean time, all the methane created by rotting garbage can be captured to create energy. These underground systems already are in place at most landfills around the world.

As one mountain grows to a large size, another could be started adjacent to the first. Eventually, there might be a circle of four or more mountains. The community could fill in the center and build a huge mountain. In northern regions, this huge mountain might become a place to ski or participate in other winter sports. Other communities might choose to build a reservoir or lake among those mountains.

So you see, garbage can create some great assets for communities, especially those in nonmountainous areas. There is no reason to haul huge truckloads of garbage hundreds of miles every day, wasting fuel and money for labor.

Garbage collection containers could be located at every gas station or grocery store. The pickup would be free to the proprietor. They could be picked up or dumped every day by waste management. Imagine how that could cut down on the millions of tons of litter that accumulate on our roads and landscapes every year.

Another issue that annoys me is that tons of useful materials are thrown away. Waste management officials will not allow citizens to take any items that are dumped at a disposal site.

I see no reason why these disposal sites cannot designate an area for items others could use. If items are not taken, then they can be scooped up and placed in the regular waste stream. I have always felt guilty for disposing of items I know others would love to have.

Sanitation and Waste Management

There was a time in my life when I had rental properties and garbage dumpsters. I often examined those dumpsters to see how often nonresidents were using my dumpsters for garbage disposal. It was frequent, and it was revealing. The dumpsters contained diapers, feces, rotting and stinking food, mold, maggots, flies, and likely vectors for disease. When the dumpsters were emptied, much of the residue remained on the sides and the bottom. It was enough to make you cringe and throw up.

Can anybody claim that these dumpsters are not the worst breeding environment for disease in our communities? However, this problem is not confined to dumpsters. People generally place clean and sanitary plastic bags in their garbage cans weekly, which allows for the safe disposal of the various substances mentioned above. Of course, many other citizens do not use these liners. As a result, the same unsanitary conditions exist in garbage cans as in dumpsters.

Now, if we could get every citizen to use garbage can liners or spray bleach into their empty garbage cans each week after they are emptied, we could remove the worst breeding ground for disease that exists in our communities.

At another point in my life, I was involved in a business that catered to apartment complexes. I occasionally had to use their dumpsters. One day, I approached a dumpster and found children playing or hiding in the dumpster. Knowing what I knew about dumpsters, it made me angry to realize that children might subject themselves to that nasty environment without knowledge of the potential danger.

I think the only way to solve this danger to society is to require waste management departments to disinfect dumpsters and garbage containers after dumping. It would not be that difficult or expensive to install a disinfectant spray system that would give garbage containers or dumpsters a quick blast of bleach after dumping.

It would be nice to think that all citizens would accept that responsibility and spray their own containers; however, we all know better. In order to protect the community and all citizens, the government should provide that service to ensure the entire community is protected from potential disease and virus contamination. You cannot depend on irresponsible and uncaring citizens to perform their responsibilities to protect public health.

Automated Garbage Collection

As I stated earlier, many citizens used garbage liners in decades past. However, with the evolution of automated garbage collection containers, that protection has disappeared. I once brought this to the attention of my local city council.

I suggested that they contact the manufacturers and challenge them to come up with a liner that would work with the automated containers. Those manufacturers must have lost a huge market when the automated collection containers came along. Why would they not wish to develop liners for modern collection containers?

Of course, bureaucrats don't like ideas unless they pay big bucks to professionals to come up with them. They detest moron citizens telling them what to do. That is exactly how they look down upon us, rolling their eyes and grimacing. It almost makes one wish to write a book to reach citizens with ideas for the betterment of society rather than letting those ideas evaporate into thin air.

Nuclear Waste and Hazardous Waste Disposal

This nation is going to have to come up with a safe area somewhere for the disposal of hazardous materials and nuclear waste. That effort needs to begin very soon, as it will be very time consuming, expensive, and politically explosive. It will likely require the federal government to purchase an entire state or a portion of a state. It will have to relocate the citizens from that area and compensate them fairly. The selected area will have to be immune to earthquakes or volcanoes. It will have to be an area from which ground waters will not flow or seep into neighboring communities. This area could then be a safe area in which to build future nuclear reactors.

There may not be a suitable area in the continental United States, so we may have to look north to uninhabited areas of Alaska or purchase a part of the Northwest Territories from Canada. There may be an opportunity to use the Arctic or Antarctic under international agreements that would allow all nations to use these areas for disposal. After all, this is a world problem.

States continue to battle one another in long and expensive suits that accomplish absolutely nothing. We damn well know that we have to come up with a long-term solution. The sooner we get started, the better.

If the world is going to be dependent on nuclear energy in the future as fossil fuels run out, then the world is going to have to work together to find an appropriate site for disposal of these materials. Ignoring the problem now is only going to cause even worse problems in the future.

Incidentally, wouldn't it be logical to build nuclear reactors deep underground, so that if failure caused a meltdown, they could easily be covered up and sealed ?

Chapter 59

Building Codes

As a do-it-yourself home remodeler and landlord for years, I have noticed several building codes I feel create dangerous situations or expensive repairs for consumers.

First of all, I will address electrical installations. I suggest that all electrical wiring in walls should be placed within conduit or hard-shelled insulation covering similar to what is required underground. The ordinary insulation on interior wire is so thin and soft that a nail or screw can easily penetrate the insulation. It may not cause a problem immediately; however, over time it can create a fire or a short within the walls. This is especially important these days when so many people are mounting televisions or other heavy objects on walls that require large screws or anchors. There is no protection for the wiring. The suggested method for mounting these objects is into studs. However, there are many wires attached to studs. If you do not hit the middle of the stud, you could easily put a nail or screw into a wire.

Wire connectors are another issue. They are unreliable as hell. You put several wires into a cone-shaped plastic connector and expect them to stay there as you bend and squeeze them into a box. Many elements can cause the wires to come loose from the connector—vibration from airplanes, motors in appliances, changes in temperature, earthquakes, etc.

Personally, I wrap every wire and the connector tight with electrical tape. I am surprised this is not a code requirement. In the mean time, why are we using this antiquated method of connecting wires? Why can't somebody come up with a simple wire connector that locks the wires into the connector?

And why are ground wires not insulated? If they make contact with a hot wire, they can cause sparking, fire, or a dead short. I suggest they coat them with a yellow insulation.

Nails versus Screws

Over the years, anyone who has paid attention to fences, siding, decking, and so on will have noticed that eventually nails come loose and boards come apart. Using a nail is like placing a needle between two boards. Wood is the most inconsistent product ever used in construction, yet it is the most common component of houses. Wood often bends, twists, and shrinks with time. When this happens, boards that are nailed together often pull apart. This causes bumps or defects in finished walls. If those studs were screwed instead of nailed, there would be little chance of those studs coming apart, twisting, warping, or bending.

This is exactly why industry invented deck screws. Deck flooring and rails no longer pop up, pull apart, and warp. Deck screws are excellent for preventing fence boards from popping loose. Personally, I use screws for everything I build. The only things I use nails for are moldings and finish work. Nothing you build will ever come apart if you use screws. Even drywall is installed with screws these days instead of nails that can work loose.

I wonder how much better homes would withstand hurricanes and tornadoes if most of their building was done with screws rather than nails. Any part of a house that is screwed together will not come apart in a hurricane. The wind would have to be tremendously powerful to blow an entire house away, especially if it were bolted to a concrete foundation.

Another great advantage of building with screws is that you can easily disassemble anything you build. If you make an error or decide to make a change, you can easily change the construction. Most contractors just rip framed walls down and throw them away, creating a huge expense in lumber. I guess spending the time to remove nails is often more expensive than buying new wood.

I realize that requiring people to use screws in all kinds of construction would be more expensive. I also realize the industry will come up with power tools that can install screws faster and more accurately than nails. The labor savings would offset the added expense of screws, homes would be much stronger, and insurance rates would decline significantly.

I will now point out what is probably the most valuable use for screws. I arrived at this discovery through personal experience. Years ago, I owned and managed an apartment building. Many times, the doors were kicked in and I had to replace the door jams. Why do you suppose the doors could be kicked in so easily? Because they were installed with nails, which have no holding power. I reinstalled the door jams using three- or four-inch steel deck screws. I also used these screws to connect the striker and deadbolt assembly to the door jam. The doors were never kicked in again.

If you want secure entry doors, simply drill holes and install these galvanized steel screws. Anything you build or reinforce with these screws will never come apart again.

Flood Solutions

People often wonder why homes are built in areas that are prone to flooding. The same communities or neighborhoods are flooded again and again. People in these areas often are unable to purchase flood insurance, or it is extremely expensive. There are also millions of homes built in areas that may not have histories of flooding but could easily flood if they experienced unusually powerful storms. It is not difficult to pinpoint neighborhoods that have the potential for flooding. If you are downhill from an area with no other drainage, then sooner or later your neighborhood will be flooded.

I believe that with a great deal of experimentation and research, we could save millions of homes from being destroyed by flooding. As we watch the news footage of homes floating down flooding rivers, there is one significant factor to consider. Those homes are buoyant. They float ! So what if we could make them more buoyant and anchor them securely?

For instance, what if these homes were built with something similar to wood beams as big as railroad ties between the concrete foundations and the floor joists? Suppose those beams were attached to the foundations with steel chains? If those beams were locked to the foundation and could be released when floods were predicted in the area, then the homes could float, and the chains would keep them anchored to their foundations. They might float a short distance; however, the huge forklifts used in construction could easily pick the houses up and replace them on their foundations. That expense would be a fraction of what it costs to replace a home wiped out by a flood.

Another issue is the lack of French drains around the foundations of new homes. Almost all foundations crack vertically eventually. Most of the cracking is the result of the ground below shifting over time.

The other cause is water collecting around foundations and freezing. When it rains heavily, the basement levels of a home can be badly damaged. It is a huge expense to repair that damage. If it is not done by competent professionals, a permanent health hazard will exist behind walls or under carpet and flooring. Repairing a foundation requires access from both sides, which means extensive excavation—a very expensive procedure.

Flood damage is by far the most expensive claim insurance companies have to pay. Most flood damage is due to the lack of codes requiring drainage systems around the foundation of homes. Pipes freezing and bursting also cause flood damage. Let me tell you, if your water pipes freeze and burst, it is because of your own negligence and irresponsibility. Can you believe that insurance companies pay billions of dollars a year in claims resulting from irresponsible homeowners?

When I see winter coming, the first thing I do is figure out how to protect my pipes from freezing. I use heat tape for pipes when it is particularly cold or a small oil type radiator heater if I am going to be away from the home for an extended period of time. *Electric heaters are too dangerous to leave unattended.*

Speaking of insurance claims, I once had a leak behind our washing machine. At first, I thought it was the hose that went into a drain basin, so I made sure it was properly installed and anchored with plastic ties. When the floor continued to be wet, I thought there must be a water pipe leaking inside the wall, so I cut out drywall behind the washing machine and found nothing. Then I did the same thing in the bathroom opposite that wall. There was still no evidence of a leak. I explored every conceivable way water might come from elsewhere in the house and perhaps traversing through floor joists.

Finally, I cut out all the drywall and continued to investigate nearly every day for months. Finally, one day I was in the laundry room when somebody ran water in the bathroom sink upstairs. Then I was able to see that the water was running out of the glue joints of the plastic sewer pipe.

So I called my insurance company and put in a claim. They sent out an adjuster, who denied the claim on the basis that the leak had been going on for a long time. Insurance companies pay claims every day because of inadequate code requirements and incompetent homeowners who allow their pipes to freeze, but they denied my claim for damage that was beyond my control. The fault was not mine but the glue manufacturer's.

I wonder how many thousands of sewer pipes fail because of glue that deteriorates after a certain number of years. You would think that the insurance industry would be interested in pursuing the manufacturer of the glue in order to prevent this problem from costing millions in the future. They were uninterested.

On another occasion, I installed a new dishwasher. Having had problems with leaking dishwashers in rental properties in the past, I wanted to install it with the strongest water supply line that I could buy, so I bought a spun-strand hose and installed it. A few years later, I woke up to a flooded house. I decided that I would always use copper supply lines from then on.

I showed the supply line with its obvious bulge and hole to the insurance claims adjuster. You would think that the insurance company would wish to go after the manufacturer. He was not interested, so I called the company's corporate headquarters and suggested that they inform the manufacturer that they sold a defective product that could cost their industry millions of dollars in claims. They sent out somebody to pick up the supply line. I asked them to keep me posted on their investigation. I called them about six months later to see what progress they had made. They had no idea what I was talking about.

Do you understand how incompetent the insurance industry is? If there were any competence, premiums would probably cost a fraction of what they now do.

You would expect the insurance industry to publish a booklet entitled *How to Maintain and Protect the Value of Your Greatest Investment.* It would contain helpful hints, such as caulking around windows to prevent water damage, using heat tape around water pipes in the winter, painting the exterior of the home before peeling occurs, cleaning out rain gutters near trees several times a year, cleaning and resealing grout in tile, checking under sinks for leaks, blowing out sprinkler systems before freezing occurs, spraying pesticides to prevent damage to valuable trees and shrubs, sealing hairline cracks in concrete driveways and sidewalks, changing furnace filters often, and using drain cleaners often.

This is just a sampling of possible suggestions or directives. Professionals could assemble a much more comprehensive list. But it is more important to show pictures of the damage that can occur and the potential costs that could be incurred if homeowners ignore these maintenance procedures.

The insurance industry can be a catalyst for teaching young homeowners how to maintain their homes in order to achieve maximum return on their investment and at the same time avoid extreme repair costs.

As you can see from everything described in this chapter, the insurance industry has the potential to remedy the tremendous expense and damage caused by lax regulations and enforcement. Weather can destroy the economy, and we have to use every weapon in our arsenal to reduce the tremendous costs to society.

Insulating Overhangs
Years ago, I lived in what was referred to as a California split-level home. There were millions of them built at that time. Many homes had rooms that extended two or three feet out from their foundations.

I could never figure out why it was so cold in that sunken living room in the winter. If you stood near the three tall windows, you could feel a very cold draft. I chalked it up to cheap windows. But it didn't make sense, because the windows were double paned. It was so cold in there that we seldom used the living room in the winter.

Then one day while painting our home, I discovered that there was no insulation under those overhangs, so I installed some Styrofoam panels. The difference was incredible. I could no longer feel a cold draft when standing or sitting near the windows, and the difference in our utility bills was significant.

Every year, our local electricity and natural gas provider gives tips on how to save electricity. I have notified them that they are missing one of the most wasteful oversights, but I have seen no mention of this problem in subsequent years. Are they really concerned about conserving energy, or are they just pretending?

Of course, I have to admit that I don't know how widespread this problem is. I do know that a few years ago, I got into an argument with a contractor who was building a three-story addition on our home. When he was insulating the floor joists that overhung the foundation, the foreman insisted that the overhang did not need to be insulated. I insisted that it be insulated even if I had to pay extra. Draw your own conclusions. But don't ever attempt to tell a contractor that he or she is wrong, because he or she will sue you. I know! Do you know what attorneys' fees can cost you? The bottom line is that I was correct.

Chapter 60

Underground Utilities

About a decade ago, our community had a severe ice storm. Trees and power lines were covered with heavy layers of ice. Power lines throughout the area were snapping. Thousands of trees fell, and many of them fell across power lines, blowing transformers and power stations out and causing massive power outages throughout the region.

In the middle of winter, with temperatures below freezing, tens of thousands were without power to heat their homes, cook, or communicate with the outside world.

We were very fortunate. Our electrical utilities were underground, and we never suffered the power outages most of the community suffered. Ever since that time, I have wondered why all power lines aren't below ground. Installing electrical lines on wooden poles is so primitive. Not only are they dangerous, but they are a blight on the skyline of any community.

I have spent a lifetime watching utility companies tearing up paved streets to make repairs to utilities. Whenever an asphalt street is dug up, the street is never again smooth. Generally, the disturbed area sinks, causing dips in the road. Patches separate from the original asphalt over time and form cracks. The cracks absorb water beneath the surface. Then the deterioration of the road begins. With each rain or winter freeze , the roads become worse. Water seeps into those cracks and erodes the ground that supports the asphalt above.

So I came up with a solution that would put an end to the destruction of our roadways, the danger of overhead power lines, the tremendous expense of digging up power and gas lines, and the inconvenience of shutting down roads for long periods of time. A huge concrete conduit beneath the roads should be installed. All utilities could run through that conduit. The sewer would be located in a plastic pipe at the bottom of the conduit. Water pipes would be above that on one side. Natural gas would be located on the opposite side. Electricity would be located above that on one side within a plastic conduit. Telecommunication lines would be located within a conduit on the opposite side.

Every fraction of a mile or so, there would be a utility entrance to the major conduit. If repairs or replacement were needed, workers could simply enter the conduit. There would be little if any deterioration from corrosion over the years. Repairs would be quick and inexpensive.

This supply line of utilities would solve the danger of long-term outages and electrocution from overhead power lines. It would reduce the tremendous expense of having to replace storm-damaged lines, transformers, and power stations. If there were a problem with components, they could be reached easily without expensive overhead line replacement or excavation.

With all these utilities within a serviceable conduit, not only would inner conduits last for hundreds of years, but as new technologies such as fiber optics emerge, they could easily be integrated into the existing infrastructure without tearing up our streets. There would be very few power outages, water shutdowns, cable outages, and so on, and there would be few expensive repairs.

I realize that some communities have to have massive sewer pipes just to serve their sewer systems. But even those should have a large concrete conduit on the outside and a durable plastic conduit within. A sewer system constructed in this manner would likely last forever. In those areas, there would be another large conduit to serve the remaining utilities.

The bottom line is that when severe weather conditions hit an area, it would not result in power outages for hundreds of thousands of citizens for several weeks during the cold of winter. And we can get rid of ugly, antiquated jungles of power lines and equipment on our skylines. Repairs and replacements could be made quickly and very inexpensively.

Chapter 61

Alcohol and Drug Taxes for Research

Why doesn't society put a tax on alcohol and drugs and use the resulting funds for research to develop drugs that make people feel good and are not damaging to physical and mental health. As it is, the government uses these exorbitant taxes as a cash cow for all its other budget items. That does nothing to solve the increasing societal problems that drugs and alcohol create.

At one point many years ago, I was using St. John's wort. I noticed that when you combine exercise and St. John's wort, you get a very natural high. I believe that the health supplement was discovered to have a negative reaction with other prescription drugs years later. However, there are millions of other plant extractions that can be researched, and it seems likely that eventually someone will discover one that delivers a natural high that will eliminate the need for damaging drugs and alcohol.

The liquor industry also needs to invest in research to find a product that will quickly remove or negate alcohol's effects from the body. Imagine being able to go out to a nightclub and drink as much as you like and then simply take a pill to be sober in a short time. It would be a great tool for bartenders and managers who encounter patrons that are out of hand and dangerous to society.

I have a serious problem with unfair taxation. I don't believe that an individual who chooses to spend his hard-earned dollars on whiskey instead of roses should be discriminated against just because some people disapprove of that product. To me it is a form of discrimination.

Now, if an added tax were directed toward solving a societal problem as described above, it might be justified. However, these exorbitant taxes always go into the general fund, and our legislators always choose to raise the so-called sin taxes whenever they get in a financial bind. They hardly ever allow the citizens to approve these taxes. The revenue stream is always there to bail them out, even if it is discriminatory. Some things in life are unfair, especially when the majority choose to discriminate against the minority through taxation. Shouldn't there be some degree of unfair taxation?

Chapter 62

Taxes on Health Supplements

Our government allows no taxes on prescription drugs. It's very noble of them indeed. However, millions of citizens fork out billions of dollars for health supplements that cure or prevent health problems. These are not luxury products. While there are thousands of fraudulent or worthless products, there are many that are very beneficial to one's health. The most popular of these are proven to alleviate pain, improve mobility, cure many health problems, and prevent many serious health incidents.

It is clear which ones are beneficial, as they are sold in the greatest numbers. Products do not sell in huge quantities unless they are effective. It is very likely that they save millions of dollars that would otherwise be spent on expensive health maintenance and surgical procedures.

It is one thing for insurance not to cover these supplements, but it is quite another for the government to chooses to tax citizens who purchase them. They are not even allowed to claim a deduction on their federal income taxes.

I suppose if the manufacturers of these products had as much money as the big prescription drug manufacturers, they could influence Congress to give their customers tax breaks. But then, why should they bother?

Even products like Metamucil are taxed. Many people (myself included) are forced to take this product daily, because otherwise we will suffer serious health problems. This can get very expensive, and yet we have to pay sales tax on it, and it is not deductible on our federal income taxes.

So let's start off with what appears to be the most evil product sold. That would, of course, be tobacco. The government approved and endorsed this product probably a hundred years ago. The government subsidized this industry for most of those hundred years. Government officials sat in smoke-filled rooms carrying on the business of the government. News anchors and almost all celebrities sat in front of millions of viewers smoking.

Now that millions of citizens are addicted, the government wants to change its position and tax the hell out of the citizens that it helped get addicted. Yeah, we all damn well know the consequences of smoking. Some can quit, and the rest of us can only wish that we could. The government has become the equivalent of a drug dealer. If you need the product, you will pay whatever price they choose.

I estimate that if it were not for the federal, state, and local taxes on tobacco products, the average price of a pack of cigarettes would be in the neighborhood of 60 cents. You also have to consider the price of the hundreds of billions of dollars of awards tobacco companies have had to pay as the result of lawsuits. That price is not paid from the companies' profits; it is paid by consumers before taxes.

It is difficult to choose who we should direct our anger at, the government or the tobacco companies. With the billions of dollars in profits they make every year, they damn well could have defended the rights of smokers and the atrocious taxes on their consumers. Currently, the level of taxation boarders on extortion. Some fairness needs to be exercised in the taxation of any product. If not, we are in for big trouble in the future. Any product the current government deems to be unsafe, environmentally damaging, unhealthy, unpopular, or undesirable in any other way can be taxed without limitation. It is not much different from mafia tactics.

One way the billion-dollar tobacco industry could have defended its consumers is by fighting for the right of bar and nightclub owners to allow smoking on their property. Before the states started enacting their laws against smoking in restaurants and bars, individual businesses could choose to be smoke free or not. That was the fair and just way to handle the problem. The government decided in favor of employee rights, and that is very fair. Nonsmoking employees migrated to nonsmoking bars and restaurants, and those who smoked migrated to smoking bars. So what was the problem? Smoke Nazis!

If smoking is so dangerous, then make it illegal. That would make it very easy for people to quit. However, then politicians would have to do without the millions of dollars the tobacco industry donates to their campaigns, wouldn't they? It's just another illustration of how democracy has devolved to become much worse than prostitution. Democracy for sale to the highest bidder! So shameful to our nation!

It seems immoral, and perhaps it should be illegal, for any tax to exceed the wholesale price of a product. But here we have a tax that is approximately 1000 percent of the wholesale price of the product. Should there not be some reasonable limit to the rate of taxation on any product?

I suggest that there should be at least some tax relief for older citizens who are the victims of the government's endorsement of this addiction. They should carry a tax-exempt card for the purchase of tobacco products.

A few decades ago, citizens decided that groceries should not be taxed. That was perhaps the greatest hit on the treasuries of state and local governments yet. This was likely the greatest source of revenue for many states. Of course, it necessitated increases in other taxes, which incensed most taxpayers, who did not realize that their states had lost their largest source of taxes. The taxation had to be shifted somewhere else.

Now many states that are struggling are beginning to realize they have to reinstate a smaller tax on groceries in order to stay afloat. This is creating much anger among the public.

I propose a solution that may kill two birds with one stone. It is a proven fact many foods contain extremely high levels of sodium, fructose, unhealthy fats, cholesterol, and other harmful ingredients. So why not put a tax on the foods that are unhealthy? I would guess that the majority of foods on the market are unhealthy. Processed foods are the greatest offenders. Do you know a dirty little secret of the processed food industry and even of many restaurants and fast-food establishments? You can make bad food taste better by adding more sodium. It's the same reasoning that leads you to grab the salt shaker at home. It's just another addiction that most of us are not aware of. I'm told by people who use little or no salt at all that when you get over your salt addiction, you actually enjoy the flavors of many foods much more.

Incidentally, I am sodium addicted. If there were a 100 percent tax on a box of salt, I would start using cayenne pepper. It is known to be a great benefit to cardiopulmonary health and a great antioxidant.

If they can tax the hell out of smokers, claiming public health as a defense, then they can also tax other products known to cause health problems. If government does not do this, isn't that discrimination against tobacco users? Fair is fair, and justification is justification. The revenue from this tax can be applied to medical care, which is a huge expense for every state. That is where the bulk of tobacco taxes go.

You cannot force people to educate themselves about the unhealthy ingredients in their food. It is shocking to examine the nutritional information of various foods. Take marinated artichoke hearts, marinated asparagus, pickles, and so on. I used to think that these items were healthy. They're vegetables, aren't they? They are the worst of the worst. I no longer indulge in these types of foods. Even things like V8 juice are loaded with sodium.

Do not allow citizens to vote on any such tax. They love their junk food, prepared food, fat-laced food, and so on. If the government and medical establishments truly wish to educate the public and encourage healthy eating habits, they will have to legislate this tax. By the way, I am not a vegetarian, and I do not insist on eating organic food. I do try to eat more fresh fruits and vegetables than other foods.

As I stated above, these taxes will have to be instituted by elected officials on the advice of professional nutrition experts and the medical community. People will be outraged; however, in the end, when they learn which foods are detrimental to their health and develop healthy eating habits, they will be pleased with the education. Just ask former smokers who were forced to quit for economic reasons. People need to learn to eat for nutrition rather than pleasure. They will then find out how much better they feel and how much good health adds to their lives.

Chapter 63

Fish and Game (Wildlife)

The state's fish and wildlife department is supported by citizen taxes. Its job is to manage wildlife in the state. Apparently, the department's employees feel that their only job is to act in the best interests of wildlife. Meanwhile, many communities are overrun with deer and other species. These animals cause many car accidents and sometimes even deaths. They destroy citizens' landscaping and gardens. As these herds grow larger each year, they become a greater problem for communities.

Yet the fish and wildlife department will not remove these animals unless they are down and can't get up. A few years ago, early one morning I counted twenty-seven does running through my yard followed by five bucks. The following winter was difficult for that herd. The ice and snow on the steep hillsides caused many of them to break their legs. A few of those deer were struggling to get around with legs dangling sideways. It was very painful to watch their suffering day after day.

I called the fish and wildlife department, and they informed me there was nothing they could do unless an animal was down and couldn't get up. They also informed me there was nothing they could do about the growing herd of deer. If we wanted to live on a ranch with cattle in our backyards, wouldn't we have purchased rural property? These deer live in dense residential neighborhoods.

Now, on the other hand, I keep reading about efforts to reintroduce the gray wolf back into some western states. I'm not a scientist; however, I try to understand the balance of wildlife in nature. It seems that everywhere the wolves are introduced, they wind up killing cattle and sheep on ranches. So the logical solution would seem to be to capture the herds of deer that are overrunning neighborhoods and release them into the wolves' habitat.

Personally, I have always tried to improve my property so that everyone can be proud of the neighborhood, and I quietly encourage others to do the same. I try to make my property as beautiful and enjoyable for my neighbors as possible by planting beautiful flowers and creating an environment I hope all my neighbors enjoy. The deer and wild turkeys appreciate my efforts too—and they eat my plants. I once thought that the department of fish and wildlife was dedicated to protecting wild animals. They are not protected when they get killed by vehicles everyday. Little did I know that they expected us to provide a habitat or ranch for these animals to graze daily in our neighborhoods.

Chapter 64

Government Employment

W hy do you suppose that every government agency is struggling with unbalanced budgets and deficits? Every year, the deficits are greater and greater, and many governments are essentially bankrupt and unable to provide basic services.

It is absolutely astonishing the pay and benefits that government employees receive compared to employees in the private sector. The voting public seems to have nothing to say about these obscene wages, salaries, and benefits.

It's almost as if government employees were holding a gun to our heads. It almost amounts to extortion.

Worst of all, all elected officials have to back government employees' demands or they will not be elected to office. Government employees represent a huge voting block. They apparently have little regard for whether the public can afford their ridiculous demands.

Where in the hell did society come up with the concept of early retirement? Why are not people required to work until sixty-five years of age? It is fine if you make private investments that enable you to retire early. However, no employer, especially the government, should finance your ability to retire after twenty years of employment at an age as young as forty-five.

So, while the majority of citizens are forced to work until sixty-five years old or older, they are also forced to pay exorbitant taxes to finance a comfortable lifestyle for government employees who live off the taxpayers during half of their productive employment years.

We need a law that prohibits any taxpayer funded retirement benefits from being paid until the recipient has reached the age of sixty-five (or whatever age at which maximum Social Security benefits are paid).

Additionally, we need to outsource many government services to the lowest bidder. If there is no competition for these services, the price of government will only continue to rise, while government employees will just smile and insinuate that they are special and entitled—entitled, I presume, to destroy the public's ability to fund government services.

I am sure all government employees will despise me for stating the facts, but sooner or later, society will realize why they can no longer fund the government. It is same reality that has put so many union employees and their industries out of business in this nation. The citizens made their votes by purchasing foreign products and sending millions of manufacturing jobs overseas. Eventually, the citizens will express their outrage at the cost of government and choose to let private companies bid on government services.

We also need to examine the concept of paid holidays. It may have been a luxury we could afford in the past, but our productivity if falling far behind in the world. Our Congress and state legislators should have the power to eliminate paid national holidays in order to save our economy in desperate times. Many conservatives constantly beg the government for tax relief to encourage economic development. Perhaps they should instead ask for the ability not to pay employees for staying home on work days. We have weekends and paid vacations. That is a hell of a lot more than millions of people in foreign nations enjoy. It is also a hell of a lot more than a lot of business owners enjoy; they give up such luxuries in order to keep their businesses afloat and provide jobs for their employees.

How much longer are citizens going to allow government employees to have unbelievable wages, benefits, and early retirement plans that put the private sector to shame? Shouldn't their pay and benefits be based on the median pay and benefits of similar jobs in the private sector? If not, shouldn't the voters have the right to vote in favor of privatizing many government services? Just as unions have driven their jobs overseas, government employees are bankrupting governments and society through their atrocious demands. They leave us little choice but to privatize government services to the lowest bidders. Where will citizens draw the line?

Many millions of private-sector employees have seen there retirement funds seriously depleted by a poor economy. However, government employees have a clause in their contracts that requires taxpayers to fully fund their pensions by making up the difference when the economy suffers. So we wind up paying more for pensions and early retirements then we pay for current employment. How long can this absurdity last?

If businesses and corporations can declare bankruptcy, then why can't governments? Perhaps these public employees will understand the situation when their employers have gone bankrupt and they are sitting home wondering what happened to their livelihoods.

Chapter 65

Census

What do you think of the federal government's cute little promotion of the census? I don't believe I've seen anything so damn stupid and ineffective in my life. They call it "a snapshot of America". What the hell does that have to do with getting through to people who don't want to have the government know what they are doing and don't want big brother in their lives?

It clearly provides no information about the importance of accounting for every citizen in each congressional district. I'd like to know how much our government paid for such an ineffective message.

Then the government mailed out over a hundred million letters stating that they would soon be mailing census forms to us. Why not just mail the damn census form to begin with? I have never seen such a stupid waste of millions of dollars. Who the hell makes these decisions? It can't possibly be one person. How could a panel of experts arrive at such incredible stupidity? Do they have no idea how bankrupt our nation is?

What would be wrong with the president, the vice-president, the Speaker of the House, or even a justice of the Supreme Court saying something like the following in a televised message:

—∞—

In order to distribute federal funding to each and every community in the nation and provide proper representation for your community, we must account for every citizen living in each district.

If you decide not to participate, you may be hurting yourself and your neighbors. There is absolutely no intention to snoop into your personal life and affairs. All facts and data are entered into an anonymous database.

The only reason we ask for names is to prevent counting one person twice. Further information that census takers ask for is only for the purpose of determining how the government should appropriate funds based on the needs of each community. You and your neighbors pay taxes, and you deserve to have your fair share of that tax money devoted to the needs of your community. Without your cooperation, you and your community will be shortchanged.

Please help your government determine the population and most essential needs of your community. Thank you for helping us to help you and your community.

—∞—

By the way, I believe that our census is an expensive and antiquated way of getting a snapshot of America. Computer programs can gather much more accurate statistics at a fraction of the costs. The census likely costs billions of dollars. Just by collecting data from tax records, drivers' licenses, Social Security cards, unemployment statistics, public assistance, utility records, and so on, we can come up with better numbers than are provided by this antiquated system of data collection. This is the computer age, people. Computer programs are capable of coming up with far better numbers than a census that cannot account for those who refuse to be accounted for. Enough of this gigantic waste of hundreds of millions of tax dollars !

One serious problem that this system cannot and never will be able to overcome is that too many citizens fear and hate their government's intrusion. That problem is likely more prevalent in some states than in others.

When they do not get total cooperation, census takers are forced to make estimates. Their job is made even harder by the fact that great numbers of citizens have moved or are traveling or overseas at any given time.

The government already has a system for providing assistance to communities suffering from dire circumstances, natural disasters, and economic decline. The census has nothing to do with those appropriations. They are based on physical damage, flooding, fires, unemployment, decease, and numerous other factors.

Census numbers are never entirely accurate. The government could provide hundreds of millions more dollars in aid to communities if they would stop wasting billions on the census.

Chapter 66

Public Meetings

Government bureaucrats came up with a cute way of suppressing public outrage about a decade ago. Instead of holding public meetings where citizens have the right to voice their opposition and inform the public of their opinions, they simply hold open houses.

In this format, the public is invited to come by any time over the course of a few hours. The government sets up stations manned by different officials where you can ask questions or state your written opinions on paper.

Unlike the previous public format, where an individual could speak up and inform others who might agree with his or her position, in the open house format, an individual's input is hidden away on paper and properly disposed of. If you have creative ideas or sound reasoning that might interest the public or know facts that might outrage the public, you are sequestered.

Another issue that should outrage us all is the time limit that officials put on citizens' testimony. Many citizens choose to state their opinions and really do not offer anything of consequence. At times, the moderator might ask for a show of hands in support of someone's testimony to avoid repetition. That is fine.

However, at times, an individual comes loaded with evidence and valuable information that we should all wish to hear. The moderator can limit that person's testimony to three minutes. That is absolute bullshit and unfair to the public. Can these morons not understand valuable input when they hear it? There are exceptions to every rule, and public officials should be intelligent enough to distinguish information that is valuable to the public from rhetoric.

Chapter 67

Air Force of Firefighters

For decades before the wars that we are currently engaged in, I felt there was a dire need for a national or even international air force of fire-fighting planes.

An American division would have air bases located in the northwest, the southwest, the northeast, and the southeast. Each of those bases would serve its sector, and if major fires broke out in a sector, all bases would dispatch a huge force of planes to any part of America.

This air force would be expensive and not financially feasible while we are engaged in wars. However, in times of peace, it would be a great investment that could save thousands of lives and billions of dollars in damage to community infrastructure and the environment. That does not even account for the loss of wildlife.

With hundreds of planes dropping water or retardant, fires could be extinguished before they become catastrophic. I'll bet Australia wishes it had such a fire-fighting air force.

It would be a better idea to have a worldwide force. It would create unity between all nations of the world. There would be no enemies among nations of this force. All nations would be invested, and all nations would be beneficiaries of the service.

All the nations of the world will have to start working together to respond to the disasters that come as a result of global warming, disease, severe weather, water shortages, and other problems. This is a good place to start and to demonstrate how much more we can achieve in this world through full cooperation. Perhaps if we can offer nations in tragic circumstances our unconditional assistance, we will be able to pull the world toward unification and the betterment of mankind.

CHAPTER 68

SPACE JUNK

There is a very serious problem developing from mankind's exploration and of space. We put thousands of satellites and other vehicles into space that will make space travel extremely hazardous in the future.

Recently, there was a collision of two satellites in space, causing thousands of pieces of space junk to litter space, much which fell toward earth. You can imagine what a serious problem we will face as the number of space vehicles and satellites multiplies in the future.

A recent report stated that there are 17,000 pieces of space junk larger than a grapefruit and tens of millions smaller pieces. If mankind does not do something to address this problem, the space around our planet will become a sea of pollution that will be difficult to penetrate in the future. How much of a gamble will nations be willing to take when billion-dollar technologies can be wiped out in a second?

Imagine a nation putting up a multibillion dollar package of expensive technology that will never have a chance to get into operational mode before it is destroyed.

Realizing the magnitude of potential problems in space, I believe that it is time for all nations to come together in a mission to clean up this mess. Almost every nation now depends on the technology involved in space exploration.

Therefore, we must all work together in an effort to solve this problem. I propose that all nations unite in an effort to round up all space junk and place it in one contained location. This will likely require a huge electro-magnetic force that will attract and hold the junk.

This mission may end up being a unifying force and will demonstrate the progress that can be achieved through worldwide cooperation in ad-dressing problems common to all nations.

All the nations of the world will be beneficiaries of present and future technologies. For example, satellites can allow cellular phones to function in even the remotest parts of the world. Soon there will be technologies that will accurately predict extreme weather conditions, earthquakes, vol-canic eruptions, tidal waves, meteors, and other potentially catastrophic events.

We cannot continue to put instruments into space without some form of management and cooperation. It is absolutely incumbent on all nations to recognize these dangers and work together to solve these problems.

I propose that the world implement a very small tax on all appliances and services that benefit from satellite technology in order to finance an international roundup of all the space junk.

Chapter 69

Traffic Congestion

Something different is going to have to be done to reduce vehicle congestion in our major metropolitan areas. Even many smaller and medium-sized cities are having serious problems relieving congestion.

I have noticed over the years that most of the commuters travel from one end of a metro area to the other end. Generally, there are residential neighborhoods of all types at both ends of the metro area.

My proposal is to offer tax incentives to these commuters to relocate closer to their jobs. In other words, we could set up a home-trading network. Commuters who could prove that by trading homes with other commuters they were shortening their commutes would be exempt from paying real estate sales taxes to transfer ownership. There would have to be much study and experimentation to arrive at the formula best suited to each community. It could be that other incentives might work better in certain areas. Certainly ride sharing should also earn tax breaks.

The government could also offer incentives for employers and employees to work weekends or nontraditional hours. I have noticed throughout my life that there are early risers and late risers. Employers should offer 4:00 a.m. or 5:00 a.m. starting times for people who prefer to start work early. There could be small tax incentives for employers to participate. Emphasis should be placed on public announcements stating that ride sharing gives drivers the opportunity to use designated lanes on freeways.

Incidentally, what ever happened to the laws requiring that window tinting be light enough to see who is driving a vehicle? For many decades before windows began to be tinted, police could easily identify criminals in their cars. There were very good reasons for this law, and yet it has gone by the wayside. What the hell are sunglasses for? There is absolutely no reason for a driver's windows to be tinted heavily. This only allows criminals to travel about in public with no fear of being discovered by police.

I'll give you another reason front windows should not be so tinted that it's impossible to see the driver's face. When you're driving down a street and you see another driver waiting at a stop sign at a cross street, you need to make eye contact with that driver to determine whether he or she sees you coming. If you cannot see the driver's face, you cannot be sure that person won't pull out n front of you. It's called defensive driving. Your legislators have taken away your best defense against inattentive drivers.

There were very good reasons for the laws limiting tinting; however, this generation of legislators has totally disregarded its responsibilities to safeguard defensive drivers and allow police officers to locate wanted criminals. Legislators have given criminals the opportunity to move about freely in society without worry. Witnesses to crimes like drive-by shootings cannot even give descriptions of the perpetrators of the crimes. It makes one wonder which side our legislators are on. Is privacy permission for criminals to operate in society without recognition or exposure?

There should be greater efforts to encourage certain employees to work from home. If their jobs are to work on computers all day, there is little reason they cannot perform those duties at home. I imagine many telemarketing jobs could be performed from home as well. Computer networks can easily monitor an employee's activity throughout the day.

In addition, an employee who needs time off for a doctor appointment or other business can easily make up for lost time in the evening or weekend if he or she works from home. That is a win for employers. Even employees who are ill may sometimes be able to work some hours from home, and doing so would cut down on the danger of contaminating others at the job site.

Chapter 70

Highway Signage

I believe that many states can do a much better job with signs on freeways. Have you ever been on a freeway with five or six lanes on a curve with signs directing you to lanes at a major interchange? Because of the curve, you can't tell which lane you should be in, and by the time you get there, you are in the wrong lane and have missed the interchange.

These kinds of problems are what cause serious accidents and bring highways to complete shutdowns for hours. Every metropolitan area has thousands of visitors every day who are new to the area and represent the potential for disaster on the local highways. These drivers, not being familiar with the local highways and interchanges, often realize too late that they are in the wrong lane and try to change lanes dangerously and cause cars behind them to slam on the brakes or swerve into other vehicles.

There is a way to make navigating through these complex interchanges much easier.

I propose that the major interstate highway through a state be given a color code. I'll use the State of Washington for an example. The most traveled highway is Interstate 5. All I-5 signs could be blue. The second most traveled highway is likely I-90, and that could be coded in purple.

I-405 might be coded green. So, as you are driving down I-5, the left lanes could be coded blue. There could be arrows painted in those lanes or colored tiles in the middle of the lanes. If you came to an interchange to I-90, there would be purple arrows in lanes directing you to the right or left lanes, whichever applied.

Color-coded highway signs and colored arrows could simplify navigation on congested highways, prevent numerous accidents, save lives, and avoid the majority of closures and delays. In other words, color coding could keep congested highways running smoothly.

Another issue that should be considered is the unnecessary congestion that spills onto adjacent roads because of people who have made errors and are trying to get back onto the freeway. Local drivers sit at congested intersections without realizing that some of that congestion is caused by drivers who are lost.

Of course, this raises another issue: the lack of signs directing drivers to the interstate or other highways. If you don't have a map of the community you happen to be lost in, you can spend a lot of time finding your way back to the highway. Some areas are well marked, but many are not. Signs are cheap compared to the cost of congestion and unnecessary pollution.

The next issue I wish to address is one I believe we can all agree on. How many times have you driven through an unfamiliar state and needed to find a place to get something to eat or refuel? You may have come upon a sign that said Smithville 1 mile. What it probably did not tell you was that Smithville was forty-five miles off the freeway.

There's no reason that information couldn't be included at the bottom of the sign in smaller letters. If these signs gave this information, drivers could better plan their food and fuel stops. In this day and age, the department of transportation should be doing everything possible to save fuel and unnecessary pollution.

Finally, there is another issue I would like to see studied seriously. I am an advocate against pollution, so I don't want to send the wrong message here. Over the decades since emission inspections became compulsory, I have seen that automotive technology has evolved dramatically, and now most automobiles run much more cleanly than they did in the past. Very few cars exceed the limits, and most of those are old. As time passes, most of those cars will disappear from our highways.

Enforcing emissions limits requires a huge bureaucracy and expensive technical equipment. I wonder how necessary it is now days. Besides, almost everybody knows that all you have to do to pass an emissions test is to make sure your gas tank is nearly empty and add a few bottles of Heet. You'll pass with flying colors.

With the high price of gasoline these days, it is in everybody's best interest to have his or her vehicle well tuned to maximize fuel efficiency. Wouldn't the public be served just as well if vehicle owners had to submit an emissions report from a tuning center within thirty days of license plate renewal? There could be serious repercussions for anyone who falsified a report. With the right technology to identify each vehicle with a computer chip, there could be absolute certification and compliance.

This could put emissions inspections back into private enterprise. It would cost little or nothing if customers were willing to take in their cars for regular tune ups. Shops do this anyway in order to determine why a vehicle is failing an emission test. If the vehicle does not require repair, the owner could simply pay ten dollars for the test. It would be a win-win situation both for the owner and for free enterprise. Finally, it would get rid of another expensive government bureaucracy.

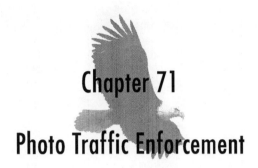

Chapter 71

Photo Traffic Enforcement

There seems to be a great deal of frustration in society about using cameras to enforce speed limits. People seem to be outraged that they cannot get away with speeding or reckless driving.

In Arizona, a judge found a loophole in the Constitution that prevents enforcement of the citations on the grounds that the accused has the right to confront his or her accuser. That is specifically why the Constitution is out of date and needs to be redone to match the realities of a modern society. They did not have the technologies we have today when the Constitution was written. The world did not have automobiles, radar, cameras, and precision instruments that are far more accurate than human judgment. It is time for amendments that fit with this technological age.

We did not have automobiles and laws against speeding then. We did not have radar either, and yet the law has accepted radar as a legal tool in the enforcement of traffic laws. Personally, I trust radar and photo technologies more than a police officer's estimate—which used to be how these laws were enforced. If an officer did not like you or your car, he or she could really create problems for you.

Cameras have become a tremendous tool for security and criminal investigations. There is nothing in the world that is more reliable. However, there are a few bugs to be worked out. Cameras located to the side of freeways or wide arterial roads present an accuracy problem. With three to six lanes of traffic all running in the same direction, how does the technology identify which vehicle is speeding? It seems that there is a possibility of error.

In order to remove that element of error, it might become necessary to string six cameras across those 6 lanes of traffic on a cable. That way, there could be no error about the identity of the speeding vehicle.

There is also another issue that has to be addressed. Apparently, people can duplicate license plates on a computer and paste them over their own plates. They do this to get revenge on somebody they dislike. This leads me to another suggestion that will make that problem disappear and at the same time solve many other problems in society.

In another chapter, I proposed that driver's licenses should become ignition devices (like hotel key cards) and that they should be issued by insurance companies. Each driver's key card would be linked to the vehicle identification numbers of the vehicles he or she driver was insured to drive.

In a similar manner, license plates could be encoded with computer chips tied to vehicle identification numbers and equipped with GPS tracking devices. If a vehicle's plates were removed, it would not start. If the plates were transferred to another vehicle with a different VIN, it would not start.

As you can see, the technology is available to track vehicles to prevent theft, misuse of license plates, and criminal activity. It will also prevent unlicensed, suspended, and uninsured drivers from operating vehicles. How can you argue with technology that will save responsible and law-abiding citizens from footing the bill for billions of dollars of damage caused by irresponsible drivers and criminals as well as saving the lives of thousands of innocent citizens?

I don't know about you, but I trust photographic evidence and electronic instrumentation more than I trust human judgment. I have found that the neighborhood radar signs displaying vehicle speed are absolutely accurate.

It seems that all the security cameras used by private individuals and businesses are okay. However, if government employs these technologies, it becomes a threat. I guess we should all have a right to disregard the rules, regulations, and laws designed to provide for our safety. Reliable evidence apparently has no place in our society.

Our police forces are already spread so thin that they cannot even respond quickly when a guy is going out your back door with all your valuables. Yet you are not allowed to shoot him. I guess we would rather have our police out issuing speeding tickets than protecting our lives and hard-earned property.

Citizens who write letters to the editor protesting photo enforcement must be criminal-minded, and so are the legislators who defend their position. Keep a close eye on them and all their dealings !

Another advantage of cameras is that they cannot discriminate. Nobody can claim discrimination or that certain races are being targeted for enforcement. This could prevent a tremendous number of lawsuits claiming discrimination.

The main reason all drivers should accept photo enforcement of traffic laws is that it will keep our highways and freeways flowing without delay. Every time a police car goes along a highway with flashing lights, the traffic comes to a crawl. Soon, the traffic comes to a halt. This destroys the functionality of the highway. Photo enforcement prevents the delays the presence of police cars creates.

Why does there have to be a sign warning drivers of photo enforcement zones? Is there ever a sign stating that a police officer is stationed down the road with a radar gun? The purpose of photo enforcement is to force drivers to develop safe driving habits. And it works well. The tools that government officials and police forces use for law enforcement are not the business of voters. Yet many states and communities have initiatives to ban these tools. Perhaps they should consider getting rid of traffic enforcement officers as well.

Some citizens argue that the lack of police on our highways is why insane, reckless drivers who speed down the freeways at speeds in access of 100 m.p.h. can get away with their driving. Well, the officers patrolling and monitoring those highways are spread so thin that there is little chance of catching those criminals. Cell phones have made it much easier for law enforcement agencies to apprehend reckless drivers. Citizens who witness these crazed drivers can notify the authorities almost instantaneously. They can then dispatch police ahead of the perpetrators or have a helicopter or plane track them.

Another problem photo enforcement has to deal with is license-plate holders that cover up the name of the state. If that vehicle is licensed in another state, then it is almost impossible to issue a citation.

The solution for this problem might be to issue plate numbers that begin with the letter or number of a particular state. That number could coincide with the order of statehood, from one to fifty. Or it might be more simplified with the first letter of the state's name. For instance: West Virginia could begin with a W1, Wisconsin with a W2, Wyoming with a W3, Washington with a W4. This could be very beneficial, because it would eliminate situations in which eyewitness of crimes are unsure of the state on a license plate but are able to get the number.

It also would give law enforcement officers the ability to issue citations to all drivers, regardless of the state their vehicles are licensed in. Currently, there are millions of drivers that potentially can get away with disregarding traffic regulations. Of course, there also has to be total cooperation between all states in withholding drivers' licenses from those who fail to show up for court and pay their fines to the issuing state.

The federal government contributes funding for the construction of highways in all states. Therefore, they have the legal ability to dictate that all states' driving laws be recognized and enforced in other states. Just as much as they control interstate commerce and the licensing and oversight of truck drivers. Driving in another state should not give you the right to ignore that state's laws and endanger the lives of the citizens of that state.

Chapter 72

Pedestrian Warning Lights

Have you ever been driving down an arterial road with multiple lanes and stopped to allow a pedestrian to cross? Suddenly, you realize that drivers in other lanes behind you might not be aware a pedestrian is crossing. You hold your breath and hope that either the other drivers will recognize that a pedestrian is crossing in front of you or the pedestrian is alert enough to make sure all lanes are clear before crossing.

Years ago, I made a suggestion to our state patrol, the state legislature, and the automobile industry that vehicles be manufactured with a flashing red light or strobe light that a driver could easily activate when stopped for a pedestrian or an accident ahead. I received zero response from them. Now you can see why I wanted to write this book.

So my question is, Is this a logical approach to this critical problem? I suppose the masses will decide. If this warning system were adopted, the law could require that drivers stop and proceed with caution whenever a vehicle ahead of them displayed a flashing read light..

A considerate citizen should not have to feel he or she is endangering someone by stopping to let a pedestrian cross the street. A flashing light atop each vehicle is the only logical way to avert this potential tragedy. It could also come in handy as a warning signal in many emergency situations, especially to warn approaching vehicles of an emergency situation ahead.

Chapter 73

Cell Phones and Technology

Recently, California's legislators were intent on passing legislation requiring all vehicles manufactured or sold in their state to install special windows capable of blocking out the intense heat of the sun. The premise was that there would be much less need for air conditioning, which decreases fuel efficiency significantly. I strongly agree. Planning was going ahead until it was discovered that this high-tech glass also blocked out cell-phone signals.

Therefore, I suggest that just as car radios used to have external antennas, it would be logical for automobiles manufactured with this type of window to have an external antenna for cell phones, GPS devices, or other electronic instruments. Manufacturers could install a tiny antenna in the roof of vehicles, and cell-phone manufacturers could install a port for an external antenna on their phones. It's not rocket science !

Numerous companies are competing to create technologies to prevent phone calls and text messaging while a vehicle is in motion. I want to offer a better solution, because it is unlikely that any of the applications they offer will be acceptable.

Convenience is the greatest selling point of technology. Being able to reach a friend or family member in an emergency situation is very valuable.

We have developed a habit of being in constant contact with our family members and friends. Some contacts are valuable, and some contacts are just nonsense. I am always concerned when people call others' cell phones without considering that the person they are calling could be driving and that their calls could result in someone's death.

Therefore, I propose that all cell phones be equipped with a button to push before driving. When the button is pushed, all callers would receive a message saying, "I am currently driving, and I don't believe you would wish to distract me or cause a serious accident. Please leave a message, and I will respond as soon as I am able to do so safely". There could also be an option to press another button that would enable the driver to respond instantly and engage the caller if the message were urgent or very important.

The bottom line is that we often feel compelled to answer our phones, and callers are unaware when their calls may be putting the lives of their loved ones or other citizens in danger. We must all learn to respect the danger we present to the people we are calling. It's too bad there is not a way to inform callers that the recipient of a call is currently driving. Then we might consider whether our calls are important enough to interrupt someone's driving or just general bullshit that could cause death or suffering for many.

It's too bad we cannot interview people who are dead as a result of talking on the phone while driving. I guarantee they would wish that cell phones had never been invented.

Actually, just the other day, I became angry with my son, who called me while he was driving a company truck. I told him never to call me while driving, especially while driving a truck. Just a few days earlier, a truck driver had killed six motorcyclists and severely injured many others because he was distracted with paperwork while driving.

Driving a vehicle requires full attention, and all callers and passengers should take that into consideration. Passengers should not argue with drivers or ask them questions when they are in high-speed traffic. Learn when to keep your mouth shut !

Chapter 74

Columbia River Diversion

Diverting some of the Columbia River's water has been a hot-button issue for many years. Many are vigilant in their defense of the river's flow to the ocean. Some threaten politicians and bureaucrats and declare they will stand with guns in hand to protect their waters.

The western and southwestern United States are experiencing explosive growth. Severe draught has plagued the southwest for years. First of all, I would like to ask of what value the river's water is when it reaches the ocean. Then I would offer the following thought: What if the southwest refused to sell the produce it grows to Northwest States? What if the farmers and distribution companies declared, "If you won't give us any water, then no produce will be shipped to Washington and Oregon"?

You see how foolish this is? We all depend on each other in this nation. We work together for the betterment of our nation and all its citizens. I'm sure the northwest is dependent on many minerals that come from the mines in the southwest for industry and commerce.

An aqueduct running from the mouth of the Columbia could create many benefits in addition to just piping water to the southwest. It could run up into the Rocky Mountains, forming reservoirs and lakes along the way. Then, on its descent, it could power dams and generate power.

It takes a small amount of power to pump water uphill compared to the power generated by dams. There could be numerous dams along the way. Additionally, this man-made river and the lakes created by dams could provide spawning habitat for salmon in the initial stretch near the Columbia River.

This would be a tremendous engineering challenge. It would likely provide millions of high-paying jobs and a much-needed boost to industry and commerce. Most of all, of course, it would provide a consistent source of water for the southwest during drought years. The entire nation depends on the produce grown in the southwest. The farmers need water, and a great deal of water is wasted when it flows into the Pacific Ocean. It's a logical solution for a problem facing the southwestern United States.

Chapter 75

Extinction of Pollinating Bees

Many times a year, I read of the mysterious extinction of pollinating bees in our nation and throughout the world. This situation, if it turns out the way the experts predict, could lead to worldwide starvation. Yet it makes no headlines, and the majority of citizens are not even aware of the problem. Most of the fruits and vegetables we eat require pollination by bees. Many orchards and farms are desperate for pollinating bees. Beekeepers are shipping bees hundreds and thousands of miles to meet the demand. Even the bee breeders are experiencing problems in raising bees. They are disappearing from their farms.

I have a few suspicions I'll throw out there, just in case the scientists have not considered them. There definitely is something in the environment that is cutting down on bee populations. It might be a popular fertilizer, fungicide, pesticide, weed killer, grass killer, or similar. It might be a popular product applied to soil to stop the development of weeds in flowerbeds and gardens. I stopped using this product when it was reported that continuous use could result in the soil's inability to sustain any plant life. It might be systemic fertilizers or pesticides. Systemic chemicals are ingredients applied to soil that are absorbed into the roots of plants and migrate up through the plants to the flowers or vegetables to ward off harmful pests.

It could be any of the above or a combination of any of the above. It could be a deterioration or evolution of chemicals. It could be any one of tens of thousands of genetically developed or altered plants, trees, shrubs, or other plants.

One thing the public needs to be educated about is the fact that bees are not offensive insects like mosquitoes. The only times bees sting are when you interfere with their hive or accidentally threaten them. I have an amazing story to tell you that to this day I cannot believe happened.

Decades ago, Pepsi was running a promotion in which the first-place prize was a luxury home in our community. There was a letter stamped on the bottom of every can of Pepsi. We had collected cans in large garbage bags for nearly a year. Suddenly, we realized we had to get our entries in soon.

I started to open the bags and found they were swarming with bees. There was no way was I going to mess with those cans. My son and I stood above on our deck as my wife went down and started sorting out the cans by letter. Bees were swarming around by the hundreds. We kept telling her that she was going to get stung. She paid no attention and continued sorting. After about ten minutes of watching, we started to feel foolish and cowardly. So we joined her and spent hours sorting the cans with the bees swarming around us. Not one of us got stung.

So take this into consideration when you decide to kill bees around your home. Consider how you might deal with not having fruits and vegetables in your diet.

People who purchase spray cans of bee-killing chemicals to wipe out hives that are high up in the eaves of homes have always bothered me. I can see that being a reasonable option if a hive is on your deck where people congregate. If that happens at our home, I simply remove the hive, but I do not kill the bees. They will find another location and start anew.

The U.S. Department of Agriculture and the media can do much to help alleviate this dire situation. They can educate the public as to what types of flowers and trees we can plant to help bees thrive. I'm confident that the majority of citizens will want to cooperate and aid in the recovery of these insects that are so vital to our food supply.

Furthermore, the government should consider banning the sale of yellow bee traps and inform citizens that they should not kill bees in hives that are in nonthreatening areas of a home or yard.

One method of keeping bees away from your family and guests while eating outdoors is to place soda pop cans with a little soda pop in them in outlying areas. Leftover barbecued meat scraps also work.

Chapter 76

Environmental and Animal Rights Extremists

Environmentalists opposed to the thinning of forests should be educated about how much space is required for a healthy tree to flourish in a natural environment and how a healthy tree can ward off disease and drought. When trees are too crowded, they do not have enough space to absorb water and nutrients essential to their health and development.

Environmentalists also should be educated about how planting other plants, such as huckleberry and blueberry bushes, among those trees can be beneficial for the forest's health as well as wildlife. Planting native grasses can benefit forests and wildlife and at the same time prevent erosion and flooding. Thinning forests and planting these different species of plants can in fact create much healthier and more stable forests. Strip-logging paths in certain areas can prevent the spread of forest fires by forming a natural fire line that protects animals and communities from devastation.

Our government does a poor job of educating the public about how much energy society can save by planting shade trees on the south and west sides of homes. The oxygen and nitrogen that trees generate also aid in the fight against global warming and greenhouse gases. At a time when energy prices are soaring, you would think that these measures would be essential.

I would rather see politicians sign off with a statement like, "Plant a tree, save our environment, and reduce our dependence on foreign oil" instead of "God bless you and God bless America".

I have been disturbed for decades by the extreme measures some PETA activists take to stop or interfere with the work of scientists who develop many life-saving technologies that prevent so much suffering for animals and humans alike.

These activists should take a few lessons from other citizen activists. Those activists take their battles to city hall. For instance, activists opposed to certain developments in their neighborhoods do not go out and blow up contractors' equipment or their headquarters. They go door to door with information and recruit others to their cause. They then go before city councils and state government hearings to present their case. Many rules, laws, and procedures have been developed as a result of the dedication of committed citizens who have worked in peaceful democratic ways for causes they believe in.

Do PETA extremists not understand that the research done on animals will likely lead to life-saving medicine and treatments that could save their lives or the lives of their loved ones in the future? That millions of lives have been saved as a result of research on animals? That animals have been spared much suffering and death as a result?

They should instead focus on making sure the animals are supplied with as much pain relief as possible. They could advocate to have representatives present in research labs to ensure that animal suffering is minimized and that research environments are as comfortable for animals as possible.

What people need to understand is that in nature, nearly every living species suffers tremendously before death most of the time unless killed instantly by something like a vehicle or electrocution. It is painful to even think about this; however, it is a sad fact of life.

I defy anybody even to suggest that I don't love animals as much as anybody in the world. I love them so much that I will not allow them to suffer in old age. When they struggle to get up, I realize that, as painful as it is, it is time to put them down. They will not suffer on my watch. It angers me to witness people prolonging the lives of their pets when they are suffering in old age. Why do veterinarians not inform pet owners that their pets are suffering severely?

So I say to PETA, please focus on the humane treatment of society's pets. Educate the public that it is cruel to allow so many pets to suffer until they die. I almost want to cry when I see people failing to recognize when their pets are in extreme agony. They are either ignorant or don't have the courage to do the humane thing. The problem is you have no right to inform another person how to treat his or her pet. If these animals could talk, they would likely beg their owners to end their suffering.

If I were king, you would have to have a license to have a pet. To get a license, you would have to complete a course on pet training and pet care and would have to actually flip the switch to put down unwanted pets at your local humane society. You would learn how many pets are euthanized each year and how people dump their pets in the country hoping that local country folk will take them in. You would learn how many dogs are chained up in yards all their lives just for their owners' security.

The cruelest thing you can do to a dog is to tie it on a leash or chain for its entire life. I wonder how these people would like to live their lives attached to a ten-foot chain. If I were king, you would not be allowed to chain up a dog. You would have to have a decent sized fenced yard in which your dog could run. Fish bowls, aquariums, and bird cages would be illegal. Zoos would be illegal except for animals not able to survive in the wilderness. No animals, fish, or birds would be imprisoned unless they were incapable of survival on their own.

Most of all, PETA members and all people need to understand that all living creatures will likely suffer before their lives end. Millions of animals in the wild sustain injuries they cannot survive, and they suffer slowly until they die. Some will be attacked and die instantly. Some will be attacked and injured and will then suffer until they starve to death. Others will simply live to old age and suffer from their inability to survive.

So I say to PETA radicals, unless you can solve the suffering of all species, don't interfere with the tedious and dedicated labors of scientists who work hard to find solutions for the suffering and death of animals and humans alike. If it were not for the miracles of science and medicine, mankind would not exist in this world.

Realize that even diseases are living species. We would not exist as a human species if it were not for the dedicated labors of scientists and doctors. Life is a balance. When things become unbalanced, it wipes out species. Which species would you rather support—an animal species, an insect species, a bird species, a disease species, or a human species?

On the other hand, I suggest you take your battle to the neglectful pet owners who should not be allowed to imprison animals by chaining them by their back doors and giving them a minimum necessary amount of food and little attention. Dogs love to run more than anything. Those who cannot provide the opportunity for a dog to run daily have no right to possess a dog.

At one time in my life, I had six dogs. They were treated better than any dogs in the world. I bought beef neck bones for them every week. I took them to parks a few times every week. They got unbelievably excited every time they knew the bones were coming out. One day, I decided I would experiment to see whether their desire for bones was greater than their desire to run in the park. I gave them fresh beef neck bones in my vehicle when we arrived at the park. They quickly abandoned their precious bones for the opportunity to get out and chase the tennis ball.

Every day, I witness people walking their dogs. Those dogs do not want to walk. They want to run ! So if you are physically fit enough to run, allow your dog to run. It's the best pleasure you can provide for your pet. Always carry water for you pet. Realize that they have fur coats and overheat much faster than humans do, even in moderate temperatures.

Actually, this craving for exercise and oxygen is also common among human beings in their youth. When we are young, we desire to get out and run more than anything. Get on that bicycle and go. It is difficult to contain children's intense desire for that oxygen high. Remember how often children have to be told not to run when they are at public swimming pools and elsewhere?

Society should promote the benefits of oxygen much more than it does. It could be said that oxygen is the most valuable medicine in the world, and it's free. Lack of oxygen causes depression, leading to obesity or a whole host of other health problems. Oxygen can offset the damage to the nervous system caused by stress. Many medical procedures, such as chiropractic care, physical therapy, and acupuncture, are based on getting oxygen to various troubled parts of the body. Oxygen heals ! Animals love it more than anything else you can give them.

Chapter 77

Newspapers

Newspapers have been a daily ritual of mine since childhood. I don't know how to start the day without reading a newspaper. I avoid all appointments and activities in the morning as much as possible. How can you make social contact with other people without knowing what's going on? When I have failed to read the morning newspaper and someone brings up something important in the news that I am not aware of, I feel stupid. It's almost as if I have failed in my duty to society.

It all started when I was a child and was just beginning to read. It started with the comics. Then, when sports started to be on television, I started reading the sports section religiously. This is what disturbs me about the way newspapers are losing popularity and in danger of going extinct. How will children in the future learn to be interested in news that affects their lives every day? Education is the comparison of past lessons to current events and discoveries. Some discoveries today negate the lessons taught yesterday. Some discoveries can capture the imagination of students and lead to greater interest in their studies. Students should be captivated by how fast science evolves and how they might be able to fit into that evolution.

With newspapers at their doors, children can be exposed to the serious problems and challenges their generation will face in the future. Every grade in school should have a current events course in the curriculum, even if it takes just five minutes a day or is incorporated into homeroom discussions.

I don't understand how a computer can replace a newspaper. If you turn it on to read the news, you are bombarded with distractions. Headlines are designed to capture your attention with misleading titles. Most often, you find that you have been duped by those misleading headlines.

How can you sit back in a comfortable chair with a computer? How can you take a computer outside or into another room in your house and sit back and enjoy your reading? How can you take it to a doctor or dentist appointment to fill the waiting period? How can you take it on public transportation to read during your long commute? How can you have it at your side while watching television to fill time during the boring commercials, especially during the endless commercials that play during sports events? Imagine getting an education while lengthy commercials are invading your life. Confession: I actually wrote a lot of this book during commercials.

Now, I do have a few major problems with newspapers. I've always counted on newspapers for more detailed versions of the stories that television mentions in fifteen-second soundbites. In recent years, I have found that newspapers have become far too brief with their reporting. They claim they do not have space for in-depth reporting. Well, my answer to that is that if you cannot provide in-depth reporting, we might as well watch television news.

How do the newspapers expect to attract talented journalists to their industry if they are not allowed to present all the facts they work so hard to investigate? It has to be a most frustrating job for hardworking, compassionate journalists.

I now wish to address a serious problem that exists in the editorial pages of every newspaper in the nation. Editorials are just as important to the readers as the news. There are not enough editorials in most newspapers. Many papers apparently have some kind of contract to run certain columnists' editorials on a regular basis, whether they have anything of value to say or not. I don't believe that newspapers serve their readers well with that approach. I believe that the editorial board should read numerous offerings from around the nation and select the ones with the most interesting perspectives. If columnists have nothing of value to offer on a particular day, then fill those pages with letters to the editor. Often, those letters are better than the nationally syndicated columns.

Editorials by foreign citizens should also be included. It is important, especially in this day and age, to know how the world views our actions.

Continuation Stories

When in the hell are editors going to figure out that the format of newspapers is an absolute pain in the ass? I have to cuss them out every damn day of my life. When you go online to read a newspaper, you do not have to finger through the pages to find the continuation of the story. It would be considerate if they at least clipped the pages like they do with some dictionaries so you could easily get to the continuation page. The problem is that when you go to the continuation page, sometimes you forget to go back, and you miss all the stories in between. I have been embarrassed a few times when talking to friends who have mentioned interesting stories I couldn't believe I missed. How could I have missed them? I thought I had read the entire newspaper that day.

They do the same thing on the sports page. I would like to know who reads just the front page of the sports section. Get a clue, you guys ! If you read the sports section, you read the entire sports section. At least you scan every page and read the articles of interest. Nobody stops on the first page. Yet sports articles always include just a few paragraphs on the front page and are almost always cut off midsentence. I'd love to do a comedy routine on how this works. The paper would be trashed from going back and forth, and the language would be X rated. Then the remnants would be sent to the newspaper office with a suggestion that they could use it for toilet paper.

Well, I think you get the message. If you are interested in government and world affairs, you are not going to read the front page only. It would be fine if they printed teasers or briefs on the front page. But don't start a story and then cut it off midsentence before picking it up again several thin, hard-to-flip-through pages later. Perhaps papers should issue instructions for flipping to the correct page: "Spit on your fingers, and good luck finding the listed page for the rest of the article". Their primitive methods may be traditional; however, in this day and age, requiring readers to go through this process is arrogance. It says to readers, "If you don't like the way we do things, too bad for you". Is it any wonder newspapers are dying?

The front page of every section should be a billboard of teasers for the stories and feature articles within. Go ahead and place some small advertisements on that page. It would likely be prime advertising space. But whatever you do, you have to end the practice of forcing readers to fumble from page to page and back again. That will only serve to drive readers to an easier read on the internet.

This is my last message to those who wish to keep seeing newspapers on their doorsteps in the morning. If you are getting dependable service, tip well. If you are getting lousy service, complain loudly. Write to your carriers and let them know you appreciate good, reliable service and will make it worthwhile for them to provide that service. If they are not dependable, they should consider another job with lower expectations.

I have experienced the worst and the best of carriers. Believe me, the reliable ones deserve a show of appreciation for their dependability. I don't know how the industry finds people who will pay the extreme price of fuel and get up at obscene hours of the morning to deliver a service many of us have been spoiled by for decades. We all have to step up if we wish to save the rag that enriches our lives and gives us direction to our future and the future of our youth.

However, newspapers and carriers can do much better.

Letters to the Editor

For a few years, my local newspaper had an award for letter writers called Letter of the Week. For some reason, they discontinued this program. I have a better idea. In reading the entire newspaper every day for decades, I have read some letters to the editor so profound and filled with enlightening ideas, I feel it is tragic they weren't shared with the entire nation.

National editorial writers do not have a patent on interesting perspectives. It just happens to be their profession. There are millions of citizens who are capable of great insight on any given day on any given subject. Society is cheated by not having access to those perspectives.

I suggest that all newspapers have the opportunity to submit letters to the editor that they feel represent outstanding insight to a national board of editors to review each day. The best might be printed on a full page of selected letters for Sunday printing nationwide. The Associated Press could be in charge of that process. I feel the editors of our nation's newspapers owe their readers the best insight and solutions to society's problems.

Keeping Newspapers Alive

As you can guess, I am a huge fan of newspapers and how they can stimulate and capture the interests of children. Therefore, I have a proposal for the industry. Launch a program where people like me can contribute a Sunday newspaper subscription to an impoverished family.

Perhaps if the recipients realize the paper is a gift, they might come to see it as valuable. The paper could include a note that the newspaper is a gift donated by Mr. and Mrs. John Smith and provide their address in case the recipient wishes to send a note of appreciation to the contributors.

The wrap on the Sunday paper should be geared for children—perhaps a cartoon page or features geared toward children and teenagers' interests. It might be packed with coupons or specials for children and teens. It could contain feature stories about local youth sports and interactions with professional athletes who connect with their communities. It could also feature stories about the achievements of local students and identify local students who have made great accomplishments in their careers. Sooner or later, every school would identify one of their own who could encourage current students.

We all recognize that something has to be done to stop the death spiral of the newspaper industry. We have to realize how those of us who value newspapers developed our love and dedication to that daily rag when we were young. We have to do everything possible to introduce our children to the habit of reading and discovering the world that exists beyond the borders of their immediate neighborhoods. If we don't at least try, then we are at fault in the dumbing down of America.

Chapter 78

California: A Trashed State

For some years now, every time I have traveled through parts of California, the freeways have been littered with tons of garbage. It almost reminds me of a third-world country, except that I have never been to a third-world country. This once prosperous and thriving state had great at one time. I understand the economic challenges and many other problems that California faces these days. However, there is no excuse for sitting at home and allowing your state to turn into a huge garbage dump. Have you no pride in your communities? Have you not heard of adopt-a-highway programs?

This past Christmas season, I visited the Palm Springs area. I almost wished that I could afford to move there and start a movement. It would be a religious movement in which the congregation would be invited to get out on Sunday and take care of the beautiful earth that God created for us. All the prayers of millions of Church members do nothing to clean up the blight that surrounds them.

I have only traveled in seven western states, so I have no idea how many more states in the United States are plagued by so much embarrassing garbage. These communities may be going through very difficult times, but there is no excuse for allowing pride in these communities to sink to such a low level. It costs nothing to form an army and get out on the roads on the weekend and clean up the mess. It would be a good learning experience for children and create a great sense of community pride.

I'm sure the government would be willing to supply staff to block off lanes and trucks to haul the garbage. It would likely save them millions. The optimism and unity created by these actions would be priceless. It would quickly get the attention of corporations and startup businesses looking for fertile ground.

Isn't that famous Hollywood sign on a hill ridiculous? With all the billions that Hollywood has pulled in, you would think that they could tear down that prehistoric sign and construct a high–tech, glitzy sign in its place—with LED lights, of course. What is the historic value of a sign that looks like the very first sign that was ever constructed? A child could be more creative than what people seem to hold in such esteem. What a blight on such a beautiful hillside.

Chapter 79

Defending Against Mass Murderers

The members of the public have received a lot of advice lately about how to defend themselves when confronted by a mass murderer. The advice is generally to run, hide under a desk, find an isolated room or closet—to get away, in other words. I must say that this is the wrong approach. I believe people would fare much better if all potential victims rushed the shooter.

Most mass murderers have launched their attacks either in classrooms or workplaces, where they were bent on destroying as many lives as possible. In this scenario, a group of people is trapped in a room or building with no apparent escape route. These situations present a choice for all. They can duck and hide and be wiped out one by one, or they can all rush the gunman at once and overcome him. A few may be killed, but not all of them. Actually, if all rush at the same time, there is not much chance any will be killed, because the shooter will not have a chance to aim at anybody. There might be a few individuals wounded, but that is a far better result than everyone being killed. And if you did happen to be one of the ones who got shot and died, wouldn't you rather go out knowing you had sacrificed your life so that many others could go on living? Following this advice would mean that the gunman couldn't just approach kill everyone as they cowered in a corner.

I am reminded of a comedy sketch by Peter Falk from a few decades ago. He was in a commanding position pursuing an enemy. He was trying to instruct his subordinate in approaching the enemy. He instructed him to serpentine (weave back and forth side to side) they were pursuing the enemy. They struggled and moved toward the enemy. However, his subordinate did not serpentine. So he made him go back and repeat his advance until he had learned how to approach properly. Essentially, I suggest that all the potential victims in such a scenario advance on the gunman by dodging, weaving, crawling, circling beside and around—anything but running in a straight line toward him. If you get close enough, dive at him. With so much commotion, the gunman will be totally confused and unable to concentrate on any one target.

This is a drill that should be taught in schools and workplaces or any other places where people are regularly gathered together. It should become an automatic response from all citizens gathered in a crowd. This is the only response that will stop a mass murderer. If ten or twenty people rush a gunman, it will be impossible for him to continue his assault. If most cower, most will die. It's simple logic. There seems to be a trend of disgruntled employees or former employees coming back to a workplace intent on killing other employees. All employees need to be prepared for this scenario. It is the only practical method for unarmed people to stop a mass assault.

Chapter 80

Japan's Nuclear Reactors

I don't know how much oversight and power the International Atomic Energy Agency has; however, it is clear that the world needs some kind of authority when nuclear contamination in one nation threatens other nations and waterways.

After two weeks of Japan failing to get control of its damaged reactors, I offered the following letter to the editor to several newspapers around the nation. The *Arizona Republic* and the *Spokesman Review* printed this letter:

> **Time for Japan to bury its reactors**
> *Isn't it overdue for Japan's nuclear-power company (Tokyo Electric Power Co.) to quit trying to salvage their nuclear reactors and bury them?*
>
> *Are they waiting until Japan in uninhabitable and millions die? Until a continuous cloud of nuclear contamination circles the world?*

I also sent the same message to CNN. The next day, Elliot Spitzer mentioned some German scientist who had suggested that Japan should bury the reactors. At the writing of this chapter, over a month later, nothing of this nature has transpired. I can't imagine that they will ever get things under control and believe that the situation will only become more catastrophic.

Chapter 81

Libya

I have never before been as depressed as I have been by all the turmoil in the Arab Nations of North Africa during the past several months. I want so badly for those millions of people to be freed from horrendous oppression and build legitimate democracies. I hang on every hourly report on CNN, hoping for victory for the oppressed. Yet the carnage and massacres continue day after day, month after month.

The United States, NATO, and the United Nations fail to understand the tactics that were able to put Mubarek out of power in Egypt so quickly and without much carnage. The military defected to the peoples' side, and it was over. So the strategy should have been to drop thousands of leaflets over Libya with a simple message: "Defect and support the protestors, or you will eventually be killed or tried for war crimes"!

Two Libyan jet fighter pilots defected to Malta. As soon as that happened, I sent the following message to four U.S. Senators, the president (through reliable channels), and other sources:

Dear President Obama:

I am writing to express my dire concern about the serious situation in Libya and to offer a solution as well. We have to do something to stop the massacre of thousands of innocent, unarmed citizens. Gadhafi must be removed before thousands more are killed. This man is a war criminal and guilty of another holocaust. You may get approval for a no-fly zone from NATO, but that will not get rid of Gadhafi or his sons. He will continue to use tanks and other heavy artillery to massacre the citizens.

I would like to suggest a perfect solution that will get rid of Gadhafi and the United States from being accused of assassinating a nation's leader. I propose that our military load up the two fighter jets that defected to Malta with bunker-busting bombs and send the pilots back to bomb Gadhafi's residence (or whatever current location can be confirmed). Our air force could supply cover for those pilots.

If President Reagan could bomb Gadhafi's residence, then why can't we? The most effective method would be to utilize intelligence to catch Gadhafi in a meeting with sons and staff. An attack on his military compound would send him and his staff into an emergency meeting quickly.

I hope that you will take this proposal seriously, as it is about the only reasonable solution to getting rid of Gadhafi and ending this carnage.

Sincerely,
Allan LeTourneau

Well, as you know, they did not accept my logical solution that could have ended this battle over night. There are likely thousands of citizens that have been tortured and killed as a result. The NATO forces could have dropped leaflets instructing Libyan military forces to head east under a white flag and promising to fly cover for them. They should also have been informed that refusing the offer would leave them vulnerable to charges of war crimes once the regime has been deposed.

As you can imagine, government officials don't want your advice or solutions. They are arrogant, and they have all the answers, regardless of how creative or logical the proposals may be.

Chapter 82

Male Circumcision

I'm amazed at the movement in this country to try to ban the circumcision of baby boys. I listened to Dr. Dean Edell for years and I respected his advice on almost every issue. However, it was very difficult to listen to his rants about circumcision. He regularly tried to convince mothers that they were mutilating their babies.

I believe that I am more qualified to address this issue than anyone else in the world. I lived my first twenty-two years uncircumcised. It was totally gross. I dreaded every day that I had to take a shower in the locker room. I was the only one who was not circumcised. An uncircumcised penis looks like that of an animal. There is a constant growth of yeast or cheese that can be washed several times a day and never goes away. It has a bad odor.

Then I would have to deal with getting it caught in my zipper often. This is very painful, and it is difficult to get it dislodged without further pain. I can see how many venereal diseases get passed around as a result of uncircumcised penises. It is likely responsible for many women having yeast infections. In addition, every woman who I have ever discussed this issue with has been turned off by uncircumcised penises, and many will not have anything to do with a man who is uncircumcised.

Finally, at age twenty-two, I had an infection that looked like it was eating away my flesh. It was not born of sexual activity, because I was not sexually active at the time. The doctor gave me an antibiotic and told me that as soon as it was healed that I should have a circumcision. I did, and I was out playing golf the very next day.

Circumcision may have originated in religious beliefs, but it is the best thing that ever happened for mankind. In pre-historic times, it was necessary for men to have a layer of protection from the elements as they roughed it in the wild. However, in these times, we have sanitation and protective undergarments that make the foreskin unnecessary. It's similar to the way men used to have beards to protect their faces from the cold and severe weather.

I have heard that men can be deprived of sensitivity by circumcision. Well, bullshit ! I have never lost an ounce of sensitivity. But I sure have felt clean and sanitary for all the decades since my circumcision. I feel that it is a crime that parents do not have their sons circumcised.

Chapter 83

Bits and Briefs

(1) Why can't electronic device manufacturers build transformers and chargers that shut off when an item is fully charged? Currently, devices create heat and waste energy twenty-four hours a day. The heat puts an unnecessary burden on air conditioning systems. It can't be rocket science.

(2) If I were king, all shoes would have to have good arch support. Flip-flops and other foot apparel would be required to have arch support. Most people do not realize how important good arch support is to the spinal column and how the lack of it can cause severe health problems. Most shoe manufacturers don't understand how important it is, or perhaps they are too cheap to build a quality shoe.

Billions of dollars in health problems could be avoided if everybody wore shoes with good arch support. It's strange that the government requires there to be certain vitamins and nutrients in bread and other foods. Yet a simple provision that could save billions of dollars and much suffering is totally ignored.

The way we sit, stand, and sleep affects our spinal columns, which in turn affects every cell in our bodies. Our nation might save billions of dollars in health care costs by educating the public about the consequences of poor posture, poorly constructed mattresses, poorly constructed living room chairs, couches with little lumbar support, and poor arch support in footwear. I have sat in few couches or living room chairs that have decent lumbar support. You would imagine that this would be a priority in building furniture.

(3) Why are real-estate investors allowed to convert apartments into condominiums? I always thought that condominiums were built with fire walls and soundproofing insulation in the walls and floors between separate living quarters. As a matter of fact, wouldn't it make more sense if all apartments had fire walls? You cannot control or prevent your neighbor's irresponsible behavior; however, you could have some level of protection from them.

(4) Can all these millions of radio waves from cell phones, radios, televisions, remote controls, and so on that invade our bodies cause confusion to our nervous systems? After all, every function of our brains and bodies is based on chemical or electric signals to and from our brains.

(5) Should owners of vacant lots in urban communities be given tax-free status or reductions in exchange for allowing community gardens and providing water for those gardens? Perhaps even greater reductions could be given to those who provide compost and other nutrients for richer soil.

(6) Should the federal government provide free, easy-to-use software or a website that allows taxpayers to fill out tax forms? After all, doesn't the taxing authority have a responsibility to determine how much we owe in taxes? Why should we have to pay exorbitant fees to figure out how much tax we should pay? The federal government could easily buy out TurboTax and provide the same service online at IRS.com.

(7) I've seen communities tear down sports arenas that could easily be used for homeless shelters. They could be supplied with rows of army cots, and the concession stands could be used for soup lines for basic nutrition. That should satisfy the requirement for food and shelter. If homeless people want privacy, they should have to work for it.

(8) Why, when unions negotiate labor contracts, do they insist on raises above and beyond cost-of-living raises? Shouldn't only cost-of-living raises be on the table ?

(9) Why is it that generation after generation, we see child geniuses on television, but we never see what becomes of them when they grow up? This would be a television series I would enjoy.

(10) When cell phone technology begins to rely on satellites instead of towers, who will be responsible for the removal of tens of thousands of cell towers? While I realize that satellite technology will provide a tremendous improvement in reception (there will be no dead spots on earth), most current cell providers will go out of business, and the taxpayers will be left to pay for the removal of the cell towers. Should those businesses have to pay a deposit to be used for the removal of those towers if the companies that built them become extinct?

(11) Shouldn't there be regulations requiring television stations and signal providers to maintain a constant level of sound? Some channels are as much as three times as loud as others. And then, of course, there are commercials that try to get your attention with sudden increases in volume. The most annoying aspect of this volume variation is that sometimes somebody is sleeping in the same room or an adjacent room, and sudden volume increases can wake them, at which point they may not be able to get back to sleep. If you are on a telephone when the volume changes, you are suddenly unable to continue the conversation. These abuses by the industry clearly show which side our government officials are on.

(12) Shouldn't there be litter barrels at all gas station pumps? And shouldn't the local garbage service provide litter collection free to the proprietor? It's a hell of a lot cheaper for the government to provide this service than to hire employees to pick up litter all over the road. Printed on those barrels should be a slogan saying, "Please keep our community and roadways beautiful". Perhaps there should be a law requiring all vehicles to have litter bags. Anyone who does not carry one clearly has no problem with littering. Police might then attach a sign on the back of the offenders' vehicle that said, "The world is my personal garbage dump".

(13) There seems to be no regulation or government authority to investigate fraudulent products that affect millions of Americans every day. Of course, the government views any enterprise that generates tax revenues as good for commerce unless it involves sex or drugs, for which there exists no legal taxing authority. There was no legal taxing authority for gambling until government determined there was a cash cow out there begging to come to their rescue. At that point, the social problems attached to gambling suddenly didn't seem to matter anymore. I have a feeling that if and when the government can devise a fool-proof method of taxing sex and drugs, they will welcome these trades with open arms these.

(14) I suggest auto manufacturers be required to install a device that would play the following message whenever the car is put in reverse: "Please back up slowly and watch for small children and people in wheelchairs".

(15) Whatever happened to the television convention of displaying the name of a performer or guest? If you have just turned on a TV or changed a channel, there is no clue as to who you are watching. Even if they were initially introduced, it's sometimes difficult to understand names. Displaying the name would help viewers to remember and register the name visually. Often, the viewer may be

engaged in conversation and miss the introduction. Is it too much trouble for the producers to display the names? I especially noticed this while viewing the Winter Olympic this past season. Note to television producers: we don't hang on your every word. Give us a break !

(16) Shouldn't the City of Washington DC be incorporated into a state, such as Virginia? Shouldn't those citizens have a representative in the Senate and House of Representatives? The federal government's buildings and properties could remain a federal reserve.

(17) Isn't it about time that the television networks became time zone appropriate? Why not play programs at the same hour in each time zone? This creates a great inconvenience for people's lives. They should not have to adjust their lives in accordance with another time zone's schedule. I believe most working people would rather have local news on at 10:00 p.m. and then hit the hay. It would certainly give people a better night's sleep.

(18) Why does the United States not have a Canadian television station in its cable network lineup? Many American citizens would be interested in what goes on in Canada, especially the millions of Canadians or former Canadians living in the United States.

(19) Why don't we either revise our national anthem to something ordinary citizens can sing or come up with a new anthem? In my opinion, Whitney Houston is the only singer who has done justice to the song. However, none of the rest of us can sing like her.

Canada has a beautiful anthem, and you'll notice that when their anthem is played, everybody sings along. You'll also notice that hardly anybody sings along when our national anthem is played. It is beautiful when a military band plays it, and it should always be a military song. However, it does contain lyrics celebrating war: "The rockets' red glare, the bombs bursting in air".

Is that the message we wish to portray to the world? A message of fear and military might? I believe that a message of pride in the richness of freedom and democracy would be much better received and respected, along with a pledge to stand by every other nation seeking the same.

We have hundreds of talented song writers in our nation. How about having a contest over several years and selecting the best offering? I'll bet we could come up with a tremendous anthem that all would be proud to sing with spirit.

(20) Isn't it puzzling that this democracy has only two major political parties? Those two parties seem to have extreme ideologies at opposite ends of the political spectrum. To me, it seems like an insult to my intelligence to identify with either party. It seems to say that I cannot think for myself. It is time for America to adopt and support a strong moderate party with an agenda of supporting independent views. All we need is for the right leader to step up and lead us in that direction. If that leader were beholden to a commitment not to receive donations from special interests and corporations, I believe American voters would rally behind him or her. Ordinary Americans want candidates who truly represent them rather than the rich, the powerful, and special interests.

(21) If Tom Brokaw or Colin Powell ran for president, wouldn't either one of them be elected in a landslide without spending a dime on their campaigns? We desperately need leaders with great integrity.

(22) Why should our president need to travel within the United States? This causes a tremendous financial burden for every community he visits, to say nothing of the expense of the Secret Service. The president has a huge staff that can study any situation and relay the necessary information back to him. His travels within the United States accomplish nothing that is worth the hardships he creates for communities. His workplace is Washington DC. The

president's job is not politicking around the nation at taxpayer expense.

(23) Life is a yacht ! You just have to figure out how to keep it afloat and bring the right people aboard.

(24) Couldn't all households save a great deal of energy if we had programmable hot water heaters? There's no need for water to be heated at night or during the day while residents are at work. I believe that hot water heaters are the single largest users of energy in our homes with the exception of air conditioners or heating systems. If we only had wall-mounted switches so we could turn off our water heaters when we are gone for a day or two, we would save a great deal of energy.

Many homes have more than one hot water heater, at least one of which is seldom used, constantly wasting energy.

(25) Will Americans ever learn to quit putting stock in the stories and rumors that proliferate on the internet? Anybody can create lies, exaggerations, and fictions on the internet. Traditional media, such as newspapers, television networks, and radio stations, are bound by strict ethical standards and must report accurately. They would be out of business if they did not. If the reports and stories you read on the internet do not originate from a reputable source like the ones mentioned above, they most likely are not accurate. Check the sources before you take seriously any of the stories and absurdities that circulate on the internet daily.

(26) It's difficult for me to understand why Britain has such adoration for its royal family. They are no different from a mafia. They have gained every damn dollar they have through robbing and plunder. Their ancestors may have been the most evil criminals in history. They took billions of dollars in resources from nations throughout the world. That wealth should be given back to the victims' descendants,

and the royal family should be thrown out on the street to fend for itself. It's time for the world to get over its fascination with fairy tales about princesses. Monarchies were nothing but vile dictatorships that robbed the poor, turned their citizens into slaves, and even killed hundreds of thousands throughout history.

(27) Why is it that United Healthcare can carry the name of the AARP? Isn't the AARP a nonprofit organization? Isn't that unfair to other health insurance companies? Did the membership of AARP vote to allow United Healthcare to use their name? It seems like there must have been some dirty politics somewhere.

(28) Isn't it foolish to display political messages on your vehicle? I have had my vehicle keyed, and once someone even shot my vehicle with a gun as I was leaving a city council meeting. My advice is never to display a message that might provoke somebody.

(29) Why is it that bananas are never sold with any indication of their species? Apparently, there are hundreds of species. Yet you never see them labeled. Most bananas have no flavor. When you are lucky enough to come across some that are delicious, it would be nice to know the variety so that you could buy that kind again. On a related matter, why do we have to buy so many lousy fruits, such as plums, nectarines, and strawberries? You never know if a fruit is good or bad by looking at it. Most bad fruit was not ripened on the tree. If you try to give unripe fruit time to ripen, it usually spoils. The reason stores keep selling bad fruit is that we don't bother to take it back and get a refund. So we are to blame ourselves. If I were a produce manager in a grocery store, I would sample these fruits as they came into the store. If they were of poor quality, I would send them back to the supplier. Yet based on many stores' marketing, you would think they sold the best and freshest produce in the world. What a joke and what bullshit. It can be a part-time job taking this crap back to the store.

(30) Why do restaurants not offer small, medium, and large portions? We are all different sizes and should eat different amounts depending on the physical energy we burn in our jobs or other activities. If you sit on your butt all day on the job, you don't need a pig's portion.

(31) We need to enact laws against physicians shaking hands with patients. There are many dangerous diseases that are passed around in medical establishments. A law would get doctors and other medical personnel off the hook by removing the obligation to shake their patients' hands.

(32) With the advent of larger homes with multiple bathrooms, some bathrooms rarely get used, especially when children grow up and leave home. So the drains in the sinks and showers might not get used throughout the year. Many dangerous things can grow in those goosenecks over time, and sewer gases rise up into that water. I recommend running some water through them once a month and pouring a small amount of bleach into the drains.

(33) Why is it that in desperate times when government budgets are stretched, local, state, and federal budgets grant money for museums and art projects? Museums are nothing but glorified junk that interests a small minority of the population. They should be supported by the people who enjoy them or shut down. The arts should not be feeding at the public trough in tough economic times. It's a luxury that we cannot afford.

Author Biography

The author is a common American citizen who has become obsessed with solving societal problems. He is sixty-eight years old and lives in Spokane, Washington, and Mesa, Arizona. He is married, with four adult children and seven grandchildren.

He has written letters to the editor nearly every month for the past twenty years. If he could publish one every day, it would not be enough to convey his insight and solutions. In addition, letters to the editor only allow him to share his ideas with one community instead of the whole world. That's why he decided to write this book. He feels obligated to share his perspective and solutions with the people who truly care about the serious problems in society and where they might lead.

He believes that we can stand together and build a strong middle class if we adopt the solutions outlined in his book. If you like ideas in this book, you should consider taking notes and/or contacting legislators.

Made in the USA
Lexington, KY
20 December 2011